A Table for Friends

To my Mamma — for teaching me so many precious life lessons, including how to lay a table properly, and that food tastes best when shared with friends.

Words and pictures by

Skye McAlpine

A Table for Friends

The Art of Cooking for Two or Twenty

BLOOMSBURY PUBLISHING
LONDON · OXFORD · NEW YORK · NEW DELHI · SYDNEY

WHY I COOK

Our table is always filled with family, friends and whoever else I've managed to persuade to join us for lunch or for dinner. Usually more people than we can easily squeeze into our kitchen, certainly more than we can comfortably fit round the table. But that is how I like it: few things in life bring me greater pleasure than to eat in good company.

When it comes to the food, I keep it simple: roast chicken, crisp potatoes, baked fruit, sweet fennel puréed and laced with Parmesan cheese, snowy-white meringue layered with whipped cream and dripping with lemon curd. The kind of food you can plonk down in the centre of the table for everyone to tuck into, towering platefuls of it, higgledy-piggledy, unpretentious, colourful and overflowing.

I don't do starters, or the kind of fiddly dishes you might find in a restaurant. I do do pudding – and usually on an extravagant scale (I have a sweet tooth) – though still never anything tricky. I decorate the table not with fancy floral arrangements, but with bowls of fruit or loaves of bread: vivid and bountiful. I have no fixed idea that this is the only way or even the correct way to host a party, but it is the simplest, most rewarding and the very best way I have found.

This is a book about cooking for friends: how to do it and how to enjoy doing it. My hope is to give you all you need to cook with the kind of relaxedness and self-assurance that will make it fun. I promise, if I can do it, you most definitely can too.

We tend to think of 'entertaining' as some kind of show, a three-course meal for which you need to wheel out the good china. I have no good china and this is not that kind of book. What you will find here, I hope, is a different way of thinking about dinner; you could call it a new philosophy for entertaining, except I don't like the word 'entertaining' or the air of rigid pretentiousness that hangs around it. While this book might offer you inspiration for the occasional birthday party, for Christmas lunch, or for any manner of happy occasions you might want to celebrate with a good meal, it's intended for you to use every day, even on week days. Most especially on week days. I believe you need no 'special' occasion to cook: if you keep things simple, if you can find a way to have friends over more often and make gatherings a regular, easy part of your life, you will feel richer for it. I'm not a trained chef. I learned to cook through some trial, a fair amount of error, a greedy desire to eat well and many hours spent happily leafing through cookbooks. But a love of sharing food with friends is why I cook, and here – tips, tricks, recipes and all – is how to do it.

It is a love of eating, the happy anticipation of sitting down to lunch and dinner, that has always driven my love of cooking. I have vivid childhood memories of my mother cooking in the kitchen, but mostly I remember how devilishly good and buttery her saffron risotto was, how indulgently rich her chocolate cake, the one she always wheeled out for birthdays. We aren't all born with an innate love of cooking; some of us – many of us – find it simply because we love to eat. Still now, cooking is not something I enjoy just for the sake of it. For me, it's not an exercise in craft, skill or precision; rather I have come to love cooking because it makes relaxing with friends over dinner not just possible, but both affordable and doable. It's the eating and the party I get excited about, the preparations are simply my way – admittedly a happy and rewarding way – of getting there.

It wasn't until I first had a kitchen of my own – in shared student digs – that I can say I really learned to cook. In my third year at college, I moved out of the old main campus and into a ramshackle student house. What my new accommodation lacked in grandeur, it made up for with access to a kitchen: only a small one, more of a glorified closet really, but blessed with a rickety oven, a sink and two hob rings. No fridge, though. So, I would cram milk and other perishables into a mini fridge in my bedroom, or in the colder months store all sorts of things I probably shouldn't have outside, along the edge of the windowsill. The kitchen had no table (certainly no space for one), so we ate meals cross-legged on the floor at the coffee table in my bedroom. When friends joined us for dinner, as they often did, I would borrow another coffee table from a room down the hall and join the two together.

I began – as most of us with an interest in food do – by reading cookbooks: earmarking those recipes I felt brave enough to try, then giving them a go. Sometimes it worked, other times it didn't. I learned a lot. I called my mother for help often: what goes well with roast pork? How do you make those peas, the ones I love that you cook at home? How do you get crisp skin on a roast chicken without drying out the meat? How can you tell when it's cooked? I turned to her to fill those holes in my own patchy knowledge that were not covered in my books, the missing pieces of the puzzle that is planning a well-rounded menu within the strict limitations of a rudimentary kitchen and the stricter-still demands of a student budget. I spent whole afternoons, when I should have been studying, staring out of the window in the library, planning supper. And when I cooked it – because it seemed pointless to just cook for myself – I picked up friends along the way to join me. Supper became a party. Little by little, I found my way to being the kind of person who cooks.

I soon learned that while to cook a risotto (wonderfully cheap to make, by the way) for two is easy, to cook it for twelve is something I have long since given up on, as the timings are too temperamental; but to cook a creamy baked pasta (also wonderfully cheap) for two or for twenty makes very little difference. So I cooked more and more baked pasta, both because food for me tastes better when shared, and because I love to live by the principle that to cook for six or for eight makes no difference at all, so if you bump into someone in the street you can happily invite them along too. I began to collect recipes that could be made well in advance, and make a mental note of dishes that create a sense of extravagant occasion while still being easy to throw together. I learned to navigate the limitations of my oven space; I became more adventurous with what I cooked on the hob, and improvised no-cook dishes, assembled entirely from raw ingredients. I developed a way of doing things that is simple and fits in with my busy life; better still, that has become a deeply gratifying part of it. You will find everything I have learned collected here in this book. Celebratory food, comfort food, beautiful food. Recipes to enjoy with whoever you are privileged to have around your table, and notes on how to use them. How to plan a menu, how to cook for lots of guests just as easily as for a few, how to present food at its best, how to lay a table beautifully, and how to do all this in an affordable fashion.

HOW TO USE THIS BOOK

Imagine we are sitting at the kitchen table together, planning a meal, choosing what to cook and scribbling down what we need to buy as we go. First we start with the main dish, what I like to call the 'star'. This is the centrepiece of lunch or dinner, the main event. It might be a plump roast chicken, a decadently cheesy frittata, or macaroni baked into a flaky pastry pie crust – you choose – but this is what sets the feel and mood of the meal. Then we think about side dishes; as a rule of thumb, we'll need two of these (three, if feeling extravagant). One should be a simple, fresh salad and perhaps you might want some potatoes (I always want potatoes). The rest is very much up to you. And pudding. Of course, we'll need pudding. Then, should we be in the mood for going that extra mile, we might consider baking a loaf of bread or making our own mayonnaise, say, or salsa verde, to complement the rest of the meal. A little something 'extra'.

I wanted the contents of this book to feel intuitive, so I wrote it just as I cook. The recipes fall into chapters that take you, step by step, through my thought process in the kitchen: stars, sides and sweets. And then, should you need them, extras. Cooking for a large crowd in a home kitchen is more about successfully juggling oven space and fitting everything you need into the fridge than it is about anything else, so you will find that each recipe section is divided according to how and where you prepare the food: recipes to 'throw together', cook 'on the hob', and bake 'in the oven'. And while these are all recipes that I love and return to time and again, it is perhaps the ones in the 'throw together' section that are my favourites. The more I cook and the more I eat, the more I realise food needn't be fussy to taste good, to feel good, or to invoke the fervent appreciation of those gathered to eat it.

Those dishes that are tricky to pull off, the kind you think you should know how to make if you're going to call yourself 'someone who cooks', are no better – no more sophisticated, nor delectable – than those which are quick and instinctive to throw together. Just different.

Time is something I never seem to have enough of, either in the kitchen, or in the rest of my life. And I assume the same applies to you. Many of the recipes here are quick to make, which helps, but speed was not my sole consideration. Some dishes do take a little longer to prepare, but only where it is really worth it. To help you plan, you will find at the top of each recipe a short note on timing: this is how long it takes me to make while pottering in the kitchen, radio on, baby gurgling in his high chair and the general chaos of life whirling around. Likely, you will be speedier than me, but my hope is that the timings will at least give you a sense of what you're letting yourself in for before you embark upon any single dish.

While a cursory glance at any recipe will give you a sense of how labour-intensive it may or may not be (most of them aren't), it is helpful, I think, to distinguish between hands-on cooking time and let-it-fend-for-itself-time in the fridge/hob/oven/what-have-you. Sometimes we crave instant gratification when cooking, and there are plenty of recipes collected here which indulge such cravings; on other occasions there is time for things to cook, just not time for you to actively be cooking them, so something like a roast chicken or snowy-white meringues – that take just moments to assemble and a good hour in the oven to bake – are what you're looking for. You will find at the back of the book a list of recipes divided by timings: these can be made six hours, twelve hours, or even days in advance, so you can choose what fits best with your day, your week and your life.

Cooking in advance doesn't buy time as such, but it can create the illusion that it does; it makes things less rushed on the day if you've done some of the work already. In almost every recipe method, you will see a line that marks the point up to which you can make the dish in advance (a tiny handful don't, either because they are dishes that don't sit well or, more usually, because they are so simple to throw together that there is no need to prepare in advance). So, for example, you might assemble a green salad in the early afternoon, set it aside, forget about it, then – just before you sit down to the table – dress it with olive oil, lemon, salt and a smattering of shaved pecorino.

AN ITALIAN(ISH) COOKBOOK

Italian food is what I know, love and cook. And Italian food, or at least my interpretation of it, is the subject of this book. When I was six years old, my family moved from London, where I was born, to Venice, where I was to spend the rest of my childhood. Much about my new life in Italy was different from what I had known before. There were the obvious things, such as the weather and the language (I spoke no Italian when we first moved, though I soon learned). Then there were the smaller details of daily life: I loved how shopkeepers would press sweets into my hand whenever I went into their store. And I loved how waiters made more of a fuss of me, aged six, than of my parents, a child's prerogative in Italy; how they would come by the table one by one to say hello, roughly pinch my cheek and give me my own bowl of grated Parmesan to spoon over my *penne al pomodoro* as extravagantly as I liked. And the food: of course, I loved the food. I've always been greedy, but what I found so enchanting about Italy is that everyone else seemed to be greedy too. From the postman to the fur coat-clad woman next to me at the bus stop, every Italian relishes talking about what they had for lunch and what they are planning on eating for dinner, just as I do.

Collected here are, for the most part at least, Italian recipes, some canonical, some less so. Favourites of mine from this and that corner of the country, from Venice, of course, which I still call home, but also from trips into the Northern hills and from sun-kissed holidays in the South. Recipes from my friends' kitchens, from their family archives, as well as from my own childhood. But this is not a book about Italian cuisine in any regional sense: it's not nearly as much about what Italians eat as it is about *how* they eat. That effortless, casual, seductive dolce vita–like quality that somehow imbues each and every meal in Italy, from a plain plate of pasta devoured at the kitchen table to the extravagant feast that is Christmas dinner. Children and *nonni* and everyone in between gathered together round the table, each meal a celebration, the simplest and most universal of pleasures.

I wasn't born Italian and yet, having spent the lion's share of my life in Italy, it is fair to say that I don't feel wholly British either. I am both. My husband, Anthony, is Australian, of Italian heritage (his grandparents emigrated from Sicily after the War): pavlova and barbecue are the cornerstones of his culinary vocabulary just as much as pasta with good tomato sauce; and with time, these have become treasured parts of my own way of cooking and eating too. The recipes collected here – from Australian damper bread to wobbly, deliciously British rhubarb jelly – reflect the higgledy-piggledy cultural make-up of our family. And so, while much of the food in this book is Italian in spirit and character, the unifying themes are simplicity, practicality and the sheer joy of a recipe, rather than any single culinary geography. Above all, this is all food that I love.

Many of the recipes are for dishes you will know well already; there is nothing new about a plain vanilla pannacotta. However, it's wonderfully useful to have a foolproof and failsafe recipe for it at your fingertips, as pannacotta is the perfect pudding to make a) in advance b) in a hurry and c) that everyone loves. Cooking should not be about reinventing the wheel, it's not about showcasing the sophistication of your palate or culinary skills, but about getting good food on the table, food that looks and tastes beautiful, that you can feel proud and excited to share with friends.

PLANNING A MENU

This is part of the fun of cooking; it's the first step towards lunch or dinner or a party, but in some ways it is also the most important step. A carefully chosen menu — that allows for the number of guests you're cooking for, the time of year, the mood of the day and how long you have to cook — is the difference between a meal that comes together effortlessly and one that feels an awful lot like work. Knowing what to cook is the secret to doing it well.

SEASON

While I am not always rigid about it, I try, broadly and where I can, to cook seasonally. And you should, too. Seasonal cooking is a matter of simple habit that, more than anything else, will transform the way you eat: the ingredients taste better, look better and cost less, and so they make the practice of cooking seductively easy. You will find at the back of this book a list of menus, divided loosely by season, to help with inspiration about what to cook when. A carpaccio of figs, for example — slivers of sweet, purple-hued fruit with lardo, rosemary and a drizzle of honey — is something I make often. It's simple to throw together, it looks stunning on the table and tastes rather as I imagine sweet ambrosia might. But it is something I make in late summer, when fig season is at its most bounteous. The same recipe, executed in exactly the same way, with costly fruit flown from halfway across the world, would taste bland and wooden were you to try to make it in winter.

Other ingredients are less temperamental: new potatoes, say, taste best when in season in spring, but are perfectly good year round too, so I cook with them all year. The simpler the recipe, the more you surrender to seasonality dictating the meal. So, as a rule of thumb, when it comes to choosing ingredients, if you're doing little to them, cook with what is in season; if, however, you're magicking up flavour by roasting or frying or making all manner of sumptuous sauces, you can be more lenient in what you choose.

NUMBERS

It is essential to think about numbers not just when planning how much to cook, but most especially what to cook. If you're catering for a large crowd, you categorically want to avoid fiddly dishes: scan recipes looking for words such as 'finely chopped' or 'best cooked in batches' and earmark those dishes for another day, perhaps when it's just four of you for dinner. Instead, choose forgiving recipes, food that will happily sit in a warm oven or on the hob for a little while once ready (when you've invited lots of guests, it's fair to assume that a few will be late), and that doesn't involve any complex techniques. To this end, from p.290 you will find a list of recipes organised by numbers − dishes that lend themselves well to cooking for four to six, eight to ten, twelve, or twenty and more − for you to use as a guide.

You also want to be mindful of how much oven space you have before settling on a menu. This doesn't mean that you can't cook for twenty out of the tiniest, most primitive, kitchen: you absolutely can and I've done so many times. But you do need the right menu. Choose a balance of dishes that you can cook both in the oven and on the hob, and that suit the idiosyncrasies of your kitchen. Fill in any gaps with recipes that don't call for heat at all, that you simply assemble. You mostly want to avoid getting to the stage of setting dishes in the oven only to discover they don't all fit (this has happened to me, and more than once). If in doubt, try fitting the empty roasting trays into the oven, but do this before you decide on a menu or start on a shopping list, rather than just as you begin cooking. Once you've gone through this practice a few times, you'll get a sense of what works for you and your kitchen. The logistics of cooking for a crowd will become as intuitive as boiling an egg.

TIMINGS

Begin by asking yourself: how much time do I have? Answer very honestly. If you're pressed, make something very simple and don't look back. Better still: don't cook at all. Throw together a plate of mozzarella and charcuterie, toss a salad with a nice peppery dressing (the one on p.260 is particularly good), buy good bread, open a bottle of prosecco and call it dinner. Serve shop-bought vanilla ice cream with a pot of strong hot coffee for pudding and style it as an affogato (p.188). What more could anyone want?

On the days when you do have some time to cook, however, always start by drawing up a mental calculation of timings. I like to do this by scribbling the menu down on paper, roughly in order of what needs doing first, with a note of what must go in the oven when. Writing everything down eases that worry of forgetting something, just as setting the alarm on your phone when you put a dish in the oven − to alert you when to check on it − allows you to turn your mind fully to other things. When deciding what to cook, be mindful not just of how long the dish takes in the oven or on the hob and how much of that is hands-on time, but also how easily shopping for the ingredients you need fits with the rhythm of your life. So, for example, meringues (p.238) bake in the oven for an hour and then ideally rest in there for a further hour after that, but take only minutes to whip up, and you make them with eggs and sugar, both of which you likely already have in your cupboard (or, if you've run out, can easily pick up from a local corner shop). Strictly speaking, they take a while to cook, but very little hands-on time. They remain one of my favourite go-to recipes for parties, big and small.

People bandy about all sorts of rules when it comes to planning a menu, most of which I can't help but feel are there to be broken: you shouldn't, they say, include cream in the main course and the pudding (I love cream and would happily have it in every course); every meal should have a balance of meat and three veg (it needn't); no fish followed by more fish, or meat followed by more meat (but why not?) and so forth. What I do find helpful, however, is to think about colour and texture when planning what to eat. If, as I firmly believe, we eat with our eyes as well as our tastebuds, then these qualities are every bit as important as flavour. In fact, colour and texture, along with taste, *create* flavour. Think about adding colour to your menu where you can. However comforting and brown a meal might be – and brown food tends to be the most comforting of all – it will always taste (and look) best when paired with a pop of something fresh. This could be as simple as a bowl of bitter leaves (p.110) or a sunny, variegated citrus salad (p.124) to go with your creamy baked pasta or your blackened juicy roast.

NO STARTERS

While we're on the subject of rules (and the exceptions that prove them), there is one that I do like to bandy about: no starters. This is not a matter of cutting corners, though I won't pretend that omitting a first course doesn't make life delightfully easier, because it does: less to think about and – crucially – to wash up. Mostly, though, I don't bother with starters because I just don't enjoy the restaurant-like formality that the serving of many courses brings to the home table. I find that just as you're sitting down to enjoy your dinner, settling into a good flow of conversation and pouring yourself a nice glass of wine, you have to jump up and whisk all the plates away (then often wash them up to make room for the main course). All of this hustle and bustle disrupts the flow of the evening.

Instead of a starter, I like to lay out olives and charcuterie, perhaps a whole chunk of cheese on a wooden board, a plate of radishes with butter and salt, or a few crostini to enjoy with a bottle or two of prosecco before dinner. Then we can drink and chat and nibble on this or that while I potter in the kitchen.

A few (low-effort) staples to serve before dinner:

- A bowl of good green olives
- A whole salami on a board with a knife, so everyone can slice pieces off
- A dish of hard-boiled quail's eggs, with celery salt for dipping
- A nice chunk of Parmesan with a knife, so people can help themselves
- A bowl of salty crisps (not chic or imaginative, but everyone loves them)
- A dish of *taralli*, those small hoop-like grissini often peppered with fennel seeds or chilli flakes

- Manchego or hard pecorino cheese, cut into slices, with a pot of truffle-scented honey for dipping
- Oat cakes with a ripe soft cheese, such as Camembert or Brie, presented whole on a board or plate, and a knife for smearing
- Whole radishes (better still if they come with their bushy green leaves) with good butter and salt

This is not to say that many of the recipes in this book could not well be served as starters – they absolutely can, if that is what you prefer – my only insistence is that you shouldn't feel you need to offer a starter in order for dinner to feel special. With that in mind, the soups, the salads, the savoury tarts, and pretty much most of the dishes in the 'throw together' portions of the Stars and Sides chapters of this book (p.34–55 and 110–125) work beautifully as a first course.

TIDYING AND WASHING UP

The bête noire of anyone who hosts a party, and the bit we all enjoy the least. There is a certain irony that what most likely prevents us from inviting friends over to eat is not the cooking, but the feeling our home isn't perfect enough to receive them. I spent many years hiding my mess away in closets and behind closed doors in spare bedrooms, before I learned to accept mess as a characterful part of my home: 'layers of life' as my friend Hugo so eloquently and affectionately describes it. And it is true that what makes home cooking so much more appealing than restaurant food is just that: its homeliness. Never feel that your home isn't ready for guests. Or, if you really can't escape the feeling, dim all the lights and scatter heaps of flickering candles around. It works a treat every time.

Conversely, once everyone has gone home, there is always the washing up to think about. Somehow this seems to be particularly troubling after dinner, when there is nothing so delightful as rolling straight into bed. For my part, I leave the clearing of the table and the washing up for the next morning. My mother, I know, will read that with horror. She could not go to sleep in the knowledge of washing up to do in the kitchen, still less that of a table half-laid and covered in the remnants of a meal. We are, of course, all different and there are no hard and fast rules, no right or wrong way to tackle this, just what suits you. I find that, were I to force myself to clear the table and wash up after a dinner for twelve late at night after all the guests have left, I would be far less likely to host dinners at all. In the morning, I am fresh, it takes me half as long as it would have the night before, and I tackle the task with the renewed energy of a morning person (which I am). I also derive an odd kind of pleasure from the table itself: if what gives a home character are the layers of life that permeate it, then the sight of a long table laden with the remnants of a decadent and cosy meal enjoyed with friends gives me the luxury of reliving the fun of the night before.

SETTING THE SCENE

Laying the table, making it look plentiful and feel welcoming, is – for me, at least – as important a part of any meal as the cooking itself. Arguably more important. If I don't feel like cooking, I'll order takeaway, but I'll always take the time to lay the table properly.

The below should not read like a shopping list. None of it is essential to cooking for friends, nor should a lack of the 'perfect' tableware stop you from inviting people over. My plates are mismatched, as is my cutlery, as are my glasses and pretty much everything else that sits on my table. Largely it's second-hand from charity shops and flea markets and much of it is chipped or worn, but everything I own I love. I have built my collection of cutlery and crockery over the years: whenever a recipe I wanted to try called for a particular plate, bowl or roasting tray, I would buy it and, over time, I find that I have all I need… though, of course, I'm still buying more. I have one rule: I own nothing that is too precious to be broken.

THE TABLE

This is the foundation of a good meal; food eaten perched, or on the hoof, does not taste as good as when it is shared around a table. My table at home is made out of old wooden floorboards that we knocked together, then laid on trestle legs; it is neither grand nor expensive, but we love it, and it is the setting for our meals together. If you need to buy a new table, I recommend something in wood or stone, a surface that is beautiful in itself and doesn't need a tablecloth to 'make it decent'. Secondly, a table should be as big as the space allows; it should fill the room, because the room in turn will then fill with people.

If you already have a table, then a tablecloth – or, more simply, a plain white cotton sheet – will go a very long way towards changing the feel of the room. Similarly, put-me-up tables (a simple tabletop, or a sheet of plywood and folding trestle legs) are a good option to store against a wall and bring out when you like, so you can seat more people. For a long time, we had a cheap flatpack pine table that we would piece together and butt up against our dinner table to double its size, then cover both with linens and white sheets. The only important thing is that it's the same height and width as your regular table, so they seamlessly become one. Though, really, it matters little if it isn't: higgledy-piggledy is a good look for house parties.

DINNER PLATES

You can go wild with plates: painted, coloured, plain, vintage… what works best on the table is really only a matter of taste. If in doubt, white plates are always a good starting point. They give uniformity, they're easy to replace if they break, and they show the food off to its best advantage. Coloured or painted plates, on the other hand, give character; these could be a whole matching set, or could theme around a single colour palette, or they could clash. It really doesn't matter, just fill the table with things that you love and you will see that it has an uncanny way of coming together. For my part, I use a mix of plain white and patterned plates that I have collected over the years from charity shops, flea markets and second-hand shops.

SERVING PLATES

When choosing plates for your table, think in terms of shapes as much as decorative design. You want dinner plates and some kind of side plate or dessert plate (or both, if you have space in your cupboards), and then you want all shapes and sizes of serving plates. Dinner plates can double up in this role, of course, but sometimes you need something a little larger or deeper. Oval dishes and shallow bowls are particularly useful for serving anything from salad to pasta and they sit nicely on the table in a way that square and rectangular serving dishes somehow just don't. I also like to use cake stands to serve savoury dishes as well as cakes – tarts, quiches and so forth – then a mix of copper pans and roasting trays for anything that's coming straight from the oven. Mix heights, shapes and textures together wherever you can, to create a bustling, abundant table. And have fun with it.

My only caveat is that plates should all be dishwasher-friendly: life is too short to wash things up by hand.

PANS

It might seem odd to include a note on pots and pans in a section so clearly focused on the table rather than the kitchen, but it is helpful, I have found, to invest in beautiful pans, so you can bring them to the table straight from the cooker. This saves on washing up and also on kitchen space, as they double up as serving vessels. I have copper pans, which are expensive (though there are some great deals to be had on second hand ones) but a wonderful investment: they are a joy to cook with, age well and (if needs be) can always be repaired. Whatever you choose, try to buy pans with heatproof handles, so they can go in the oven as well as on the hob.

NAPKINS

There is nothing quite so pleasing as unfolding a nice, pressed linen napkin over your knees before dinner: it feels deeply luxurious. Good linen will last a lifetime: my mother still has linens from her wedding, a little worn and darned in places, but all the more charming for that. If anything, I find napkins only improve with age, as the fabric will soften with wash and use. For practical reasons, I like white napkins: it's simple enough to bleach away any stains and it's easy to keep them looking pristine. That said, any cloth napkin will do; neatly pressed and folded tea towels are particular favourites of mine, as are vintage linens collected from charity shops and flea markets, or unfinished cuttings of pretty patterned or plain fabric. Fold neatly and lie them either on top of each dinner plate, on top of the side plate (if you've laid one), or under the fork to the left of the plate. If you're feeling fancy, you could decorate the napkins with rosemary or lavender sprigs, or tie them up with big silk bows.

CANDLES

These add a certain ethereal magic to a meal. Everything from faces to food looks dreamy in the soft glow of candlelight. And candles – lots and lots of them – are likely the simplest and most inexpensive way to create an opulent table. My personal preference is for taper candles in old-fashioned candlesticks. I like to use beeswax candles when I can, because of their indulgent honey colour and that very delicate waxy scent they have. But you could mix in pillar candles and tea lights to vary the height of the table setting and bring even more life to it. If sitting outdoors, hurricane lanterns on the table are charming (and essential protection against wind, unless it's a very still evening). I also like to dot scented candles around the living room to make it feel more cosy and welcoming, but I never use them at the table, as their perfume distracts from the even more heavenly aromas of food.

FLOWERS

Flowers on a table set the scene. They create a sense of occasion, and, if they're arranged casually in a jug, a jar or an unassuming vase, they frame a meal as blissfully relaxed from the outset. Keep arrangements low, so that you can see whoever is sitting across from you at the table. And make them look like they haven't been arranged.

Flowers from the garden, of course, are always the most charming. They smell sweet and, by nature, they have that ramshackle quality which is so very irresistible. Nonetheless, it's easy enough to create the illusion of a garden with shop-bought flowers. A trick I have learned is to buy white roses from the supermarket (they are more affordable than florist blooms, and seem to last longer), cut the stems short and at different lengths, and arrange them in tumblers and small jugs. Then roughly prise open the petals of each flower to give them that overblown-garden-rose feel. Dot lavender sprigs (fresh if you can find them, otherwise dried will do just fine) and small bunches of rosemary and sage here and there in the arrangement. This breaks the flowers up and makes the posy smell delicious.

FRUIT

Flowers are beautiful and indulgent and a very spoiling treat, but they're not the only way to create a dramatic or festive tablescape. I love a table that is laden with fruit. This tends to be less costly than flowers, as well as less wasteful, because you can eat it (or cook it) when you're done. Put bowls, dishes, plates, even cake stands down the centre of the table and pile them high with whatever is in season: grapes, apples, pears, lemons (the big gnarly ones with leaves), cherries, peaches, plums, even piles of asparagus, red onions or purple-hued artichokes. The odd pineapple works beautifully, too. In all, pretty much anything you can get your hands on that you like the look of.

Part of the charm of doing the table this way is to create a scene that feels both opulent and un-done at the same time: dot a few candles in there, if you can, and scatter some of the fruit directly on the table, as if spilling out of its vessel. More is very much more in this instance: it's all about over-the-top abundance. It works best if you stick to a colour palette: shades of green, mixed in with fresh, lemony citrus; or warming reds and autumnal hues. Above all, what I love about laying the table this way is not only the picturesque quality of the fruit – the colours, the tones, the textures – but the way, after dinner while lingering over coffee, everyone breaks into the decorations and helps themselves.

BREAD

Towards the back of this book (p.252–259) you will find three simple recipes for making your own bread. These are for you to play around with – and enjoy – if and when you have time. Sometimes I make my own bread, more often I get it from the shops, but I never lay the table without it: a dining table feels bare without bread. If you can, try to buy from a good bakery. Something crusty and rustic-looking is ideal, not just because it's good to eat, but also because it doubles as decoration. Better still if you can pile up a few loaves: it might seem extravagant, but there is no better (nor comparatively inexpensive) centrepiece to a table and bread will always get eaten, especially if you leave a knife with it to encourage everyone to help themselves. What you don't get through at dinner can be repurposed happily as toast or panzanella (p.50–55) the next day.

STARS

The first thing I learned to cook in the first kitchen I called my own was a roast. Not 'a roast' as in all the elaborate trimmings that the two words 'Sunday' and 'lunch' conjure up. But, more literally, just roast lamb. This is the recipe: rub down a leg of lamb with olive oil and salt, then wedge a few garlic cloves, peeled but still whole, and a rosemary spriglet or two into its layer of fat. Cook it in the oven for an hour or so, in the comfort of my mother's assurance that you can't really go wrong with lamb. Undercooked and you serve it pink, overdone and you call it 'slow-cooked'. Nothing fancy, but I remember feeling very happy with it. Pleased that it had turned out well, happily surprised that this cooking-a-nice-meal business was far simpler than I had imagined it to be.

Roasts remain one of my favourite things both to cook and to eat: they're comfort food, simple, yet innately ceremonial. But over the years, my repertoire of favourites has grown, and you will find here very many other dishes that share a roast's same heart-of-the-meal quality. There are baked pastas: tagliatelle gratin with crisp pancetta, layered with decadent, cheesy bechamel; penne doused in a creamy saffron sauce and baked into a buttery puff pastry crust. Both are showy to look at and comforting to eat. There are soups, and panzanella - stale bread tossed with juicy tomatoes, basil and a good tin of fish - to make a delectable meal from leftovers. There is Sicilian couscous laced with lemon, saffron and raisins, which takes moments to throw together. And the list goes on: the common theme is that this is all food that works well for a crowd.

You could call the recipes in this chapter 'main courses', but they're also dishes that feel, look and taste extravagant and impressive, so I like to call them 'stars'. Should you find yourself pressed for time, you could choose a recipe from these pages, serve it with a well-dressed green salad (from a bag) and follow with fruit and mascarpone, for a meal you could proudly serve to anyone. Should you, on the other hand, be in the mood for something a smidgen more elaborate, there are plenty of sides and sweets from which to take your pick in the chapters that follow.

BURRATA WITH PRESERVED LEMONS, MINT & CHILLI

HANDS ON TIME
5 minutes

FOR 6
2 preserved lemons
5-6 burrata cheeses
A drizzle of extra
    virgin olive oil
A few mint sprigs
¼ tsp chilli flakes

The preserved lemons here are an exquisite contrast – sharp, tangy and moreishly salty – to the extravagantly rich burrata cheese, which is halfway between milky-white mozzarella and something akin to clotted cream. The sprinkling of mint leaves and fiery chilli flakes are by no means necessary – you'd do just as well with torn sweet basil leaves or aromatic thyme instead, if that's what you have on hand – but they are a nice touch, both for colour and the warmth of flavour they bring.

This is the kind of dish that it is easy to scale up, depending on how many people you are feeding, calculating just less than a ball of burrata per person. Hold off until the last minute to tear open the cheeses and scatter over the embellishments, as this doesn't sit particularly well on the table.

Coarsely slice the rind of the preserved lemons (discard the flesh) and set aside. Arrange the balls of creamy burrata on a serving dish.

—

Just before sitting down at the table, roughly tear open the burrata with your fingers. Top with the lemon rind and drizzle with olive oil. Roughly tear the mint leaves and scatter them over the plate, then sprinkle with the chilli flakes.

SERVE WITH…
I will happily eat this on any occasion. For a lighter summer meal it works alongside something colourful, such as CARPACCIO OF FIGS WITH LARDO, HONEY & ROSEMARY (p.42), and bread: lots of it. You could even bake your own (p.252, 254 and 256-7). In colder weather, it's nice alongside a dish of WILD RICE & LENTIL SALAD (p.132) with a few shimmering pomegranate seeds, a deliciously nutty contrast to the over-the-top creaminess of the cheese. Add a little colour with a BLOOD ORANGE, RED ONION, BLACK OLIVE & BASIL SALAD (p.124).

AND FOR PUDDING…
In summer, try DRUNKEN STRAWBERRIES (p.194) swimming in sweet red wine juices, with or without a generous helping of clotted cream on the side. In the depths of winter, I love RED WINE POACHED PEARS (p.212) or, as we nudge towards spring, a wobbly, delectably PINK RHUBARB & PROSECCO JELLY (p.222).

MOZZARELLA WITH CELERY, OLIVES & PINE NUTS

HANDS ON TIME
15 minutes

HANDS OFF TIME
20-30 minutes resting

FOR 6–8
12 black olives, pitted
6-8 anchovies
25g pine nuts
2 tbsp extra virgin
   olive oil
1-2 celery sticks
6 mozzarella cheeses,
   ideally buffalo

A lighter, slightly less decadent version of the burrata recipe on the previous page. You can pair mozzarella successfully with most things, though I find that celery, with its distinctive mineral flavour, works particularly well with the salty black olives here, while the pine nuts add an unexpectedly creamy note.

The success of this dish depends upon the cheese. Buffalo mozzarella, if you can get your hands on it, is my favourite; it's lighter and a little tangier than mozzarella made from cow's milk.

One of the joys of this dish is that the mozzarella can be sliced a little in advance and left on its serving dish for a couple of hours, though of course the longer it sits, the less fresh it will taste.

Finely chop the olives, anchovies and pine nuts together. Spoon them into a bowl, pour over the olive oil, give everything a good stir and set aside. Thickly slice the celery.

Slice the mozzarella thickly, roughly 1cm thick, and arrange on a serving dish. Sprinkle the chopped celery over the cheese, then spoon over the olive mixture with all of its flavoured oil. Set aside – ideally in the fridge, or if fridge space is at a premium, somewhere cool – for 20–30 minutes before serving, so the cheese becomes imbued with the flavour of the oil.

—

Bring the cheese to room temperature before serving.

SERVE WITH...
Mozzarella goes well with pretty much anything and everything, but there are few more delightful lunches than this served alongside ROAST STUFFED TOMATOES (p.156), a big dish of BABY ARTICHOKE, FENNEL & PECORINO SALAD (p.122), and perhaps - if feeding a hungry crowd - an ASPARAGUS WITH LEMON & TOASTED ALMOND GRATIN (p.138). If you want to really spoil your guests, add a dish of SICILIAN COUSCOUS SALAD (p.46) or a generous serving of TUSCAN PANZANELLA (p.50).

AND FOR PUDDING...
Fresh fruit, either with or without MERINGUES (p.238), but most certainly with a healthy dollop of mascarpone.

CHILLED ALMOND SOUP

HANDS ON TIME
10 minutes, at most

HANDS OFF TIME
1–2 hours chilling,
  or longer

FOR 6
150g stale white bread
1 litre chilled water,
  plus extra if needed
200g blanched almonds
2 garlic cloves, peeled
100ml sunflower oil
2 tbsp balsamic vinegar
1 tsp fine sea salt

**OPTIONAL EXTRAS,
  TO SERVE**
Apple, figs or grapes
A little lemon juice
A drizzle of extra
  virgin olive oil
Crusty bread

I inherited this recipe for *ajo blanco* from my Spanish friend Gola. I don't believe it could be improved upon, so I have replicated it here in its unadulterated and unadapted form, just as she gave it to me. It is a dish of pure, inviting, elegant white and could not be easier to make: assuming you own a food processor, you simply put all the ingredients in it and blitz. Nothing more to it. Though, if you want to elaborate on perfection, top it with a few shimmering grapes, chunks of sweet apple or slivers of fig, alongside a drizzle of golden oil.

Put the bread into a mixing bowl, pour over the measured chilled water and leave to steep for a few minutes until the bread is soft and most of the liquid has been absorbed.

Now combine the rest of the ingredients in a blender, add the bread and any remaining soaking water and blitz until smooth and creamy. Add a little more chilled water, if you want the soup to be more liquid, bearing in mind that it will thicken a little in the fridge. Chill for a couple of hours.

—

Before serving, if you like, quickly slice an apple (you can do this a few hours in advance, just dress it with lemon juice to stop it browning, then chill), or a few figs or grapes, and serve alongside the ice-cold soup, with a drizzle of olive oil and good bread, if you want.

SERVE WITH...
In summer, you'll need lots of bread and plenty of colourful salads, such as BEETROOT & MINT SALAD (p.118) and WATERMELON, FETA & PISTACHIO CARPACCIO (p.120), a riot of fuchsia pink topped with salty feta and candy-green pistachios. In the winter months, when the appetite is more robust, this works best alongside another dish. A few years ago, I made it on Christmas Eve, followed by ROAST PORK WITH HONEY-ROAST PERSIMMONS (p.96), so deliciously vibrant in colour and glistening in their sweet juices, and A REALLY GOOD CHICORY SALAD WITH CREAMY MUSTARD DRESSING (p.110).

AND FOR PUDDING...
In summer, try a fabulous over-the-top confection, such as SUMMER BERRY CLOUD CAKE (p.240) topped with a carpet of berries and edible fresh flowers. In the colder months, go for PISTACHIO PANETTONE CAKE (p.198), smothered in soft Italian meringue, ever-so-slightly burnished, so it is chewy.

GAZPACHO

HANDS ON TIME
15 minutes

HANDS OFF TIME
1–2 hours chilling

FOR 4
1kg tomatoes, chopped
2 large carrots, chopped
3 small sweet red
   peppers, ideally
   Romano peppers,
   deseeded and chopped
1 medium apple, cored
   and chopped
¼ red onion, chopped
2 tbsp balsamic vinegar
2 tbsp extra virgin
   olive oil, plus extra
   to serve
1 tsp fine sea salt,
   plus extra to taste
Freshly ground
   black pepper

This riot of flavour and colour is another recipe from my friend Gola; it's a particularly good gazpacho, made with apple rather than the traditional bread. Deliciously light and summery, it's also excellent for friends with gluten intolerance. All you do is blitz everything in the food processor, then chill. If I have time, I push it through a sieve to make it smoother, but if you're happy with the texture, feel free to skip this step.

Boiled eggs, chopped into tiny pieces, or shavings of apple, or torn parsley leaves, are all sublime sprinkled on top to add texture. Or try small chunks of bread lightly browned in a pan, or toasted in the oven, with a generous glug of olive oil.

Combine all the ingredients (except the seasoning) in a blender and blitz until smooth. Add the 1 tsp salt, blitz again to combine, then taste. Season with pepper and more salt, if you like. Pass the mixture through a sieve if you want. Chill the smooth, vibrant soup in the fridge for a couple of hours.

——

Serve the ice-cold gazpacho drizzled with oil and scattered with a little more seasoning, if you like.

SERVE WITH...
I most feel like eating this in summer. It works well on picnics, kept chilled in a vacuum flask with small enamel mugs for serving. To go with it, try TORTA PASQUALINA (p.76), a spinach and ricotta pie with whole eggs baked into it, cold cuts, and crudités of peppers, fennel and peppery radishes to eat dipped in olive oil and salt. At home, if you feel you should offer meat, then BRESAOLA E GRANA (p.44) will give a little oomph. And you can't go wrong with a plate of ASPARAGUS WITH LEMON & TOASTED ALMOND GRATIN (p.138), served at room temperature.

AND FOR PUDDING...
On a picnic, pack LAVENDER HONEY PANNACOTTA (p.208), made in small glass yogurt pots or jars, covered with their own lids if they have them, or with greaseproof paper and sealed with an elastic band. At home, try EASY-PEASY LEMON MERINGUE PIE (p.182), or a simple tower of cloud-like MERINGUES (p.238) with a big bowl of sharp raspberries.

CARPACCIO OF FIGS WITH LARDO, HONEY & ROSEMARY

HANDS ON TIME
10 minutes

FOR 6
150g lardo, finely sliced
10 ripe figs
2 tbsp runny honey
A few rosemary sprigs

It is, of course, wildly inaccurate to call this a Carpaccio, which – strictly speaking – is a dish of finely sliced raw beef. But I can't help but feel that the moment you see the word 'salad' you think rough and tumble, whereas this dish, bejewelled with its delicate, finely sliced figs, is anything but. So let's revel in the fact that this recipe still boasts all the sumptuousness and subtle sophistication of a good Carpaccio and call it that.

You should find lardo – strips of pork fat, cured with herbs including rosemary, and very finely sliced – in any good Italian delicatessen. It's like eating well-seasoned butter, and pays the loveliest compliment to the sweetness of the figs here. If you can't get hold of it, try adding thin slices of prosciutto crudo, or even fine shavings of salty Parmesan cheese, instead.

Drape a layer of lardo over a serving dish. Finely slice the figs lengthways from top to bottom and arrange the slices over the lardo. You can do this up to a couple of hours before you want to sit down to eat, just cover and store in the fridge until you are ready.

—

Just before serving, drizzle over the honey and sprinkle liberally with rosemary sprigs.

SERVE WITH...
You must eat this in late summer, when figs are at their ripest. Serve it with a COURGETTE BLOSSOM & TALEGGIO GALETTE (p.160), and a verdant, sweet PANZANELLA WITH GARDEN PEAS & BABY ARTICHOKES (p.52) for a simple lunch in the garden (or kitchen), or a quick weeknight supper.

AND FOR PUDDING...
You will want something wildly extravagant, such as LEMON MERINGUE CAKE (p.244), layered with sharp curd and whipped cream.

BRESAOLA E GRANA

HANDS ON TIME
5 minutes

FOR 6
50g rocket
Juice of ¼ lemon
A generous drizzle of
    extra virgin olive oil
300g bresaola,
    finely sliced
40g Parmesan cheese,
    shaved
Sea salt flakes
Freshly ground
    black pepper

Bresaola – that tissue-thin sliced air-dried Italian beef – with shavings of Parmesan cheese. This dish follows the same deliciously simple principle as those other Italian classics prosciutto-and-melon or tomato-and-mozzarella, in that it is fundamentally a matter of assembling two or three extremely good ingredients. Buy the best Parmesan you can afford and make sure it comes in a large chunk that you can shave fine slivers from.

This isn't a dish that sits well for too long, as the green leaves wilt a bit: broadly, it tastes best when made at the last minute. That said, this is so easy and intuitive to make that I happily throw it together while chatting with guests in the kitchen.

Heap the rocket leaves high on a large serving dish. Squeeze over the lemon juice, drizzle with olive oil and add a generous pinch of salt, then toss the leaves lightly to dress them (I do this with my fingers).

Arrange the ruby-red bresaola over the top, overlapping the thin slices so the leaves are hidden underneath. Top with the shavings of Parmesan. Season with a little more olive oil and some black pepper just before serving, if you like.

SERVE WITH...
I would happily offer this for a quick lunch, just as I would for a more elaborate dinner party, with something warming such as a dish of ROAST NEW POTATOES WITH BAY LEAVES (p.152) or a TIMBALLO OF BAKED COURGETTES (p.162) to go with it. And, depending how hungry you are, either a dish of CREAMY BAKED LEEKS WITH MUSTARD & PARMESAN (p.164) or of BEETROOT & MINT SALAD (p.118), swimming in its crimson juices... or, indeed, both.

AND FOR PUDDING...
SVERGOGNATA (p.202): thick ricotta cream, laced with candied peel, bitter chocolate and pistachios, with sweet biscotti for dipping.

SICILIAN COUSCOUS SALAD

HANDS ON TIME
15 minutes

HANDS OFF TIME
15 minutes, for the
   couscous to swell

FOR 6
300g couscous
1 vegetable stock cube
400ml boiling water
70ml extra virgin
   olive oil
20g flaked almonds
10-12 caper berries,
   halved
1 small fennel bulb,
   finely sliced
400g tinned tuna,
   drained
A handful of rocket
Juice of 1 lemon
Sea salt flakes
Freshly ground
   black pepper

If you were being pedantic, you would cook couscous in a *couscoussière*, a Moroccan clay pot in which you slowly steam the grains over a bubbling stew. The way I do it is rather less romantic and utterly inauthentic, but it is quick and convenient without compromising either on the flavour or the delightful fluffy texture of the cooked grains.

You could of course serve couscous plain, dressed with a little oil and lemon juice, even a smattering of aromatic spice – cinnamon, nutmeg and so forth – to go with pretty much anything. But, inspired by the way they cook it in Sicily, I throw in salty caper berries, a good tin of oily, almost meaty tuna and sweet aniseedy fennel. This makes for a vibrant centrepiece more than substantial enough to serve on its own.

Pour the couscous into a large heatproof bowl. Dissolve the stock cube in the measured boiling water, then pour the boiling stock over the grains, cover and set aside for 10–15 minutes to swell up.

When all the liquid has been absorbed, use a fork to fluff up the grains, then douse generously with one-third of the oil. Now add the almonds, caper berries and fennel and toss everything together well.

Add the tuna, breaking it up with a fork and mixing it through the salad. This will happily keep for a day in the fridge.

—

Lastly throw in the rocket (if it sits in the dressing, it will wilt). Squeeze in the juice of the lemon and dress with what is left of the oil. Toss again and add salt and pepper to taste.

SERVE WITH...
This is perfect picnic food alongside some good hard cheese, cold ham or salami and a loaf of bread; I favour DAMPER BREAD (p.252), wrapped neatly in a clean tea towel and served with lots of salty butter. I don't think you'd want for much more.

AND FOR PUDDING...
Strawberries with a pot of clotted cream and a good solid picnic cake such as PISTACHIO BUTTER CAKE WITH MARZIPAN ICING (p.232)... but on this occasion leave it uniced; instead, just dust it with icing sugar.

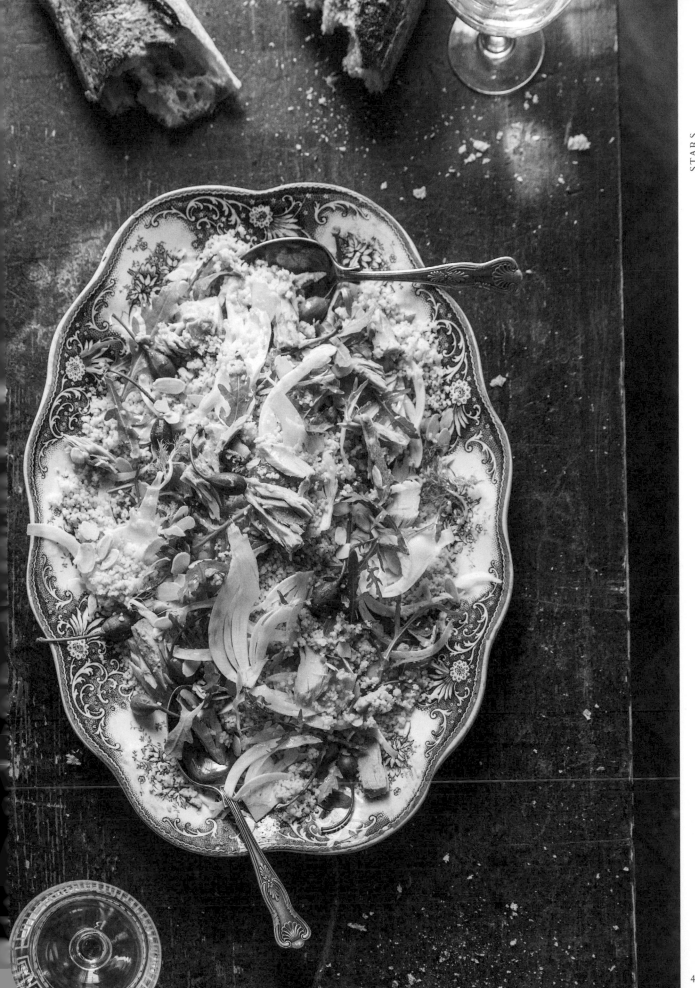

WINTRY SAFFRON COUSCOUS

HANDS ON TIME
10 minutes

HANDS OFF TIME
15 minutes, for the
couscous to swell

FOR 6
1 tsp saffron strands
300g couscous
120g raisins
Finely grated zest of
 ¼ lemon, plus extra
 (optional) to serve
1 vegetable stock cube
400ml boiling water
A generous drizzle of
 extra virgin olive oil
80g pomegranate seeds,
 plus extra (optional)
 to serve
60g pine nuts
Sea salt flakes
Freshly ground
 black pepper

So much of what we eat and crave in the colder months is brown – roasts, golden potatoes, nourishing lentils and so forth – that the deep lemony colour of this dish is a welcome break.

I always keep saffron in my spice drawer, but if you don't have any knocking around and don't have the time or inclination to seek it out, feel free to go ahead and make the recipe without it. Instead add ½ tsp each of ground cinnamon and mixed spice to the grains; you won't get that wonderful colour, but they will give a seductive, subtle spiced aroma to the dish.

Put the saffron in a mortar with a generous pinch of salt, then grind it into a fine powder.

Pour the couscous into a large heatproof bowl with the saffron, raisins and lemon zest. Dissolve the stock cube in the measured boiling water, then pour it over the couscous, cover and set aside for 10–15 minutes.

When the grains have absorbed all the liquid, fluff them up with a fork. Dress generously with olive oil and taste. Season with a little salt and pepper, if needed, then add the pomegranate seeds and pine nuts and toss everything together to combine.

——

This will happily sit for a day, even 2 days, in the fridge. Scatter with a few pomegranate seeds and a bit more lemon zest to serve, if you like.

SERVE WITH...
As with the recipe for the more summery couscous salad on the previous page, this will - served generously - stand happy alone for any supper or lunch party. For a true riot of colour on the table, serve alongside BLOOD ORANGE, RED ONION, BLACK OLIVE & BASIL SALAD (p.124), some ROAST RED ONIONS (p.166) - deliciously caramelised in the oven - and BUTTERY CARROTS WITH CHESTNUT HONEY (p.142), cooked until tender and sweet.

AND FOR PUDDING...
If it's around Christmas, I don't think you can improve on PISTACHIO PANETTONE CAKE (p.198), smothered in snowy-white soft meringue. Or, if in a hurry, affogato: a generous scoop of ice cream - made weeks in advance (p.184, 186 or 188), or good shop-bought - drenched in espresso.

TUSCAN PANZANELLA

FOR 6

1 small red onion,
    finely sliced
550g baby tomatoes,
    halved
1 fennel bulb, trimmed
    and roughly sliced
2 tbsp red wine vinegar
6 tbsp extra virgin
    olive oil
50g stale crusty bread,
    such as baguette
    or ciabatta
A handful of black
    olives, pitted
A handful of basil
    leaves, roughly torn
Sea salt flakes

The virtues of a good Tuscan bread salad are manifold: you can make it well in advance and, in fact, it's one of those blessed recipes where the flavours improve and intensify after a day spent in the fridge. You use leftover bread (and pretty much whatever else you have sitting around), so it's also the kind of food you can plausibly throw together for friends (or yourself) at the last minute. And, most importantly, everyone enjoys it: there is something about the way the crusty bread soaks up the grassy oil and sweet tomato juices that always proves irresistible.

The recipe here is for a traditional panzanella, except that I prefer to use fennel in place of cucumber, because I love the crisp texture alongside the juicy tomatoes and I also find it to be more sweetly flavoursome.

Put the onion in a bowl, cover with water and set aside for 10 minutes to mellow the pungent flavour. Meanwhile, chop the fennel.

Drain the onion and pat dry with kitchen towel. Toss the tomatoes, onion and fennel into a large bowl. In a second bowl, combine the vinegar and oil with a generous pinch of salt and whisk lightly to combine. Drizzle over the tomatoes and toss so everything is well coated in the dressing. Roughly tear the bread into pieces, throw it in and toss, so it soaks up all the good juices. Add the olives and toss again.

—

Throw in the basil leaves just before serving, or they wilt in the dressing.

SERVE WITH…
This is lunch-outside-in-the-garden food, or, if you don't have a garden, it's for when you want to create that same relaxed, sunny atmosphere in your kitchen or dining room. To go with it, try something equally light and summery, such as a CARROT, CUMIN & MINT SALAD (p.144), refreshing and crisp, and A REALLY GOOD CHICORY SALAD WITH CREAMY MUSTARD DRESSING (p.110), with torn parsley leaves and peppery radishes (I have a soft spot for the watermelon variety) thrown in. And if you're feeding a small army, then add a SPINACH, MINT & MELTED CHEESE SYRIAN FRITTATA (p.80), just warm and still dripping with melted cheese.

AND FOR PUDDING…
MERINGUES (p.238), dusted in bitter cocoa and piled on a cake stand or a serving dish, with a large bowl of MELON IN GRAPPA SYRUP (p.196).

PANZANELLA WITH GARDEN PEAS & BABY ARTICHOKES

HANDS ON TIME
10 minutes

FOR 4
200g stale crusty bread,
    such as baguette
    or ciabatta
6 tbsp extra virgin
    olive oil
Juice of 1 lemon
150g shelled sweet
    garden peas
6–8 baby artichokes,
    or chargrilled
    artichokes in a jar,
    finely sliced
2 spring onions,
    finely chopped
2 Baby Gem lettuces
A handful of mint
    leaves
A handful of basil
    leaves
Sea salt flakes

Panzanella, in most of its incarnations, is a riot of colour, but this variation is an ode to the verdant plenty of spring: a sumptuous green salad, only amplified. I use those tender baby artichokes that are so small and sweet you can eat the choke, or else the chargrilled kind you find packed in glossy olive oil in jars. Feel free to add to the mix as you please: a few stems of slender asparagus either raw or lightly chargrilled (great for using up any leftovers from p.138), shavings of fennel, or just-blanched, podded broad beans. You could also slip in a few oily, salty anchovies.

Whereas most panzanella will keep – indeed improve in flavour – with time, lettuce tends to wilt if left sitting around for more than 30 minutes. If you want to prepare this in advance, leave out the leaves and soft herbs, then throw them in just before serving.

Roughly tear the bread into pieces and throw it into a large bowl. In a second bowl, combine the olive oil, lemon juice and a generous pinch of salt, whisk vigorously with a fork, then drizzle over the bread. Now add the peas, artichokes and spring onions, then toss together well to dress all the ingredients. (To prepare baby artichokes, if using, see p.58.)

———

When you're ready to go to the table, roughly tear the lettuce leaves, mint and basil, throw them in the bowl, then toss one last time before serving.

SERVE WITH...
Piled high on a pretty serving plate, this is such a pleasing burst of colour and works well as a centrepiece for a light vegetarian lunch. To go with it, maybe something just-warm, like a dish of ROAST STUFFED TOMATOES (p.156) with their buttery gratinated breadcrumbs, and a COURGETTE BLOSSOM & TALEGGIO GALETTE (p.160) with heaps of oozing, melted cheese. If you're in the mood for a more substantial meal, serve this with a tray of HONEY-ROAST POUSSINS (p.94).

AND FOR PUDDING...
After a lighter meal, something quick and easy to throw together, like a large dish of FROZEN BERRIES WITH SAFFRON WHITE CHOCOLATE SAUCE (p.182) would make a lovely fresh choice. And to follow a heartier spread, try something delicate, such as a LAVENDER HONEY or SALTED CARAMEL PANNACOTTA (p.208 and 210).

PANZANELLA WITH TUNA & ANCHOVIES

HANDS ON TIME
15 minutes

FOR 6
1 small red onion,
    finely sliced
500g baby tomatoes,
    halved
2 tbsp red wine vinegar
6 tbsp extra virgin
    olive oil
100g stale crusty bread,
    such as baguette
    or ciabatta
250g tinned tuna,
    drained
4-5 anchovies,
    roughly chopped
A handful of black
    olives, pitted
A handful of mint
    leaves, roughly torn
A handful of parsley
    leaves, roughly torn
Sea salt flakes

I am a big fan of this heartier variation of bread salad. The addition of a tin of tuna – the really good, expensive kind that comes swimming in olive oil – along with a few salty anchovies is what gives this its oomph, and makes it every bit as suitable for a proper supper as a light lunch.

Put the sliced onion in a bowl and cover with cold water, then set aside for 10 minutes or so; this will help mellow its pungent flavour. Drain the onion and pat it dry with kitchen towel, then toss it into a large bowl with the tomatoes. In a second, smaller bowl make the dressing: combine the vinegar and olive oil with a generous pinch of salt and whisk lightly with a fork until well combined. Drizzle over the tomatoes and onion and toss to make sure they're well coated in the juices.

Roughly tear the bread into pieces and throw it in with the tomatoes, tossing together so the bread soaks up all the dressing. Add the tuna, anchovies and olives and toss again.

—

Throw in the mint and parsley leaves as you sit down to eat, then toss for the last time before serving.

SERVE WITH...
The quasi-magical charm of this panzanella is that you really don't need much - if anything - to go with it: a nice bottle of wine and you're pretty much done. But to make a particularly sumptuous meal, add A REALLY GOOD GREEN SALAD (p.112) and perhaps something else green and crisp, such as a plateful of ASPARAGUS WITH LEMON & TOASTED ALMOND GRATIN (p.138).

AND FOR PUDDING...
I love COFFEE MASCARPONE BISCUIT CAKE (p.190), which can also be prepared well in advance. And should figs be in season, you can't go wrong with a HONEY, FIG & WALNUT SEMIFREDDO (p.218).

CARROT & CINNAMON SOUP

HANDS ON TIME
10–15 minutes

HANDS OFF TIME
15–20 minutes simmering

FOR 4
2 tbsp extra virgin
    olive oil, plus extra
    (optional) to serve
1 onion, roughly
    chopped
800g carrots, roughly
    chopped
1.2 litres vegetable
    stock
1 tsp ground cinnamon,
    plus extra (if needed)
Fine sea salt
Freshly ground
    black pepper

For this, you need a bag of carrots, a single onion and a splash of stock made up with a cube (certainly nothing fancy). And yet, by some alchemy, what you end up with is a luxurious velvety soup the deep colour of a Tuscan sunset. Carrots are in ready supply year-round in even the humblest corner shop, making this a gratifying solution to last-minute cooking when you're too busy with the business of life to give proper thought to the shopping.

This can be made in advance and will keep happily in the fridge for up to three days. Otherwise, it freezes like a dream.

Heat the oil in a large saucepan over a medium heat. Add the onion and a generous pinch of salt, then fry gently for 3–5 minutes until soft and translucent. Add the carrots, pour in the stock and bring to the boil. Reduce the heat, cover and simmer for 15 minutes or so, until the carrots are tender. You should be able to insert a butter knife with no resistance.

Take the soup off the heat and blend until creamy and smooth: you can either do this in the pan with a hand-held blender, or pour the soup into a food processor (or blender) and blitz until smooth. Depending on the capacity of your blender, you may need to do this in batches. Pour the soup back into the pan, add the cinnamon and stir until well combined. Taste and season as you fancy with salt, pepper, or more spice.

—

Just before serving, reheat gently, then serve, drizzled with oil if you like.

SERVE WITH…
I have absolutely no shame in serving a soup supper, in fact I rather like it. There is a nourishing, comforting cosiness about it, especially when served with warm bread, such as DAMPER BREAD (p.252). And possibly a plate of charcuterie and/or a few cheeses. You could make it more of a feast, if you like, by adding a salad of sorts (plenty to choose from on p.110 onwards), but to be honest, as long as the soup is plentiful and the bread comes with good salted butter, I don't think you need to. The charm of a soup supper is its very simplicity.

AND FOR PUDDING…
Indulge in a FLOURLESS CHOCOLATE, CHESTNUT & ROSEMARY CAKE (p.234), made from velvety, rich, sugared chestnut purée and dusted in a cloud of icing sugar, and maybe a dollop of clotted cream.

TUSCAN SPRING VEGETABLE SOUP

HANDS ON TIME
15 minutes

HANDS OFF TIME
10-15 minutes simmering

FOR 6
2 tbsp extra virgin
   olive oil
150g chopped pancetta
2 spring onions,
   finely chopped
4 baby artichokes
125g asparagus spears
1.2 litres hot chicken
   stock
100g frozen or fresh
   podded petits pois
100g frozen or fresh
   podded broad beans
Parmesan cheese,
   to serve
Sea salt flakes
Freshly ground
   black pepper

I plonk this down at the centre of the table in an old-fashioned soup tureen, or just the pot it is cooked in, still steaming, for everyone to help themselves. There are few things more warming and comforting than this spring-green broth, bursting with chunky vegetables and rich with flavour. If you can get your hands on them, baby artichokes – so small and tender you eat the choke – are lovely in this soup, but, if you can't find them, just add a few more peas, broad beans or asparagus.

In a large saucepan, heat the olive oil over a medium heat and add the pancetta. Fry for 3–5 minutes until the bacon has crisped slightly. Now add the spring onions and cook for 2–3 minutes until they have softened.

Tear away the tougher outer leaves of the baby artichokes, cut the top 2–3cm off the heads and trim the stalks, halve each one from top to tail, then cut into wedges, if they are larger. Pop these into the pan with the pancetta and spring onions and give everything a good stir. Now chop the asparagus into 3–5cm-long pieces and add them to the pan, too.

Cook for 5–10 minutes until the vegetables are lightly coloured but still quite tough. If they're browning too much, add a little stock. Now toss in the peas and broad beans and pour in the stock. Simmer for 10 minutes or so, until the vegetables are tender. Taste the soup and season as you like.

——

Make this up to a day in advance, store it in the fridge, then gently reheat. Serve piping hot with bread and copious quantities of shaved Parmesan.

SERVE WITH...
Soup, in my view, categorically needs bread, and if you make your own so it is still warm and the butter melts as you smear it on, it will go a long way towards making an otherwise quite humble meal memorable. My friend Sarah's **WALNUT SODA BREAD** (p.254) is particularly good for this: it's improbably easy to knock up (no need for yeast or proving) and you can plausibly make it when you walk in after work, then cook the soup while the bread bakes (unless you made it that morning).

AND FOR PUDDING...
You can, I feel, afford to be extravagant with pudding in this instance. As it is spring, serve the three creamy tiers of **SUMMER BERRY CLOUD CAKE** (p.240).

SPAGHETTI WITH CREAMY LEMON SAUCE

HANDS ON TIME
20-25 minutes

FOR 4
2 lemons
4 tbsp extra virgin
    olive oil
220ml single cream
1 egg yolk
350g spaghetti
A small bunch of thyme
Fine sea salt
Freshly ground
    black pepper

I don't often trust myself to cook pasta for more than four people, because the timings are too delicate. As they say in Naples: 'people wait for pasta, not the other way round.' Overcooked pasta is a cook's worst nightmare, while pasta eaten cold when it should be hot is not much better. But this recipe – like eating a bowl of sunshine – is so simple that even I can happily chat and bring it together at the same time. I prepare the sauce in advance and leave it covered on the hob, then, while the pasta is bubbling, slice the lemon, shuffle everyone to the table and assemble the dish once they are sitting down, so they eat it hot.

Bring a large saucepan of water to the boil. Meanwhile, finely zest both the lemons and toss the zest into a deep frying pan, then add the olive oil and set it over a medium heat. Gently fry the zest for a few minutes until it begins to take on a deep, vibrant yellow colour.

Now pour in the cream and the egg yolk, mix well with a wooden spoon, then reduce the heat and leave to gently cook for 5–10 minutes, giving it a stir every now and then.

—

Add a generous pinch of salt to the boiling water, and, when it begins to gallop, add the spaghetti and cook until *al dente* according to the packet instructions. Finely slice one-third of a lemon.

When the pasta is cooked, drain in a colander, reserving a little of the cooking water (roughly ¼ cup). Squeeze the juice of the remaining lemons into the sauce, add salt and pepper to taste, then toss the pasta into the frying pan. Add the reserved cooking water, throw in the lemon slices and toss everything together so the pasta is well covered with sauce. Tear up the thyme sprigs, sprinkle generously over and serve immediately.

SERVE WITH...
You need little more with this, as it's pretty much a meal in itself.
Perhaps a nice green salad with OLGA'S PEPPERY VINAIGRETTE (p.260).

AND FOR PUDDING...
Something easy-going, such as a LAVENDER HONEY PANNACOTTA
(p.208), or STRAWBERRIES IN LEMONY SYRUP (p.192).

TAGLIATELLE WITH GORGONZOLA, PEAR & WALNUT

HANDS ON TIME
15–20 minutes

FOR 4
350g tagliatelle
80ml single cream
450g Gorgonzola cheese, chopped
1 large or 2 small pears
A handful of whole walnuts
Fine sea salt
Freshly ground black pepper (optional)

If the Spaghetti with Creamy Lemon Sauce on the previous page is innately summery, this is its warming winter counterpart: an indulgently rich balm to soothe body and soul in the bitter cold. The pear and walnut are by no means essential, in fact a plate of tagliatelle drenched in just the creamy, peppery cheese sauce is pure joy. However, the chunks of fruit add a delicate sweetness that cuts through the intense richness of the sauce and it's little extra effort to throw them in.

This dish breaks all my rules of stress-free cooking for friends, as it can in no way be prepared in advance. But it's so simple to make that I feel comfortable and happy serving it to company, though I would baulk at cooking it for more than six, because the delicate timings of the pasta become too unwieldy for my peace of mind.

Fill a large saucepan with water, add a generous pinch of salt and bring to the boil. When the water is galloping, add the pasta and cook until *al dente* according to the packet instructions.

Meanwhile, pour the cream into a small saucepan and add the cheese, then set over a medium-low heat and stir occasionally until the cheese has almost completely melted. Core the pear(s) and slice finely, then roughly chop the nuts.

Drain the pasta in a colander, reserving a little of the cooking water (roughly ¼ cup), toss in the cheese sauce and reserved cooking water, then, just before serving, toss through the pear and walnut pieces. Add a little black pepper, if you like, and serve immediately.

SERVE WITH...
The pasta needs nothing to go with it and its one-pan-ness and nursery food-like simplicity are a great part of its charm, for both cook and guest. But, if you really want, you could offer a plate of BRESAOLA E GRANA (p.44), either to start or to follow.

AND FOR PUDDING...
CHOCOLATE CHESTNUT MERINGUE CAKE (p.242), like a towering pavlova filled with whipped cream and sugared chestnuts. Or, in that magical moment when winter is at its last burst and spring is burgeoning, make the most of the pinker-than-pink – almost fuchsia coloured – rhubarb, and make a blushing PINK RHUBARB & PROSECCO JELLY (p.222).

RIGATONI WITH MASCARPONE & PANCETTA

HANDS ON TIME
15-20 minutes

FOR 4
350g rigatoni
1 tbsp extra virgin
    olive oil
120g pancetta, chopped
100g mascarpone
2 egg yolks
40g Parmesan or
    pecorino cheese,
    grated
Fine sea salt
Freshly ground
    black pepper

This is halfway to a carbonara, but with a generous dollop of creamy mascarpone mixed in, so richer and – if possible – even more comforting to eat. You could also make this with a coarsely chopped piece of prosciutto cotto in place of the fried pancetta, if you don't want to use (and wash up) a second pan, or leave out the meat entirely and increase the quantity of cheese a little, then top with an extravagant flurry of black pepper.

Bring a large, generously salted pan of water to the boil and cook the pasta until *al dente* according to the packet instructions.

Meanwhile, heat the oil in a frying pan over a medium heat, then toss in the pancetta and fry for 5 minutes or so, until crisp. Combine the mascarpone, egg yolks and grated cheese in a mixing bowl and stir until smooth. Season to taste with salt and pepper, bearing in mind that the pancetta is salty.

When the pasta is cooked, scoop out about half a cup of the cooking water. Drain the pasta in a colander, then toss it back into the saucepan. Add the mascarpone cream and the reserved cooking water and give everything a good stir. Now add the pancetta, season again to taste and serve immediately.

SERVE WITH...
This is fast food in every sense. Its joy lies in its immediacy and simplicity, so you want to keep the rest of menu as simple as possible too. A plate of good pasta and a nice salad, in my view, is enough, but if you wanted to do something more, then throw together a dish of BRESAOLA E GRANA (p.44) to put at the centre of the table. And make sure there is plenty of bread, whether DAMPER BREAD (p.252), or WALNUT SODA BREAD (p.254), or good shop-bought.

AND FOR PUDDING...
PINE NUT ICE CREAM 'AFFOGATO' (p.188) drenched with hot, bitter coffee, or affogato made with good shop-bought ice cream.

SAUSAGES WITH GRAPES

HANDS ON TIME
10 minutes

HANDS OFF TIME
25-30 minutes

FOR 4
1 tbsp extra virgin
   olive oil
8 pork sausages
500g red grapes
240ml white wine
1 tsp cornflour

The recipe for this comes from Pellegrino Artusi's classic *Science in the Kitchen and the Art of Eating Well,* via Colman Andrews's wonderfully nostalgic book, *The Country Cooking of Italy*. Like the pasta dishes before this, it's one of a handful of recipes in this book where all the cooking happens at the last minute. I have included it nonetheless, because the ingredients – sausages, grapes and a bottle of wine – can easily be picked up pretty much anywhere, and because it lends itself so well to last-minute cosy kitchen suppers.

Andrews's recipe calls for Italian sausages, but I prefer humble British sausages, which, made with a healthy dose of breadcrumbs, are not quite as rich and fatty to eat. Any kind of good pork sausage will do, but buy the very best quality you can find.

Heat the oil in a deep frying pan or heavy-based casserole over a low heat, then add the sausages. Cook for 5–6 minutes, turning occasionally, until browned all over. Now add the grapes, snipped into small bunches, then pour in the wine, increasing the heat to medium-high as you do so.

Bring to the boil, then reduce the heat to low and simmer gently, uncovered, for a further 15–20 minutes until the sausages are cooked through and the wine has evaporated by half. Using a slotted spoon, lift the sausages and grapes from the pan and set on a serving dish.

To make a sauce, mix the cornflour with 1 tbsp of the cooking liquid in a small bowl, then add this to the juices in the pan. Bring to the boil, stirring, and simmer for 2 minutes until thickened, then serve with the sausages and sweet grapes.

SERVE WITH...
This is comfort food and it needs almost nothing to go with it apart from A REALLY GOOD CHICORY SALAD WITH CREAMY MUSTARD DRESSING (p.110) and some good bread for either mopping up the juices, or even for improvising a hot sausage sandwich with the meat and the sweet grapes. If you feel the need for some warming vegetables as well, try FENNEL & PARMESAN PURÉE (p.136), akin to mashed potato but rather more delicate in flavour.

AND FOR PUDDING...
PISTACHIO, MASCARPONE & SALTED CARAMEL CHEESECAKE (p.214) is an absolute dream.

ALLEGRA'S POT-ROAST BEEF

HANDS ON TIME
10 minutes

HANDS OFF TIME
35-60 minutes cooking,
   to taste
15-20 minutes resting

FOR 4
1kg silverside of beef
4 tbsp extra virgin
   olive oil
1 onion, finely chopped
1 carrot, finely chopped
1 celery stick,
   finely chopped
1 vegetable stock cube
A few thyme sprigs
100ml white wine
Sea salt flakes
Freshly ground
   black pepper

My friend Allegra swears by this way of cooking beef, which is what she grew up with as a child in rural Tuscany. The novelty of her recipe lies in the fact that you roast the meat gently on the hob rather than in the oven: it comes out browned at the edges, deliciously juicy at its centre and imbued with the flavours of the wine and stock throughout.

Rub the beef with 2 tbsp of the olive oil, salt and pepper. Put a large frying pan over a very high heat and sear the beef for 1–2 minutes on all sides. Take it out of the pan and set aside on a plate.

Heat the remaining 2 tbsp of olive oil over a medium-high heat in a large, deep, heavy-based saucepan, add the onion, carrot and celery with a pinch of salt and cook gently for 5 minutes or so, until translucent and softened. Lower the joint of beef into the pan over the chopped veg. Crumble in the stock cube, add the thyme sprigs and pour over the wine. Cover the pan and cook for 35 minutes for medium-rare, 45 minutes for medium, or 1 hour for well done.

———

Allow to rest for 15–20 minutes before carving. Serve with the vegetables and juices from the pan.

SERVE WITH...
Beef, I always feel, works particularly well with A REALLY GOOD TOMATO SALAD (p.114), as the acidity of the tomatoes complements the fatty richness of the meat. For the rest, you need lots of mustard, and I like mayonnaise (even TRUFFLE MAYONNAISE, p.264), which is by no means a canonical combination with beef, but great nonetheless. And then potatoes: baby ROAST NEW POTATOES WITH BAY LEAVES (p.152), cooked until the skins turn golden.

AND FOR PUDDING...
A bowl of poached AMBROSIAL APRICOTS (p.224), tender and soft, swimming in a syrup of sweet honey and peppered with verdant pistachios, are divine on their own, or, if you want to go all out, even better alongside a LAVENDER HONEY PANNACOTTA (p.208).

OSSOBUCO WITH SAGE & LEMON

HANDS ON TIME
30 minutes

HANDS OFF TIME
2–2¼ hours

FOR 4
4 ossobuco pieces
25g plain flour, to dust
8 tbsp extra virgin
  olive oil
50g salted butter,
  plus extra to reheat
  (if needed)
¼ onion, finely chopped
1 fennel bulb, finely
  chopped
2 celery sticks,
  finely chopped
3 pared strips of
  lemon zest
A small bunch of
  sage leaves
200ml white wine
200ml chicken stock
Sea salt flakes

This recipe defies ossobuco convention by omitting the rich tomato sauce you would usually expect; instead I prefer a delicately flavoured *soffritto* of fennel, onion and celery, with a few strips of lemon zest and copious sage. The result is heavenly, buttery and means that, while meaty, this version translates equally well to spring, late summer or full-blown winter suppers. The key to making ossobuco well is not to overcrowd the dish; depending on how big the pieces of meat are, you should be able to squeeze four or five into a large casserole dish. If you want to cook it for ten, you'll need two casseroles bubbling away on the hob.

Dust the meat in flour. Add half the oil to a casserole dish wide enough to hold the pieces of ossobuco in a single layer, set it over a high heat, add 2 pieces of meat and brown on both sides for roughly 5 minutes, until golden and crusted. Set aside and repeat with the rest of the oil and meat.

Reduce the heat to medium. Add three-quarters of the butter and, when it melts, the onion, fennel, celery and a generous pinch of salt, then cook until soft. Add the lemon zest and sage leaves and cook for a few minutes more. Increase the heat to high and pour in the wine. Lay all the meat back in the dish over the vegetables and let the wine bubble away until reduced by half. Pour in the stock and return to a simmer. Cover the dish, reduce the heat to low and leave to simmer for 2–2½ hours, turning the meat every 30 minutes or so, until the ossobuco is tender enough to cut with a spoon.

——

Add the last of the butter to the dish and leave it to melt before serving. You can make this up to 3 days ahead and store, covered, in the fridge. Just reheat it very gently with a little more butter before serving.

SERVE WITH…
The Milanese eat ossobuco with saffron risotto… a little too rich for my taste and rather too labour-intensive. I prefer it with a lighter FENNEL & PARMESAN PURÉE (p.136), that you can also make in advance. And then a sharp citrusy salad, such as BLOOD ORANGE, RED ONION, BLACK OLIVE & BASIL SALAD (p.124) is just the right sweet tanginess to cut through the fat of the meat. You could also, if cooking for a crowd, treat them to a dish of ROAST NEW POTATOES WITH BAY LEAVES (p.152).

AND FOR PUDDING…
Sweet snowy white MERINGUES (p.238), drenched with bitter cocoa.

POULET ANGLAIS

HANDS ON TIME
20-25 minutes

HANDS OFF TIME
15 minutes

FOR 6–8
1 litre chicken or
    vegetable stock
6 skinless chicken
    breasts
250g plain yogurt
1 tsp poppy seeds
1 medium cucumber,
    peeled, deseeded
    and finely chopped
2 shallots, finely
    chopped
A small bunch of
    tarragon, leaves
    roughly chopped,
    plus extra to serve
Sea salt flakes
Freshly ground
    black pepper

The name of this dish rolls off the tongue with a nostalgic, Constance Spry-esque quality that I find oddly pleasing. It is a relic from my childhood, my mother's go-to dish for light lunches when I was growing up. It is somehow very soothing to eat and, laid out on a large plate with the sauce either on the side or splashed casually over the chicken, has the kind of inviting, relaxed quality that I love.

Because the meat is served cold, delicately and thinly sliced, then smothered in a refreshing yogurty sauce, it is a dish that I associate with summer. My mother always made it for picnics: the yogurt sauce in one jar, for dipping, and the chicken breasts still whole and swimming in a generous dousing of their cooled cooking juices, in a second, larger jar.

Bring the stock to the boil in a large saucepan over a medium-high heat. Reduce the heat to a gentle simmer, add the chicken breasts and poach for 15 minutes, until cooked through and tender. Remove the chicken from the stock and set aside while you make the yogurt sauce. When it is cold, douse it in some of the cooking juices and store, covered, in the fridge.

In a large bowl, combine the yogurt, poppy seeds, cucumber, shallots and tarragon and stir until blended. Season with salt and pepper as you like, then store covered in the fridge until you're ready to serve.

—

Just before sitting down to eat, slice the chicken breasts and arrange on a serving dish, then drizzle over the creamy sauce and scatter with a little more tarragon.

SERVE WITH...
The fact that it can - in all its parts - be prepared well in advance makes this ideal for larger gatherings, whether low-key or more extravagant. Serve with a big dish of NEW POTATOES WITH LEMON & SAMPHIRE (p.126) and perhaps something crisp and green such as a BABY ARTICHOKE, FENNEL & PECORINO SALAD (p.122).

AND FOR PUDDING...
You might want to go for a celebratory cake, such as COFFEE & WALNUT CAKE (p.236), layered with mascarpone buttercream icing, for the full retro experience.

WHOLE POACHED COLD SALMON

HANDS ON TIME
5 minutes, plus
    10 minutes if you
    decorate the fish

HANDS OFF TIME
15-20 minutes cooking
4-5 hours cooling

FOR 10, WITH LEFTOVERS
1 whole salmon
    (2.5-2.75kg)
1 lemon, cut into
    wedges, plus extra
    to serve
1 quantity Home-Made
    Mayonnaise (p.262,
    optional)
1 quantity Salsa Verde
    (p.266, optional)
Finely sliced lemon
    and cucumber,
    to decorate (optional)
Fine sea salt

The recipe for this comes from Arabella Boxer's wonderful *Book of English Food: A Rediscovery of British Food From Before the War* and indeed there is something nostalgic, utterly classic, about it. The dish is blissfully simple. Traditionally, you decorate it with fine slices of cucumber and lemon, though I tend to just skin the fish, set it on a dish or board and serve with sharp lemon wedges and a big bowl of thick mayonnaise or salsa verde.

Arrange the whole fish in a fish kettle (or roasting tray) so that it fits comfortably. If the pan is too big for the fish, or if it fits it too tightly without enough space for the right amount of water, it will affect the cooking time. Cover with cold water, add a generous amount of salt and throw in the lemon wedges. Cover (either with a lid or – if you don't have one that will fit – foil will do fine), set over a low heat and bring to the boil on the hob. When the water is boiling, turn off the heat and leave the fish to sit in the water until completely cooled; this will take 4–5 hours.

While the fish rests, you can make the mayonnaise or salsa verde, or both. When the salmon is cold, remove it from the water and allow it to dry.

—

Shortly before eating, peel the skin from the salmon and decorate the fish with finely sliced lemon and cucumber, or simply offer lemon wedges, as you prefer, and serve with the mayonnaise and/or salsa verde.

SERVE WITH...
This really is designed for big parties, because, while impressive to look at and eat, it's so simple to make that you will have plenty of time to get on with other things. Serve with GREEN BEANS WITH BABY TOMATOES (p.140), and a salad of NEW POTATOES WITH LEMON & SAMPHIRE (p.126) and the HOME-MADE MAYONNAISE (p.262) or SALSA VERDE (p.266) - or both - on the side.

AND FOR PUDDING...
Definitely SUMMER BERRY CLOUD CAKE (p.240).

TORTA PASQUALINA

HANDS ON TIME
30 minutes

HANDS OFF TIME
1¼ hours in the oven
10 minutes resting

FOR 6
2 tbsp extra virgin
    olive oil
750g frozen spinach
2 × 320g sheets ready
    rolled, all-butter
    puff pastry
4 eggs, plus
    1 extra for glazing
250g ricotta
120g pecorino cheese,
    grated
A good grating
    of nutmeg
3 anchovies
Fine sea salt
Freshly ground
    black pepper

Italian custom dictates that you eat this pie at Easter, hence the name, which literally translates as 'Easter cake'. The recipe, which dates back to the 15th century, is rich with symbolism: the eggs represent rebirth and the onset of spring. And it is the eggs – cooked whole in the pie, so when you slice into it, a riot of verdant green with a circle of white and a second of sunny yellow yolk awaits you – that make it so special. The anchovies are not traditional, but I love that extra touch of saltiness; they melt into the background and you will find that even those who profess not to like anchovies enjoy it.

You can eat the pie warm, in which case you should prepare it up to the point at which you brush it with a glaze of yellow egg, cover and store it in the fridge for up to a day, then bake when you need to. Or, after baking, store in the fridge and eat at room temperature (it will keep for up to two days).

Heat the oven to 190°C/fan 170°C/Gas 5.

Pour the oil into a large, deep frying pan and set over a medium heat. Add the spinach and cook for 5–10 minutes, or until completely defrosted. Set aside until cool enough to handle, then drain the spinach and squeeze out any excess liquid with your hands. This is important, as otherwise the liquid from the spinach will seep into the pastry as it cooks and give your pie a soggy bottom.

While the spinach is cooking, roll out the first sheet of puff pastry into a circle large enough to line a 23cm springform cake tin with a little overhang. Using the rolling pin, drape it into the tin, pressing it into the bottom. Prick it all over the base with a fork (this stops the pastry from puffing up too much), cover with baking parchment, fill with rice or baking beans and blind bake for 15–20 minutes, until the edges are very lightly coloured. Remove the parchment and the baking beans from the tin and return it to the oven for a further 5 minutes, until the pastry is dry to the touch and still only lightly coloured. Leave to cool.

Reduce the oven temperature to 180°C/fan 160°C/Gas 4.

Crack 1 of the eggs into a mixing bowl and beat lightly with a fork, then add both cheeses and whisk again with the fork until well combined. Spoon in the spinach and give everything a good stir. Now add the grated nutmeg, season with salt and pepper to taste and stir again until well combined.

Spoon the spinach filling into the cooled pastry case and spread it out evenly. Using the back of a spoon, make 3 deep indentations, equally spaced apart, in the spinach. Lay an anchovy in each of the nooks, then carefully crack in a whole egg, so it sits nestled in there.

Take the second sheet of pastry, drape it over the top, trim away any excess and press the edges together with those of the pastry base to seal. Use a sharp knife to cut 2–3 slits into the pastry to allow the steam to escape, then decorate – if you like – with the pastry offcuts.

—

When you're ready to bake the pie, crack the last egg into a small cup, whisk lightly with a fork, then brush it over the top of the pie.

Bake the pie for 45 minutes. To test if it's done, the top should be crisp and golden and – if you slide a knife through a steam hole right down to the base – its tip should feel hot to the touch. If the pie is browning too fast during the cooking time, and it looks like the pastry might catch, just cover the top with foil. Remove from the oven and allow to cool for 5–10 minutes, then release the sides of the tin, place it on a plate and serve slightly warm, or at room temperature. Once cooled, cover and keep in the fridge for up to 2 days.

SERVE WITH...
Traditionally you eat this at Easter, as part of your celebratory feast alongside a roast. I'd add ASPARAGUS WITH LEMON & TOASTED ALMOND GRATIN (p.138) and a verdant dish of AN EMBARRASSMENT OF SPRING VEGETABLES (p.146). Or it would make a lovely centrepiece for a picnic on Easter Monday. It is, in fact, perfect picnic food, as each slice is almost a complete meal. To go with it, pack a selection of cheeses, some charcuterie and a chilled soup such as GAZPACHO (p.40) in a vacuum flask.

AND FOR PUDDING...
A tin of crisp white MERINGUES (p.238) and a tub of clotted cream to go with them.

Pictured overleaf →

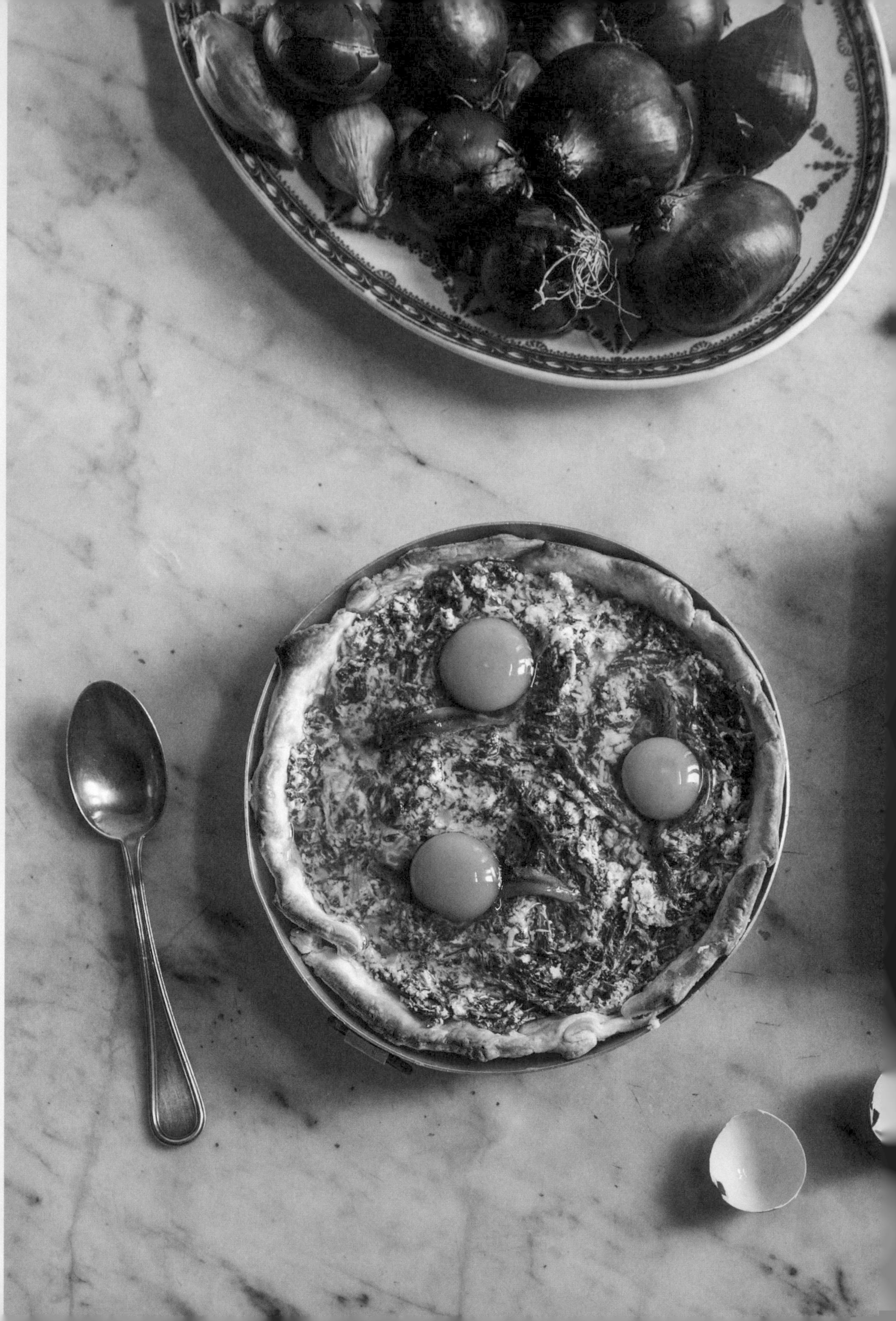

SPINACH, MINT & MELTED CHEESE SYRIAN FRITTATA

HANDS ON TIME
20 minutes

HANDS OFF TIME
40 minutes

FOR 6–8
2 tbsp extra virgin
    olive oil
1 red onion, roughly
    chopped
500g frozen spinach
5 eggs
125g mozzarella cheese,
    roughly chopped
100g feta cheese,
    roughly chopped
350g provolone cheese
    (or mild Cheddar
    cheese), grated
150g cottage cheese
Leaves from a small
    bunch of mint,
    roughly chopped
Fine sea salt

This is the most blissfully cheesy concoction, rather like the very middle (the creamiest bit) of a good quiche. And while it might look unassuming, much like any other frittata, it is the absolute embodiment of comfort food, served still in its frying pan. The recipe comes from Poopa Dweck's wonderful book on Syrian food, *Aromas of Aleppo,* barely adapted other than to add even more cheese and a mix of different kinds.

Heat the oven to 190°C/fan 170°C/Gas 5. Pour the oil into a large, deep frying pan and set over a medium heat. Throw in the onion and cook for about 5 minutes, until it softens and becomes translucent. Add the spinach and cook for a further 5–10 minutes, until completely defrosted.

Meanwhile, crack the eggs into a large mixing bowl and beat lightly with a fork. Add all 4 cheeses and stir with a wooden spoon until well combined.

Take the spinach and onion mixture off the heat and allow to cool for a few minutes (or completely), then mix it in with the eggs and cheese and add the mint. Finally add a pinch of salt; take care not to overdo it, as the feta is already quite salty. Spoon the mixture back into the frying pan (if it's ovenproof), or into an ovenproof baking dish, ready to go in the oven. It will keep in the fridge like this, covered, for 1–2 days.

——

When you're ready to cook the frittata, bake it in the middle of the oven for 40 minutes, until lightly golden on top. Serve warm. It really does taste best straight out of the oven, when it is still gooey and cheesy in the middle, although I would not turn my nose up at leftovers heated up again the next day, perhaps with a crunchy green salad or some fresh tomatoes.

SERVE WITH...
I like to add a couple of side dishes of FRIED BROCCOLI WITH BLACK OLIVES (p.128) and A REALLY GOOD TOMATO SALAD (p.114), for a light summer lunch or quick midweek supper.

AND FOR PUDDING...
The ambrosial PISTACHIO BUTTER CAKE WITH MARZIPAN ICING (p.232) pays homage, in a small way, to the frittata's Middle Eastern heritage.

TORTA DI MACCHERONI

HANDS ON TIME
30-40 minutes

HANDS OFF TIME
30-40 minutes
  in the oven
10 minutes resting

FOR 6
2 × 320g sheets ready
  rolled, all-butter
  puff pastry
250g short pasta, such
  as macaroni or penne
2 tbsp extra virgin
  olive oil
1 red onion, finely
  chopped
100g finely chopped
  pancetta
280ml single cream
1 tsp saffron strands
80g Parmesan cheese,
  grated
80g Gruyère cheese,
  grated
120g Taleggio cheese,
  chopped
1 egg
Fine sea salt
Freshly ground
  black pepper

I have long fantasised about the *torta di maccheroni* described in such mouth-watering detail at the beginning of Giuseppe di Lampedusa's *The Leopard*. Lampedusa's pie is a magnificent affair filled with steaming-hot pasta, chicken livers, hard-boiled eggs, sliced ham, chicken and truffles. My recipe, undoubtedly and unabashedly, is a simpler concoction of macaroni, cream, golden saffron, salty-fatty pancetta and oozing melted cheese. But I love it.

This really does taste best straight from the oven, so the buttery pastry melts in your mouth and the creamy filling drips with melted cheese. For peace of mind, I usually assemble the pie in advance, keep it in the fridge for up to a day, then glaze it and bake when needed, allowing ten minutes more in the oven to account for it coming straight from the fridge.

Heat the oven to 190°C/fan 170°C/Gas 5. Roll out the first sheet of puff pastry into a circle large enough to line a 23cm springform cake tin with a little overhang. Using the rolling pin, drape it into the tin, pressing it into the bottom. Prick it all over the base with a fork (this stops the pastry from puffing up too much), cover with baking parchment, fill with baking beans or rice and blind bake for 15–20 minutes, until the edges are very lightly coloured. Remove the parchment and the baking beans from the tin and return it to the oven for a further 5 minutes, until the pastry is dry to the touch and still only very lightly coloured.

Meanwhile, bring a large saucepan of heavily salted water to the boil. When the water begins to gallop, add the pasta and cook until very *al dente* (roughly 3 minutes less than it says on the packet; you want the pasta slightly undercooked, as it will cook more in the oven when it bakes).

Set a saucepan over a medium heat and spoon in the oil. Toss in the onion with a generous pinch of salt and cook for 3–5 minutes, until soft and translucent. Now add the pancetta and fry for 3–5 minutes, until cooked through and crisping a little. Take off the heat, add the cream and saffron and give it a good stir so the sauce takes on a majestic deep yellow colour.

When the pasta is cooked, reserve half a cup of its cooking water and drain the rest in a colander. Throw the pasta back into its saucepan and pour over the sauce with the reserved cooking water. Add the Parmesan and Gruyère and stir until each little pasta tube is coated in cream and melted cheese. Season with black pepper to taste. Let cool to room temperature or thereabouts, bearing in mind that if you try to assemble the pie while the pasta is hot, it tends to melt the pastry and make it hard to work with.

Spoon the cooled pasta into the par-baked pastry shell, filling it right up to the edge, and dot the little chunks of Taleggio here and there, nestling them in among the pasta. Now take the second sheet of pastry, drape it over the pie, trim off any excess and press the edges together with those of the pastry base to seal. Use a knife to cut 4 slits into the pastry to allow steam to escape. Collect any spare bits of pastry and use to decorate the pie, if you like, then cover and set in the fridge for up to a day.

—

When it's coming up to time to eat, crack the egg into a small bowl, lightly beat it with a fork, then use a pastry brush to paint a sunny glaze over the top and edges of the pie. Set in the oven and bake for 30 minutes (40 minutes if straight from the fridge), until golden brown and the filling is completely heated through. To test if it's done, the top should be crisp and golden and – if you slide a knife through a steam hole right down to the base – its tip should feel hot to the touch. Remove from the oven and allow to cool for 5–10 minutes, then release the sides of the tin, place the torta on a plate and serve warm.

SERVE WITH…
This feels like birthday party food. And indeed it is exactly the kind of thing I might prepare two of (perhaps one without pancetta, for any vegetarian guests) for a birthday dinner for up to fourteen people. The pies are so rich that they need little to go with them; perhaps try dishes of shimmering BEETROOT & MINT SALAD (p.118), swimming in scarlet-hued juices, and a plate of good cheeses and some nice bread, if you want. Add a peppery, crisp salad such as A REALLY GOOD CHICORY SALAD WITH CREAMY MUSTARD DRESSING (p.110) and you're pretty much done.

AND FOR PUDDING…
Birthday cake, of course. COFFEE & WALNUT CAKE (p.236), layered with rich mascarpone cream and topped with an extravagant posy of seasonal flowers… and birthday candles.

Pictured overleaf →

TAGLIATELLE GRATIN

HANDS ON TIME
20-30 minutes

HANDS OFF TIME
35 minutes

FOR 4-6
FOR THE PASTA
350g tagliatelle
60g salted butter
100g chopped pancetta
90g Parmesan cheese,
    grated
Fine sea salt

FOR THE BÉCHAMEL
40g salted butter
40g plain flour,
    preferably type '00'
330ml whole milk
A good grating
    of nutmeg
Freshly ground
    black pepper

This recipe is very loosely adapted from the tagliolini baked in a sumptuous Parmesan béchamel that they serve at Venice's iconic Harry's Bar. I first made this at home after I ate it at the restaurant and found myself craving more. What I have discovered since is that it also – like most baked pasta dishes, for that matter – lends itself wonderfully well to large gatherings. Firstly, it's the kind of food that everyone loves. And secondly, it can be made well in advance – even a day or so ahead – covered and stored in the fridge, then simply warmed in the oven until golden and bubbly. If you have vegetarians among your number, leave out the pancetta, which is salty and delicious but not integral, and season the already cheesy sauce with a more generous dash of Parmesan.

Heat the oven to 220°C/fan 200°C/Gas 7. Fill a large saucepan with cold water, add a generous pinch of salt and bring to the boil.

While the water heats, make the béchamel: spoon the butter into a small saucepan set over a very low heat, stirring until melted. The moment it becomes liquid, add the flour and stir vigorously until a thick paste forms, then continue to stir over the heat for a minute, for the flour to cook. Add a splash of the milk and keep stirring until it becomes a thick cream. Keep stirring constantly as you slowly pour in the rest of the milk, then keep going until the sauce begins to thicken to the texture of a soft custard. Take it off the heat, season with salt, pepper and nutmeg and set aside.

When the water is boiling, add the tagliatelle and cook until *al dente* (5–6 minutes), bearing in mind that the pasta will cook more once it is in the oven. Meanwhile, spoon one-third of the butter into a large frying pan set over a medium heat. As the butter begins to melt, add the pancetta and fry until cooked through.

When the pasta is ready, drain it and add to the frying pan. Add another one-third of the butter and sprinkle with half the Parmesan, then toss together until the pasta is well coated in cheese, with crisp pieces of pancetta running through it.

Spoon into an ovenproof casserole dish (about 1.5-litre capacity) and spread it out evenly. Pour the béchamel over the pasta and sprinkle with what is left of the cheese, then cut the remaining butter into small pieces and scatter them over the top. Cover and set in the fridge for up to a day.

———

When you want to eat, place the dish at the top of the oven and cook for 15–20 minutes (or a little longer, a further 10 minutes or so, if you've taken the dish from the fridge), until golden brown and bubbling on top. To test if the pasta is warmed through, insert a knife to the very centre of the dish: when you take it out, the tip should feel hot to touch. Serve immediately while still hot.

SERVE WITH...
All this needs is a crisp, fresh green salad dressed with a sharp, mustardy dressing such as OLGA'S PEPPERY VINAIGRETTE (p.260), or olive oil and a squeeze of lemon juice as on p.112, whichever you prefer. You could of course cook more, but that would be to over-gild an already magnificent lily.

AND FOR PUDDING...
Something light to compensate for all that richness: DRUNKEN STRAWBERRIES (p.194) in a sweet red wine syrup or, for special occasions, LEMON MERINGUE CAKE (p.244). Or - frankly - both.

Pictured overleaf →

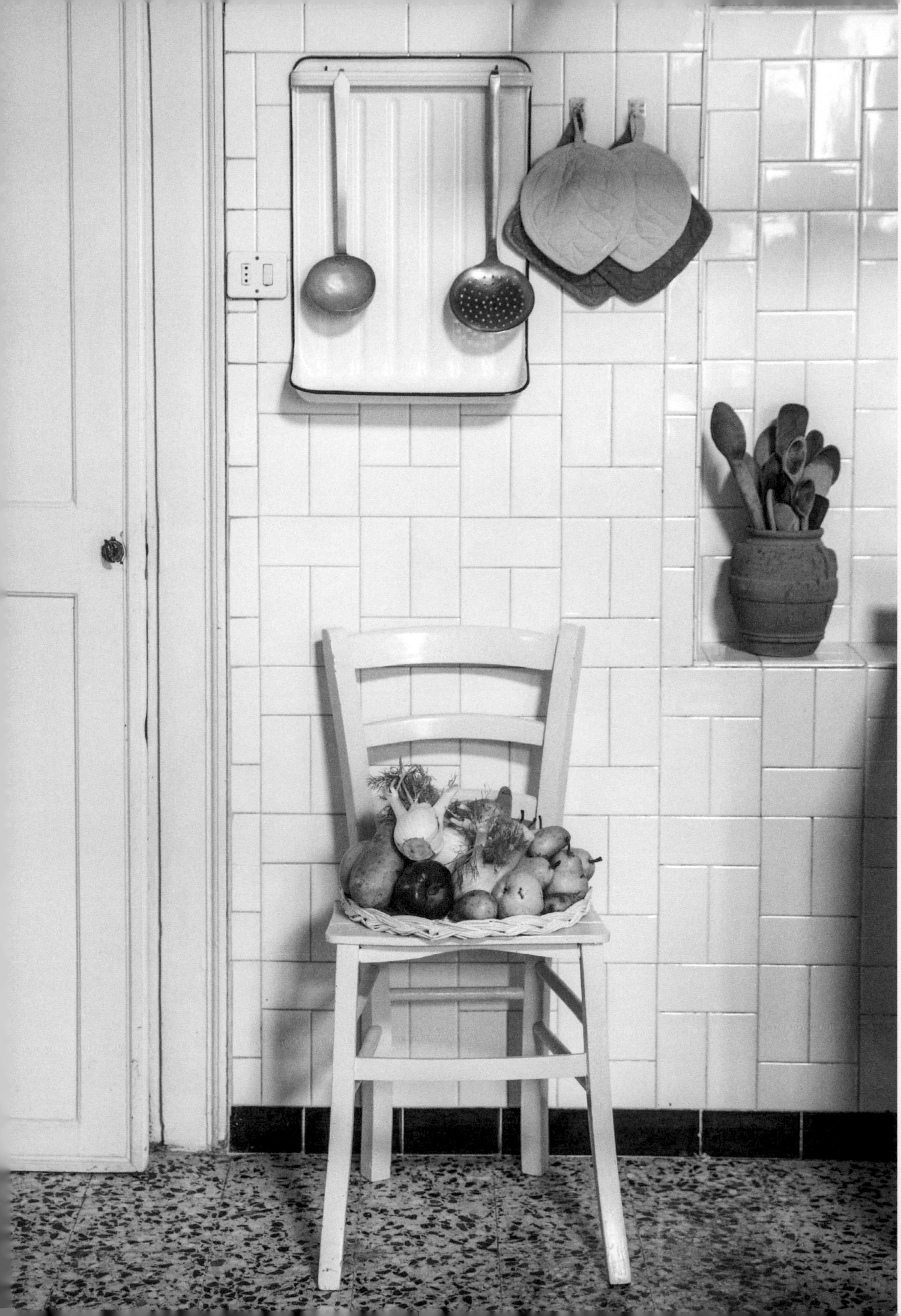

APHRODITE'S ROAST CHICKEN

HANDS ON TIME
10-15 minutes

HANDS OFF TIME
1 hour 10 minutes
   cooking
10 minutes resting

FOR 4
4 potatoes
4 tbsp extra virgin
   olive oil
1 small chicken, about
   1.4kg, preferably
   organic
1 lemon
A large bunch
   of rosemary
2 garlic cloves
Sea salt flakes
Freshly ground
   black pepper

This recipe comes from my mother's friend, Aphrodite, and is to my mind (smallest of puns intended) truly food of the gods. Its charm lies in its simplicity: the bird roasts on a bed of very finely sliced potatoes, which crisp to golden around the edges of the tin, while those directly under the chicken are soft and deliciously imbued with the rich cooking juices. The trick is to make sure that you get a little bit of both kinds of potato on your plate.

You can happily prepare this a few hours before you're ready to roast the chicken, cover and store in the fridge. Just don't slice the potatoes more than four hours or so ahead, as they may brown or curl.

Heat the oven to 200°C/fan 180°C/Gas 6. Finely slice the potatoes into rounds 3–5mm thick, using a mandolin if you have one. Arrange in a single layer over the bottom of a large roasting dish, overlapping them. I do this in a round 32cm tarte Tatin dish, but whatever you have to hand will do. Drizzle with 1 tbsp of the olive oil and season generously.

Set the chicken in the dish, nestled over the potatoes. Prick the lemon all over with a fork and stuff it into the cavity along with half the rosemary. Drizzle the remaining oil over the chicken, then rub it into the skin with a very generous dash of salt. Lightly crush the garlic cloves (unpeeled) and scatter them over the potatoes, along with what is left of the rosemary.

—

Now set the roasting dish in the oven and cook for 60–70 minutes, until the skin is crisp and the juices run clear when you stick a knife into the thickest part of the bird (between the leg and the body). Allow to rest for 10 minutes before carving, then eat with the potatoes.

SERVE WITH...
The magic of this dish is that it's nearly a one-pot wonder. All you really need to add is a salad, whether A REALLY GOOD TOMATO SALAD (p.114), or A REALLY GOOD CHICORY SALAD (p.110). ROAST PLUMS (p.170) – juicy and sharp – are great on the side.

AND FOR PUDDING...
This is the kind of food I cook when I crave simplicity and ease, so go with ice cream (whatever flavour you have in) with either a dousing of hot, strong Italian coffee, as in my PINE NUT ICE CREAM 'AFFOGATO' (p.188), or a dollop of soft EASY SALTED CARAMEL SAUCE (p.268).

BUTTERY LEMON ROAST CHICKEN

HANDS ON TIME
15 minutes

HANDS OFF TIME
1¼ hours roasting
10 minutes resting

FOR 4
A large bunch of sage
1 lemon
50g salted butter,
    softened
1 tsp sea salt flakes,
    plus a generous pinch
1 small chicken, about
    1.4kg, preferably
    organic

Recipes for roast chicken are ten a penny, yet it is the one recipe most of us need. This one is my failsafe, the meal everyone loves, that I can dress up or down with sides and pudding as the occasion demands. The skin becomes crisp and the butter, stuffed under the skin, melts into the flesh, giving the plumpest, most tender and flavoursome meat. Don't be intimidated by the thought of squeezing butter under the skin, as it's simple enough… and oddly satisfying. You can prepare the bird up to twelve hours in advance of roasting: just cover, store in the fridge and return it to room temperature two hours before cooking.

Heat the oven to 200°C/fan 180°C/Gas 6. Finely chop half the sage and finely zest the lemon. In a small bowl, mix the butter, chopped sage, zest and the 1 tsp salt, mashing it to a lemony, buttery paste (I use my hands).

Put the chicken in a roasting tray. Cut the lemon in half and squeeze some juice into the cavity, then stuff the 2 halves inside with the remaining sage sprigs. Gently lift the skin flap on the right breast and smear one-quarter of the butter mixture under it, using your fingers to press it down as far and as evenly as possible and taking care not to tear the skin. Repeat on the left breast. Now rub the rest of the butter over the chicken, on the breasts, legs and wings. Sprinkle all over with an extra pinch of salt.

—

When you're ready to cook, roast the chicken for 1¼ hours, until the skin is golden and crisp and the juices run clear when you stick a knife into the thickest part (between leg and body). Leave to rest for 10 minutes before carving and serving with a spoonful of the delectable juices.

SERVE WITH...
When cooking for more than four, roast two chickens and pile them on a bed of gnarly rosemary and thyme. It is beautiful and smells every bit as delightful. You'll want an extra-large tray of ESPECIALLY GOOD ROAST POTATOES (p.150), as everyone always wants seconds, a CARROT, CUMIN & MINT SALAD (p.144) and A REALLY GOOD GREEN SALAD (p.112). I pop a tray of ROAST GRAPES (p.168) in the oven as the bird rests, to serve – sweet and bursting from their skins – with the meat.

AND FOR PUDDING...
Something classic and comforting such as APPLE & WALNUT CRUMBLE PIE (p.246) with either a scoop of SALTED HONEY ICE CREAM (p.186) or, more simply, thick, runny double cream.

HONEY-ROAST POUSSINS

FOR 6
6 tbsp extra virgin
    olive oil
6 tbsp clear honey
2 lemons
1 tsp mixed spice
¼ tsp ground cinnamon
6 poussins
4 garlic cloves,
    unpeeled
Sea salt flakes

Poussins look spectacular piled high on a serving dish, their skins crisp and tantalisingly blackened. As far as I'm concerned, they bring all the joy of a roast chicken to the table, but without the hassle of carving. I generally offer one bird per person, plonked satisfyingly whole on each guest's plate, though half is actually plenty. And because you roast them snugly together in the pan, I can easily squeeze six small birds in my standard enamel roasting trays, and two to three of those trays in my oven, which means that poussins lend themselves surprisingly well to catering in large numbers, where a whole chicken (which on average serves four) simply doesn't.

The birds can sit, covered, in the marinade in the fridge for hours, actually improving in flavour with time, so you can prepare them in the morning before work and pop them in the oven when you get home.

Heat the oven to 200°C/fan 180°C/Gas 6. In a small bowl, combine the oil, honey, lemon juice and both ground spices. Beat lightly until you have a sweet, syrupy marinade.

Place the birds in a roasting tray in which they sit snugly, nestled up next to each other. Drizzle the honey mixture over them, covering as much of the birds as possible (use your fingers to smear it over their sides and legs). Sprinkle generously with salt and toss in the unpeeled garlic cloves.

If you are preparing the poussins in advance, cover and store in the fridge for up to a day, then return them to room temperature before roasting.

—

When you're ready to eat, roast for 45–60 minutes, until the skins are golden and the juices run clear when you stick a knife into the thickest part (between leg and body). Serve with the juices from the tin.

SERVE WITH...
If cooking for a crowd - or if you're simply feeling greedy, as I often am - then serve the poussins with a dish of creamy, cheesy POMMES DAUPHINOISE (p.154). You could add a couple of vibrant vegetable dishes: a green salad and perhaps a BEETROOT & MINT SALAD (p.118).

AND FOR PUDDING...
Something rather extravagant, such as a COFFEE & WALNUT CAKE (p.236) layered with rich mascarpone buttercream.

ROAST PORK WITH HONEY-ROAST PERSIMMONS

HANDS ON TIME
10 minutes

HANDS OFF TIME
3 hours chilling
1 hour 40 minutes
    roasting
10 minutes resting

FOR 6–8
1.8kg piece of pork
    loin, rolled and tied,
    skin scored
4 persimmons, halved
2 tbsp clear honey
4 star anise (optional)
Sea salt flakes

In Italy, from late October until Christmas, you will find persimmons on sale: plump and round orange fruits, so full and ripe they look like they're going to burst out of their fine, translucent skins. They are so sweet and so good that it's best to eat them as they are, with a spoon. In Britain, I find persimmons, sometimes also called sharon fruit, are quite different. They're bright orange, yes, but hard to the touch, more like an apple. These cook beautifully in a syrup of honey with just a hint of star anise, if you like, and make a glorious accompaniment to most roast meats, but to roast pork in particular. Think of them as serving the same role as apple sauce, but sweeter, more vibrant in colour and more richly flavoured. I find the cooking method below infallibly gives the very best and crispest crackling for pork.

Rub the scored pork skin with salt and leave it to dry out in the fridge, uncovered, for at least 3 hours, for wonderfully crisp crackling.

——

Heat the oven to 180°C/fan 160°C/Gas 4. Place the pork in a roasting tray and set it in the oven. Roast for 1 hour 10 minutes, then increase the oven temperature to 230°C/fan 210°C/Gas 8 for another 30 minutes to crisp up the crackling. The joint is done when the juices run clear when pierced through the thickest part with a knife, and should register 68°C (154°F) on a meat thermometer. Leave to rest for 10 minutes.

Meanwhile, roast the persimmons. Place them in a second roasting dish, cut sides up. Dissolve the honey in half a cup of boiling water, add the star anise, then pour this light golden syrup over the fruit. Seal the dish with foil and bake for 45 minutes or so, until tender. When you crank the oven temperature up for the crackling, remove the foil, spoon the juices over the fruit and roast for 10–15 minutes until caramelised. Serve with the pork.

SERVE WITH...
THE SIMPLEST ROAST POTATOES (p.148) seem essential with roast pork, and I love ROAST RED ONIONS (p.166), ever-so-slightly burnt and deliciously sweet. I like SAFFRON FENNEL (p.134) with this too, braised in wine and sunny, yellow spice, and – as always – A REALLY GOOD CHICORY SALAD WITH CREAMY MUSTARD DRESSING (p.110).

AND FOR PUDDING...
COFFEE MASCARPONE BISCUIT CAKE (p.190), served with a pot of strong Italian coffee.

CONFIT DUCK PIE

HANDS ON TIME
20 minutes

HANDS OFF TIME
45 minutes

FOR 6–8
1.2kg Maris Piper
    potatoes, peeled
    and cut into chunks
100g salted butter
70ml single cream
1 Pink Lady apple,
    cored and chopped
    into 1cm pieces
100g raisins
3 × 765g tins of confit
    duck legs (6 legs)
Fine sea salt

Inspiration for this dish came from a tiny brasserie in Brussels where we ate *parmentier* for lunch some years ago, an elegant dish with layers of cooked apple, buttery mashed potato and melting confit duck. My recipe is a more rustic incarnation that loosely resembles shepherd's pie. It has that same nursery-food quality, with the richer, more extravagant duck (which you can buy in tins from some supermarkets or specialist shops) in place of lamb.

The recipe can be assembled a day or two ahead of eating and stored, covered, in the fridge. Then just cook it in the oven when the moment comes. The tiny pieces of apple in the mash are almost imperceptible, they sort of melt into the buttery potato, but don't think of leaving them out; like the raisins, they add a touch of sweetness that is sublime with rich duck.

Heat the oven to 180°C/fan 160°C/Gas 4. Bring a large saucepan of generously salted water to the boil. When the water begins to gallop, add the potatoes and cook for 10–15 minutes, or until tender. Drain, then mash them with the butter and cream. Add the apple and raisins and stir so they're evenly distributed through the fluffy white mash.

Peel away the skin from each duck leg. Now tear the meat off the bones and, where it comes off in chunks, rip it into smaller pieces. Arrange it in a 30 × 20cm ovenproof dish. Spoon over the mash and spread it out evenly. At this point you can either cook the pie straight away, or cover and leave in the fridge for a day or so. Just bring it to room temperature before cooking, or allow a slightly longer cooking time.

—

Set the dish in the oven and cook for 25–30 minutes, until the potato is golden on top. To test if it's cooked, stick a knife in the middle of it, right to the centre: it should come out warm to the touch.

SERVE WITH...
This needs something crisp: I always do A REALLY GOOD CHICORY SALAD WITH CREAMY MUSTARD DRESSING (p.110) and then something sweet and fresh, too, such as a CARROT, CUMIN & MINT SALAD (p.144), the carrots barely blanched, then dressed with oil, lemon and spice.

AND FOR PUDDING...
In late winter, when rhubarb is in season, I can't resist serving a wobbly PINK RHUBARB & PROSECCO JELLY (p.222).

PORK WELLINGTON WITH APPLE & SAGE

HANDS ON TIME
30 minutes

HANDS OFF TIME
40 minutes

FOR 4–6
30g salted butter
2 small apples
    (preferably Pink
    Lady), peeled, cored
    and finely sliced
A small bunch of sage,
    roughly chopped
2 tbsp demerara sugar
1 pork tenderloin
    (roughly 450g)
2 tbsp extra virgin
    olive oil
2 sheets filo pastry
6 slices of prosciutto
2 × 320g sheets ready
    rolled all-butter puff
    pastry (you'll have
    some leftovers)
1 egg

Truthfully, this is nothing more than a glorified sausage roll: pork loin stuffed with slices of apple that have been cooked in butter and sage until sweet and meltingly tender, then enveloped in buttery puff pastry (categorically shop-bought; life is too short to make your own). I can't tell you how good it is. It might seem fiddly to wrap the pork loin in puff pastry, but in fact it's far simpler than it looks and – importantly – can be done well in advance, as the whole concoction will sit happily in the fridge for up to a day. The key, as with any Wellington, is to seal the parcel well so the juices from the cooked meat don't leak.

Heat the butter in a frying pan over a medium heat and melt it gently, then add the apples and sage and sprinkle with the sugar. Leave to cook for 10–15 minutes, until the fruit has softened, turning the apples every so often so they don't burn.

Take the pork and cut it open as you would cut open a baguette to make a sandwich. Flatten it out and put it in a large frying pan with the olive oil over a medium heat to sear the meat. Cook for 1–2 minutes on the first side until lightly coloured, then turn over and do the same on the second side.

Heat the oven to 190°C/fan 170°C/Gas 5. Now for the pastry. Unroll 1 sheet of the filo pastry on top of 2 sheets of cling film (this stops the filo sticking to the kitchen surface, and helps you roll the meat in the pastry) and arrange the slices of prosciutto over it, covering the filo completely.

Gently lift the pork out of the pan and set it on a board or plate, still splayed open like a baguette. Spoon the cooked apples down the centre of the meat and fold the tenderloin over, as if closing the sandwich. Then place the stuffed pork at the edge of the prosciutto-lined filo pastry and roll it up, as tightly as you can, using the cling film to help. This is much easier than it sounds. A doddle, really. Then wrap your parcel in a second sheet of filo pastry, making sure you cover the seams of the first sheet and folding the ends tightly underneath. This will keep the puff pastry crisp as it cooks, and stop any cooking juices from the meat escaping.

Now roll out your first big sheet of puff pastry. Place the pork parcel in the middle and wrap it as you would a present: close the top by gently pressing the pastry together and the ends by folding the excess pastry into a triangle and cutting off the corners. Check that the Wellington is sealed everywhere and move it on to a baking sheet.

Now roll out the second sheet of puff pastry (roughly half the packet will do) and cut it in a lattice shape. You can do this with a lattice cutter (if you have such a thing), or quite simply by hand, by tracing a diamond-shaped pattern with a sharp knife, for a more rustic look. Gently lift the lattice sheet up, stretch the holes out so they are as even as possible – embracing any imperfections – and lay it over the Wellington. Leave to rest in the fridge for up to 1 day, if you like.

—

When you're ready to cook the Wellington, crack the egg in a small bowl, beat lightly with a fork, then paint egg wash lightly all over the pastry. Set the baking sheet in the middle of the oven and bake for 40 minutes until golden all over.

SERVE WITH...
This works well with most variations on the theme of fennel: the FENNEL & PARMESAN PURÉE (p.136), particularly, has that soft, creamy, quasi-nursery quality that is a dream with the crisp golden pastry and rich meat. BUTTER-&-SAGE ROAST PUMPKIN (p.158) suits the autumnal character of the apple-stuffed pork, as does a tray of ROAST APPLES (p.172). For the rest, you can't really go wrong with ROAST NEW POTATOES WITH BAY LEAVES (p.152), cooked whole in the oven until golden brown and stuffed with aromatic bay leaves, then some kind of crisp salad to counterpoint the soft roast meat and vegetables.

AND FOR PUDDING...
While there is nothing strictly Christmas-y about this dish, it has a certain ceremonial quality about it, so I often end up making it around the festive period: you could go over the top with a PISTACHIO PANETTONE CAKE (p.198), with thick swirls of soft Italian meringue.

Pictured overleaf →

COLD ROAST TOPSIDE OF BEEF

HANDS ON TIME
5 minutes

HANDS OFF TIME
45-55 minutes in
    the oven
At least 2 hours cooling
Up to 2 days chilling

FOR 6
1.3kg topside of beef
1 tbsp extra virgin
    olive oil
1 heaped tbsp sea
    salt flakes
1 quantity Salsa Verde
    (p.266, optional)

Topside works out at roughly the same price as good-quality chicken, and I've found the method for roasting here to be failsafe. I cook the meat in advance, then keep it wrapped in the fridge. To serve, bring it to room temperature, slice finely and drizzle generously with peppery salsa verde to cut through the marbled fattiness beautifully. Sometimes I serve it with a dish of Home-Made Mayonnaise (p.262), though that is not a combination for the faint of stomach. This recipe has become a favourite for larger gatherings, especially when I don't have the time or inclination to cook much on the day. Leftovers are delicious in a sandwich, smothered with what is left of the eggy mayonnaise and lashings of English mustard.

Bring the beef to room temperature; I take mine out of the fridge 1 hour or so before cooking.

Heat the oven to 230°C/fan 210°C/Gas 8. Set the beef in a roasting tray, drizzle with the olive oil, then rub the salt all over.

Roast for 15 minutes, then reduce the temperature of the oven to 180°C/fan 160°C/Gas 4 and cook for a further 30 minutes for rare, or 40 minutes for medium-rare. To test how well-cooked the meat is, gently press it with your finger: if it feels pillowy, it is rare; if it springs back, it is medium; if it is solid, it is well done. Bear in mind that the meat will go on cooking while it rests, so don't panic if it feels undercooked when you take it out of the oven.

Leave to cool, then wrap in foil and store in the fridge for up to 2 days.

—

When you're ready to eat, slice the beef as finely as you can, arrange on a large platter and serve with the salsa verde.

SERVE WITH...
It's nice to pair the cold meat with something warm: you can't go wrong with a dish of NEW POTATOES WITH LEMON & SAMPHIRE (p.126) and something with a little texture and crunch to it, such as WILD RICE & LENTIL SALAD (p.132). Good bread, whether home-made DAMPER BREAD (p.252) or a baker's loaf, is essential for mopping up the juices.

AND FOR PUDDING...
I love SALTED CARAMEL PANNACOTTA (p.210), which has a decadently classic feel about it.

SIDES

This chapter, perhaps more than any other in this book, is all about the table. The recipes here, which I have loosely grouped together for want of a snazzier title as 'sides', are quick and easy to make. Broadly speaking, they call for little time or effort in the kitchen, but truly come to life at the table or, better, these are recipes that bring life to the table. Colourful, vibrant, rich food: food that is made for sharing, the kind you serve in big dishes and pass merrily round for all to help themselves. Crunchy salads; potatoes laced with fresh herbs that you douse in oil, shove in the oven and allow to fend for themselves until crisp and golden; lentils peppered with pancetta that you leave to simmer in broth on the hob, then serve steaming-hot straight from their saucepan; vegetables – whatever is in season and looks good – fried, grilled, roasted or baked in a decadent cheesy sauce. For all the pretty plates, the flowers, the soft candlelight and the delicate shimmering glasses that you can use to decorate your table, it is food that will make it beautiful: it is food, piled gloriously high, that will draw you in.

Of course, everyone has their own style and way of doing things, but I believe strongly that when it comes to the art of the table, more is absolutely more. Perhaps this is because I simply love to eat, and it brings me pleasure to see a colourful spread laid out, dishes butting up against each other, so many plates on the table that they end up perched precariously around the edges; but more so, I think, because a generous table always makes you feel welcome.

This isn't necessarily as extravagant a business as it sounds, most especially if you know what to cook: neither lentils nor potatoes, for example, are costly to buy, nor do they call for any great effort in the kitchen, certainly no skill. Salads take moments to throw together, yet they bring colour, texture and a delectable freshness to any meal. In practical terms, to go heavy on the recipes in this chapter, to choose two – perhaps even three – of these side dishes to serve alongside your star, is the simplest and thriftiest way to create a deliciously full table; to make lunch feel like a feast and dinner feel like a party.

A REALLY GOOD CHICORY SALAD
WITH CREAMY MUSTARD DRESSING

HANDS ON TIME
5 minutes

FOR 6
1 heaped tbsp
    mayonnaise
1 heaped tbsp Dijon
    mustard
1 heaped tbsp
    wholegrain mustard
2 tbsp red wine vinegar
3 tbsp extra virgin
    olive oil
4-5 heads of chicory
Sea salt flakes

I like to serve some kind of salad with every meal; it's quick to throw together, adds colour to the table and is – simply put – a very easy way of stretching out the rest of the menu. This chicory, with its bitter leaves and ridiculously moreish dressing, is perhaps my favourite, as you might have guessed from the number of times it crops up across the pages of this book. You can make it with the common-or-garden variety of chicory, or the kind with beautiful scarlet leaves, it's up to you; simply pile the leaves high in a wide shallow dish a few hours in advance if you need to, or as I do, once your guests have arrived, as you chat to them in the kitchen. The real magic of this salad is the dressing – heavenly, creamy, just peppery enough – which comes from Julia Turshen's brilliant book *Small Victories*.

The salad is plenty in itself as is, but you could toss in a handful of crisp walnuts if you like. Or, in the warmer months, paper-thin slices of radish (I love the pinky-hued watermelon variety) and heaps of bushy parsley. My only caveat is that you must use a good-quality mayonnaise, rich in colour and flavour, rather than regular shop-bought. (There's a recipe on p.262, if you want to go the extra mile.)

Make the dressing; you can do this anytime, even the day before if you don't want to have to think about it when your guests are there. In a small bowl, combine the mayonnaise and both mustards, add the vinegar and whisk lightly with a fork until well combined. Then pour in the olive oil and whisk again until you have a creamy, velvety dressing. Season with salt as you like.

Tear the leaves off the heads of chicory and toss them in a generous salad dish.

—

Just before serving, pour the mustardy dressing all over the leaves and toss together.

SERVE WITH...
Absolutely anything and everything. I do.

A REALLY GOOD GREEN SALAD

HANDS ON TIME
5 minutes

FOR 6
A bag of mixed green
    salad leaves (rocket,
    baby spinach)
A handful of
    watercress, coarse
    stalks removed
2 Baby Gem lettuces,
    leaves roughly torn
¼ fennel bulb,
    finely sliced
2 tbsp extra virgin
    olive oil
Juice of ¼ lemon
Sea salt flakes

This is my other go-to salad, and one I make almost every bit as often as the chicory with mustard dressing on the previous page. It is a muddle of crisp, green leaves, either dressed with a glug of olive oil, a squeeze of lemon juice and salt, as here, or drenched in Olga's Peppery Vinaigrette (p.260). There is of course no fixed recipe for salad, but there are certain rules: you want a mix of leaves, some sweet and tender, such as baby spinach; others peppery, such as rocket or watercress; others still crisp and crunchy, such as Baby Gem or Romaine. To this, I add more green (and categorically no other colours) with a few shavings of fennel, as I love the sweetness and crunch. And if you really want to dress the whole thing up, you could throw in a handful of parsley leaves or flaked almonds, or, when in season, sweet garden peas are a lovely touch.

Combine the green leaves in a large salad bowl or pile them high in a wide, shallow dish. Toss the fennel through the leaves.

——

Just before serving, drizzle the olive oil over the leaves and toss until they're well coated throughout. Squeeze over the lemon juice and sprinkle generously with salt, then toss again. Serve immediately, as, once dressed, the leaves will wilt quickly.

SERVE WITH...
I throw together a salad to go with pretty much whatever I'm eating: it takes me minutes to make and adds a welcome pop of vibrancy on the table. I find a green salad works particularly well with richer dishes, as well as to follow on from a plate of pasta.

A REALLY GOOD TOMATO SALAD

HANDS ON TIME
10 minutes

FOR 6–8
1.25kg baby tomatoes
    and tomatoes of mixed
    sizes and colours,
    as you prefer
A generous glug of
    extra virgin olive oil
A handful of black
    olives (preferably
    Taggiasche), halved
    and pitted
A handful of basil
    leaves
Sea salt flakes
Freshly ground
    black pepper

I like to make this with a few baby tomatoes, as they tend to be sweeter and more flavoursome, but a mix of shapes, sizes and colours is really what you want: they look so pretty and give an exquisite appearance to an otherwise simple dish. To dress tomato salads, I've tried any number of vinaigrettes — laced with balsamic, sugar, honey — but I don't believe you can improve on a good glug of olive oil and a dash of salt, so that is what I suggest here.

Halve the baby tomatoes, cutting them from top to toe to show their pretty, seeded interiors, and slice the mixed tomatoes. Pile high in a shallow serving dish, drizzle over the olive oil, add the olives, then season with salt and pepper.

——

Just before serving, tear the basil leaves and toss them in with the tomatoes.

SERVE WITH...
By rights this is a summer dish, because that is when tomatoes are at their most flavoursome. I like tomato salad with COLD ROAST TOPSIDE OF BEEF (p.104), sliced tissue-thin and ruby-red at its centre. To go with it a nice dish of POMMES DAUPHINOISE (p.154), swimming in cream, topped with a golden layer of melted Parmesan, and A REALLY GOOD CHICORY SALAD WITH CREAMY MUSTARD DRESSING (p.110).

AND FOR PUDDING...
Something wonderfully indulgent, such as CHOCOLATE & RUM PUDDING (p.226) and a big bowl of sharp berries.

TOMATO, RED ONION & MINT SALAD

HANDS ON TIME
10-15 minutes

FOR 6–8
1 red onion
1.25kg juicy tomatoes,
    mixed sizes and
    colours, as you prefer
A glug of extra virgin
    olive oil
A handful of mint leaves
Sea salt flakes
Freshly ground
    black pepper

I tend to make this with large, firmer tomatoes, either sliced into rounds or cut into juicy wedges, but you could just as well make it with baby tomatoes if you prefer. This is a proper 'meaty' tomato salad, pungent and fresh, with sweet red onion and a smattering of mint.

Finely slice the red onion and put it in a small bowl. Cover with cold water and leave for 10–15 minutes, to help mellow the pungent sharpness. Meanwhile, slice the tomatoes and arrange on a serving dish.

Drain the onion and pat it dry, then sprinkle the spirals over the tomatoes. Drizzle generously with olive oil and season with salt and pepper.

——

Scatter the mint leaves over just before serving.

SERVE WITH...
This is particularly good alongside a TORTA PASQUALINA (p.76), either as part of a picnic feast, or a light lunch at the kitchen table. You don't need much else, but you could serve a BABY ARTICHOKE, FENNEL & PECORINO SALAD (p.122) too, if you wanted to stretch the meal out further.

AND FOR PUDDING...
AMBROSIAL APRICOTS (p.224), poached in syrupy lemony honey and smattered with pistachios, either with shop-bought vanilla ice cream, chilled double cream, or a generous dollop of mascarpone.

BEETROOT & MINT SALAD

HANDS ON TIME
10 minutes

HANDS OFF TIME
1 hour marinating

FOR 4–6
4 tsp caster sugar
4 tbsp balsamic vinegar
Juice of 2 lemons
4 tbsp extra virgin
  olive oil
12 cooked beetroots, a
  mix of colours if you
  prefer, finely sliced
  into rounds
A small bunch of
  mint leaves
Sea salt flakes

This is just such a beautiful dish: slivers of beetroot swimming in crimson, glossy juices. I am quite generous with the sugar in the dressing, which is otherwise just a mix of balsamic vinegar, olive oil and lemon juice, because I find the sweetness a moreish complement to the earthy beetroot. You could of course roast and peel your own beetroot, then leave them to cool before dressing, but the ready-cooked kind in those vacuum-sealed packets are what I turn to most often.

Once dressed, you can leave to marinate happily for a day, or two at a stretch, in the fridge.

In a small bowl, combine the sugar, vinegar, lemon juice and olive oil with a generous pinch of salt and whisk lightly with a fork.

Throw the sliced beetroot into any old bowl; I usually let the salad marinate in a mixing bowl for a few hours, then transfer it to its serving dish after, as the crimson juices can stain. Roughly chop half the mint leaves, throw them in with the beetroots and pour the dressing over. Sit in the fridge – or in a cool spot – for an hour or so, to help intensify the flavours.

——

To serve, drain off some of the excess marinade, arrange the beetroot slices on a serving plate and scatter over the last of the mint leaves.

SERVE WITH...
This dish works year round. For a weekend lunch when the days are still bright but the air is cold, serve alongside BUTTERY LEMON ROAST CHICKEN (p.92), BUTTER-&-SAGE ROAST PUMPKIN (p.158) – caramelised at the edges so it's almost sweet – and a tray of THE SIMPLEST ROAST POTATOES (p.148). Come the depths of winter, you crave something a little more rich and indulgent, such as the salty, crunchy, fatty crackling of ROAST PORK WITH HONEY-ROAST PERSIMMONS (p.96), also with those roast potatoes (p.148) and A REALLY GOOD CHICORY SALAD WITH CREAMY MUSTARD DRESSING (p.110).

AND FOR PUDDING...
APPLE & WALNUT CRUMBLE PIE (p.246) in autumn, with its exquisitely crumbly cinnamon and golden sugar topping. In winter, I treat myself (and my guests) to CHOCOLATE CHESTNUT MERINGUE CAKE (p.242).

WATERMELON, FETA
& PISTACHIO CARPACCIO

FOR 4–6
¼ small watermelon,
   chilled
100g feta cheese
A handful of shelled
   pistachios, very
   coarsely chopped
2–3 tbsp extra virgin
   olive oil
Sea salt flakes
Freshly ground
   black pepper

I first tasted this – or a variation of it – with my friend Lydia Forte in Sicily, and was utterly seduced by the combination of grassy olive oil and salty pistachios. The secret is to cut the watermelon finely, then pile it on the plate in delicate layers, as you would a beef Carpaccio: the whole affair has a wonderful summer-by-the-seaside feel about it with its slightly naff shades of ice-cream pink and pistachio green.

It goes without saying that you should use a good watermelon: sweet and not too watery, vibrant in colour and flavour. It should be heavy, with a skin that is a uniform dark, forest green, and, when you tap it, it should sound hollow.

Cut the thick green skin away from the watermelon, then slice it in large rounds as finely as you can. Slice these in half and arrange the juicy deep pink pieces of fruit on a large serving dish. You can do this in advance, then cover and store in the fridge for up to a day.

—

Before serving, crumble the snowy white feta cheese over the fruit, scatter over the pistachios, salt and pepper and drizzle generously with the oil.

SERVE WITH...
This magnificent pop of colour is heaven for lunch with a nutty WILD RICE & LENTIL SALAD (p.132) and a large dish of milky MOZZARELLA WITH CELERY, OLIVES & PINE NUTS (p.36). Somehow it's the sort of menu that works every bit as well for a small, intimate gathering as for a large crowd. For dinner, it goes particularly well with HONEY-ROAST POUSSINS (p.94), cooked in a sweet, spiced honey glaze so the skin is sticky and crisp, then a TIMBALLO OF BAKED COURGETTES (p.162), sweet, fresh and swimming in olive oil. You could throw together A REALLY GOOD GREEN SALAD (p.112) too, with a dash of OLGA'S PEPPERY VINAIGRETTE (p.260).

AND FOR PUDDING...
SVERGOGNATA (p.202), a sugary, smooth ricotta layered with chunks of dark chocolate and sweet candied peel. And perhaps – for the sake of variation – you might substitute its pistachios for coarsely chopped blanched almonds.

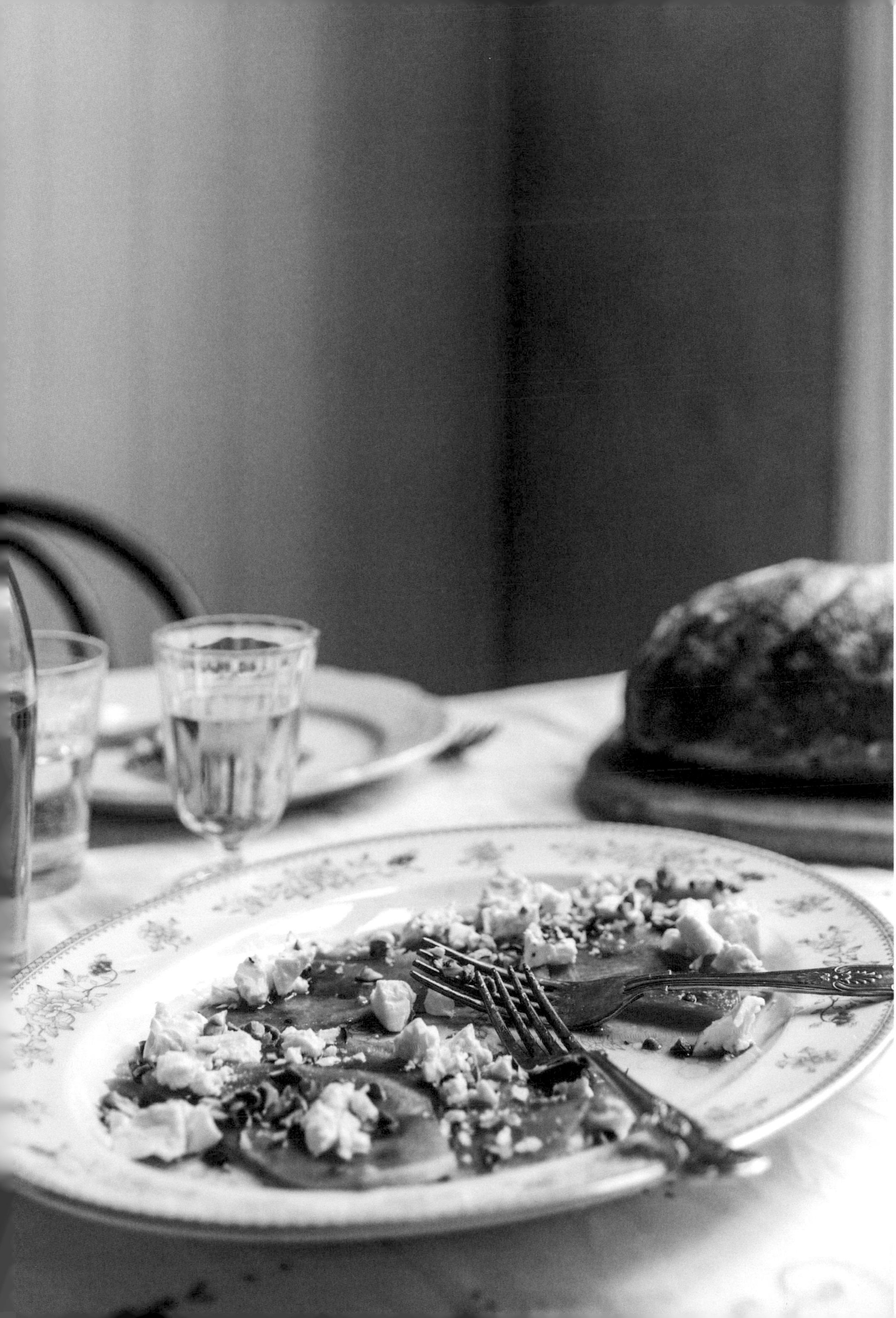

BABY ARTICHOKE, FENNEL & PECORINO SALAD

HANDS ON TIME
10 minutes

FOR 6

10 baby artichokes
    in oil

1 fennel bulb

Juice of 1 lemon

2 tbsp extra virgin
    olive oil

A handful of parsley
    leaves

100g pecorino cheese,
    or Parmesan cheese

Sea salt flakes

Freshly ground
    black pepper

The principle here is simple: fine slices of baby artichoke and shavings of sweet fennel, then some peppery pecorino to round it off, or Parmesan if that's what you have on hand. When tender baby artichokes are in season, I use those: just tear away the outer leaves and, where the petals start to turn that blushing shade of pink, finely slice the whole thing from top to toe, toss into the salad and dress everything with a little more oil than recommended below. The rest of the year, I use the artichokes that come in jars, already preserved in oil.

Quarter the artichokes. Remove the fennel fronds and save to dress the salad. Finely slice the fennel bulb. Toss the artichoke and fennel slices into a salad bowl, squeeze over the lemon juice and drizzle with the olive oil. Toss, then add the parsley, season with salt and pepper to taste and toss again. Cover and keep in the fridge until you are ready to serve.

——

Bring to room temperature, then top with shavings of pecorino and the bushy green, sweet fennel fronds.

SERVE WITH...
For a quick, improvised summer lunch, serve this with a generous bowl of SPAGHETTI WITH CREAMY LEMON SAUCE (p.60). For a slightly more elaborate affair, when you are blessed with a little more time to potter in the kitchen, this is good with HONEY-ROAST POUSSINS (p.94), ROAST NEW POTATOES WITH BAY LEAVES (p.152) - so pretty on the plate and so exquisitely salty to eat - and magenta-hued ROAST PLUMS (p.170), soft and tender, to eat with the meat.

AND FOR PUDDING...
For a quick lunch, you'll want something equally and deliciously low-effort, such as STRAWBERRIES IN LEMONY SYRUP (p.192). For a fancier gathering, a large dish of variegated FROZEN BERRIES WITH SAFFRON WHITE CHOCOLATE SAUCE (p.204), swimming in caramel-like molten chocolate.

BLOOD ORANGE, RED ONION, BLACK OLIVE & BASIL SALAD

HANDS ON TIME
10-15 minutes

FOR 6

1 small red onion,
  as finely sliced
  as you can
1.2kg blood oranges
5 tbsp extra virgin
  olive oil
120g black olives
  (preferably
  Taggiasche), halved
  and pitted
A handful of basil
  leaves
Sea salt flakes
Freshly ground
  black pepper

You can make this Sicilian dish with any old oranges, but the almost theatrical burst of colour that you get with good blood oranges when they're in season (from January through to the beginning of March) is like nothing else. There is some degree of labour involved in peeling and slicing the fruit, I admit, though I find it oddly therapeutic; the kind of mindless, repetitive action that you can relax into while listening to the radio or chatting.

Fill a small bowl with cold water and add the red onion. Let it rest in the water for 10–15 minutes: this will mellow its flavour so the salad doesn't taste overpoweringly of raw onion.

Cut away the peel and pith from the oranges, then slice them across into rounds roughly 1cm thick. Spoon the olive oil into a small bowl along with ¼ tsp salt and a generous dash of pepper. Whisk lightly with a fork.

In a bowl, combine the orange slices, olives and red onion (taking care to drain and pat them dry first). Dress everything with the seasoned olive oil. The salad will keep nicely for a day in the fridge.

—

Add the basil and toss together with your hands before serving.

SERVE WITH...
This goes particularly well with OSSOBUSO WITH SAGE & LEMON (p.70), cooked in its delicate sauce, the sharpness of the orange providing a delicious respite from the butteriness of the meat. Round the meal off with a crisp, regally coloured REALLY GOOD CHICORY SALAD WITH CREAMY MUSTARD DRESSING (p.110) and a dish of warm FENNEL & PARMESAN PURÉE (p.136), so comforting, but still light and delicate, or WINTRY SAFFRON COUSCOUS (p.48).

AND FOR PUDDING...
A devilishly rich FLOURLESS CHOCOLATE, CHESTNUT & ROSEMARY CAKE (p.234), no icing needed, just a light dusting of powdered sugar.

NEW POTATOES WITH LEMON & SAMPHIRE

HANDS ON TIME
10 minutes

HANDS OFF TIME
25 minutes

FOR 6
1kg baby new potatoes
70ml extra virgin
    olive oil
1 lemon, sliced into
    very fine rounds
90g samphire
A large bunch of
    parsley, leaves
    roughly chopped
Sea salt flakes

I adore samphire, fresh and intensely salty like the sea, and that *al dente* texture it has when cooked just right. I find it pays the most perfect compliment to the buttery new potatoes in this dish. The trick to making this well is to drench the potatoes in olive oil while they're still warm, so they soak up the flavour, and to have the finely sliced lemon ready to go before the potatoes are cooked, so when you toss it in with the warm spuds, it tenderises ever-so-slightly with the heat, and infuses them with that sharp citrusy flavour.

You could serve this dish warm, but you don't have to. Mostly, I cook it a day ahead and serve at room temperature, to ease my to-do list when it comes to getting supper (or lunch) together on the day.

Boil the potatoes for 20–25 minutes in a large pan of generously salted water, until they feel tender when pierced with a fork. When cooked, put them in a large bowl, drizzle generously with the oil and sprinkle with salt. Toss well, so all the potatoes are coated and absorb the lovely grassy flavour. Be mindful that the samphire is quite salty, so err on the side of caution when you season: you can always add more salt later.

Add the lemon slices to the potatoes while they're still piping hot, so the fruit tenderises a little from the heat of the potatoes and releases some of its tart juices. Meanwhile, steam the samphire for 4–6 minutes until tender, but not wilted, then add it to the potatoes. Toss everything together well.

—

When the potatoes have cooled a little, add the parsley to the mix. Serve warm or at room temperature.

SERVE WITH...
These work particularly well with COLD ROAST TOPSIDE OF BEEF (p.104), sliced and served with a generous dollop of peppery SALSA VERDE (p.266). Or - if you want to keep things really simple - English mustard. I love A REALLY GOOD TOMATO SALAD (p.114) with cold beef, just juicy, ruddy tomatoes with black olives, and I might throw in a handful of slivers of red onion too.

AND FOR PUDDING...
Some kind of frivolous concoction that speaks of long midsummer days (even when the weather doesn't): LIMONCELLO SEMIFREDDO (p.220).

FRIED BROCCOLI WITH BLACK OLIVES

HANDS ON TIME
5 minutes

HANDS OFF TIME
15 minutes

FOR 4–6
3 tbsp extra virgin
    olive oil
1 garlic clove,
    finely chopped
3 anchovies
¼ tsp chilli flakes
    (optional)
400g Tenderstem
    broccoli, or 2 large
    heads of regular
    broccoli, chopped
    into florets
50ml water
A handful of black
    olives, halved
    and pitted

Once you have tried this, you will never want to eat broccoli any other way. The hint (just a hint) of saltiness from the anchovies and oily black olives is just what you need with the bitter greens. You could also throw in a dash of chilli flakes, if you like. Any kind of broccoli works: purple-sprouting, Tenderstem, plain old common-or-garden... My preference is for Tenderstem and purple-sprouting, when it's in season, with its extravagantly coloured flowers. This is, in part, because I love the ease of simply tossing the florets as they come from the shop straight into the pan, but mostly because the crispy bits – those slightly burnt edges – are my favourite part, and the flattened shape of the longer stems seems to crisp better than the chunkier variety.

Heat 2 tbsp of the oil in a large saucepan over a medium heat. Add the garlic, anchovies and chilli flakes (if you're using them) and fry gently for 2–3 minutes, until the garlic colours slightly and the anchovies begin to melt away. Now add the broccoli and measured water. Cover and cook for 10–15 minutes, until the water disappears and the broccoli is just tender (it will become vibrant green). Throw in the olives. At this point, you can leave it on the hob for a day (any longer and it's better kept in the fridge).

—

When you are ready to serve (this is fine to eat at room temperature, but really does taste best warm), uncover the pan, increase the heat to high and fry for 3–5 minutes with the remaining 1 tbsp of oil, turning the glistening green florets now and then, until lightly crisp and golden.

SERVE WITH...
Purple-sprouting broccoli is cold-loving and in season from November to early April, so you'll want something warming and indulgent to go with it, such as CONFIT DUCK PIE (p.98) and perhaps some BUTTERY CARROTS WITH CHESTNUT HONEY (p.142). Part of the charm of this recipe, though, is that some kind of broccoli is available year round. In the summer, it makes for a lovely pop of vibrancy alongside APHRODITE'S ROAST CHICKEN (p.90), cooked on its bed of potatoes.

AND FOR PUDDING...
In cold weather, RED WINE POACHED PEARS (p.212), slowly cooked until a deep, seductive shade of burgundy, with a scoop (or two) of SALTED HONEY ICE CREAM (p.186). In warmer weather, try A VERY GOOD VANILLA PANNACOTTA (p.206), sumptuous and silky-smooth, with a big bowl of STRAWBERRIES IN LEMONY SYRUP (p.192).

BRAISED LENTILS WITH PANCETTA

HANDS ON TIME
10 minutes

HANDS OFF TIME
1 hour

FOR 6
3 tbsp extra virgin
   olive oil, plus extra
   (optional) for
   dressing
2 shallots, finely
   chopped
1 small fennel bulb,
   finely chopped
150g finely chopped
   pancetta
1 tsp fennel seeds
300g Puy lentils
1.2 litres vegetable
   stock, plus extra
   if needed
Sea salt flakes
Freshly ground
   black pepper

In Italy we eat lentils for luck: a bowl enjoyed as the clock strikes midnight on New Year's Eve brings you good fortune in the coming year. This tradition dates back to Roman times, when lentils were associated with money, each little lens representing a small coin.

In winter – when I long for warmth, nourishment and comfort in my food – I find myself craving this dish in all its earthy, buttery glory. Crisp, salty pancetta is heaven with the lentils, but if you're cooking with vegetarians in mind, feel free to leave it out: the pulses with the aniseedy fennel and fennel seeds are plenty flavoursome enough.

Heat the oil in a large, heavy-based saucepan over a medium-high heat. Add the shallots, chopped fennel, pancetta and fennel seeds and cook for 3–5 minutes, stirring occasionally, until the vegetables are beginning to soften and the pancetta is becoming crisp.

Rinse the lentils in cold water, then add them to the pan and cover with the stock. Bring to the boil, then reduce the heat and simmer gently for 1 hour, until the lentils are tender. If the liquid looks like it's drying out, just add a little more water or stock to the pan: you want the dish to be moist, but not brothy. Once cooked, take off the heat and let sit, covered, on the hob for up to 1 day, or store in the fridge for up to 3 days.

—

Before serving, reheat gently on the hob for a few minutes, adding a splash more water or stock if the lentils look dry, then season with a little more salt, pepper and a dash of oil, if you like. Best served a little warm.

SERVE WITH…
In winter – for a Sunday roast or a cosy weekend supper – there are few things more comforting than ROAST PORK WITH HONEY-ROAST PERSIMMONS (p.96), with indulgently crisp, salty crackling and burnished fruits, alongside a big dish of these lentils. You don't really need much more, other than perhaps some BUTTER-&-SAGE ROAST PUMPKIN (p.158), caramelised just at the edges, and A REALLY GOOD CHICORY SALAD WITH CREAMY MUSTARD DRESSING (p.110).

AND FOR PUDDING…
An explosion of vibrant colour in the form of a WINTER FRUIT & MASCARPONE TART (p.180).

WILD RICE & LENTIL SALAD

HANDS ON TIME
15 minutes

HANDS OFF TIME
25-30 minutes (15 of
   which you're busy
   doing other things)

FOR 4-6
200g wild long-grain
   rice, rinsed and
   drained
1 litre water
2 tbsp extra virgin
   olive oil, plus extra
   for seasoning
120g Puy lentils, rinsed
   and drained
500ml vegetable stock
1 onion, finely sliced
120g pomegranate seeds
A small bunch of
   mint, leaves picked
Sea salt flakes

ON THE HOB

Loosely adapted from Charlotte Wood's brilliant book *Love and Hunger*, this light, nutty recipe works equally well as a centrepiece or a side dish. I like it best with wild rice, which you often find sold as part of a mix with basmati or brown rice and that works too, just adjust the cooking times accordingly.

You can cook the components – rice, lentils and crisp fried onion – ahead of time in stages, if that makes life easier, then simply assemble everything on the day you want to eat it. Once assembled, it will sit happily in the fridge for a day or two. Better still, you can buy the lentils (and rice, if you like) in sachets ready-cooked, so all you need do is toss it all together and dress.

Toss the wild rice into a saucepan. Cover with the measured water and add ½ tsp salt. Bring to the boil over a high heat. When the water begins to gallop, reduce to a simmer, cover and cook over a gentle heat for 25–30 minutes. The rice should be chewy and some grains may burst open like exotic flowers in bloom. Drain off any liquid, then tip into a large bowl, seasoning generously with olive oil and a little salt while the rice is warm.

While the rice cooks, toss the lentils into a separate saucepan. Cover with the stock and bring to the boil over a high heat. Reduce the heat, cover and simmer gently for 25–30 minutes until just cooked: you want them to hold their shape nicely and have a little bite to them. Drain away any liquid and add to the bowl with the rice. Fluff together with a fork and season with a little more olive oil.

Lastly, cook the onion: heat the 2 tbsp of olive oil in a saucepan over a medium heat, add the onion and fry until very crisp and dark. Combine the onion and pomegranate in a serving dish with the grains and pulses.

—

Before serving, tear in the mint leaves, toss, check for seasoning and serve.

SERVE WITH...
This is an absolute dream for picnics, with a tub of hard-boiled quail's eggs in their little speckled shells, and celery salt for dipping. And a good selection of crudités with a jar of deliciously rich home-made TRUFFLE MAYONNAISE (p.264), charcuterie and a nice loaf of bread.

AND FOR PUDDING...
Punnets of strawberries and a tin of rose-scented MERINGUES (p.238).

SAFFRON FENNEL

HANDS ON TIME
10 minutes

HANDS OFF TIME
30 minutes

FOR 6–8
4 fennel bulbs
2 tbsp extra virgin
    olive oil
1 onion, finely sliced
200ml white wine
1 tsp saffron strands
2 tbsp hot water
¼ vegetable stock cube
20g salted butter
Fine sea salt
Freshly ground
    black pepper

The magic of this dish lies in its magnificent, rich colour as much as in its exquisitely buttery flavour. You can make it in advance and serve at room temperature, piled high on a serving dish and topped with sweet fennel fronds or parsley, if you like. Otherwise, reheat it and serve warm.

Cut each fennel bulb into about 8 wedges. Heat the oil in a frying pan, then add the onion along with a generous pinch of salt and fry for 3–5 minutes, until soft and translucent. Add the fennel and fry for 2–3 minutes to colour a little, then pour in the wine. Put the saffron in a small bowl, add the measured hot water and infuse for a few minutes, then pour the golden liquid into the pan with the fennel. Give everything a good stir.

Crumble the stock cube over the fennel, stir again, cover and simmer gently for 30 minutes, until the fennel is soft, tender and a light golden colour, but still holds its shape nicely. Take off the heat, add the butter and stir until melted. Season and eat warm, or at room temperature.

——

If you like, you can store this in the fridge, covered, for up 24 hours, then just gently reheat on the hob with a splash more water, if necessary.

SERVE WITH...
This, much like the fennel purée overleaf, works wonderfully well with meat and fish alike: I'm particularly fond of this vibrant, summery dish with WHOLE POACHED COLD SALMON (p.74). To make a full meal of it, throw together a watercress salad, dripping in OLGA'S PEPPERY VINAIGRETTE (p.260), and a big, sweet bowl of A REALLY GOOD TOMATO SALAD (p.114).

AND FOR PUDDING...
A bowl of AMBROSIAL APRICOTS (p.224), swimming in chilled honey-and-lemon syrup.

FENNEL & PARMESAN PURÉE

HANDS ON TIME
10 minutes

HANDS OFF TIME
20 minutes

FOR 6
2 litres vegetable stock
5 medium fennel bulbs
50g salted butter
1 tbsp double cream
70g Parmesan cheese,
   grated, plus extra
   shavings (optional)
   to top the dish
Sea salt flakes
Freshly ground
   black pepper

Fennel purée shares the same irresistible comfort-food quality as mashed potato, only it's more delicate in flavour and less stodgy in texture. For me, a great part of this recipe's charm lies in the fact that there is no need for peeling or mashing of anything by hand, two tasks I find tedious. You simply chop the fennel – and roughly at that – poach it until tender, then whizz through a food processor and add lots of Parmesan. If you want to prepare it in advance, you can do so up to three days ahead, then simply warm through in a saucepan just before serving.

Bring a large pan containing the stock to the boil over a medium heat. Trim the fennel, reserving the leafy green fronds, and quarter the bulbs.

When the stock comes to the boil, add the fennel and cook for 15–20 minutes until tender. Drain the fennel and blitz until smooth in a blender. Stir in the butter, cream and Parmesan. Add salt and pepper to taste.

——

If making ahead of time, reheat gently on the hob for a few minutes, then spoon into a serving dish and top with the sweet, leafy fennel fronds and a few shavings of Parmesan, if you like.

SERVE WITH...
You can eat this purée with pretty much anything: fish, poultry, or fattier meats such as pork. Try it with SAUSAGES WITH GRAPES (p.66) for an extravagant supper-party variation on sausages and mash, together with a light, ruddy and autumnal REALLY GOOD CHICORY SALAD WITH CREAMY MUSTARD DRESSING (p.110).

AND FOR PUDDING...
APPLE & WALNUT CRUMBLE PIE (p.246), with its custard-like fruit filling baked into a buttery, flaky pie crust.

ASPARAGUS WITH LEMON & TOASTED ALMOND GRATIN

HANDS ON TIME
20 minutes

FOR 6–8
800g asparagus spears
7-8 tbsp extra virgin
  olive oil
Juice of 1 lemon
1 garlic clove, peeled
50g stale bread
40g flaked almonds
Fine sea salt

My most favourite way to cook and eat asparagus is lightly blanched, then served at room temperature, drenched in olive oil and seasoned with a generous dash of salt and pepper. This recipe is a simple variation on that theme with a little extra something, in the form of lightly toasted almond flakes and golden breadcrumbs scattered over the green stems. You can cook both the asparagus and the gratin a day ahead of when you plan on eating them. As a side note: asparagus cooked this way, then topped with a fried egg, makes for a very spoiling supper for one.

Bring a large saucepan of generously salted water to the boil. Snap off the woody ends of the asparagus and discard. When the water begins to gallop, gently lower the asparagus into the pan and cook for 6–7 minutes, or until tender but not soggy. You can test to see if they're cooked by inserting a knife into the thickest part of the stem: it should slip in with no resistance. Carefully drain the asparagus, arrange on a plate and dress with 2–3 tbsp of the olive oil and a squeeze of lemon juice.

Meanwhile, heat the remaining 5 tbsp of olive oil and the whole garlic clove in a large frying pan over a medium heat for 6–7 minutes until the garlic turns golden. Blitz the stale bread in a food processor to coarse crumbs. Remove the garlic clove from the frying pan and add the breadcrumbs and flaked almonds with a generous pinch of salt. Fry for a minute or so, until the crumbs and nuts turn golden. Take off the heat.

—

Before serving – either warm or at room temperature – sprinkle the toasted almond crumbs over the green stems.

SERVE WITH...
POULET ANGLAIS (p.72), tender poached chicken breast served cold with a gloriously delicate yogurt sauce, is an absolute favourite of mine in the summer months, and this asparagus is sheer bliss with it. To go with the greens and the chicken, a big dish of NEW POTATOES WITH LEMON & SAMPHIRE (p.126) and, if you feel you need it, you might as well toss together A REALLY GOOD GREEN SALAD (p.112).

AND FOR PUDDING...
Smooth, velvety PINE NUT ICE CREAM 'AFFOGATO' (p.188), drenched in bitter black espresso.

GREEN BEANS WITH BABY TOMATOES

HANDS ON TIME
15 minutes

FOR 4
360g green beans,
   trimmed
2 tbsp extra virgin
   olive oil, plus extra
   for dressing
1 garlic clove, peeled
150g baby tomatoes
   (ideally red and
   yellow), halved
¼-½ tsp chilli flakes
Sea salt flakes

Green beans are a vegetable that is too often disappointing, either overcooked and bland, or undercooked and unappetisingly squeaky when you bite into them. But I absolutely adore beans cooked this way; the juice of the tomatoes and the olive oil almost melt into the greens and imbue them with an exquisite umami flavour. I could happily eat these as they are – warm or cold – by the bowlful, with just some bread for mopping up the juices.

Bring a large saucepan of generously salted water to the boil. When the water begins to gallop, add the green beans and cook for 4–5 minutes until crisp-tender. You want them *al dente*, as they will cook a little more in the pan with the tomatoes.

In a large frying pan, heat the oil and the garlic. When the garlic starts to brown, throw in the tomatoes. Cook for 3–4 minutes until they begin to soften and release their colourful juices. Now drain the beans and add them to the pan, give everything a good stir and dress with a splash more olive oil. Sprinkle with the chilli flakes and salt to taste. Cook for a further minute or so to let all the flavours intermingle nicely, then serve warm straight from the pan, or at room temperature.

—

Leave in the pan for up to a day (or store for 2 days, covered, in the fridge), then either serve at room temperature as a salad, or reheat for a few minutes in the pan.

SERVE WITH...
I love these with the cheesy SPINACH, MINT & MELTED CHEESE SYRIAN FRITTATA (p.80). There is something about the two together that has an almost nursery-food quality about it... in a good way. For the rest, you don't need much: bread for mopping up the delectable juices, and, if really hungry, a WILD RICE & LENTIL SALAD (p.132).

AND FOR PUDDING...
CHOCOLATE & RUM PUDDING (p.226), gloriously rich and chocolatey, with a big bowl of raspberries.

BUTTERY CARROTS WITH
CHESTNUT HONEY

HANDS ON TIME
10 minutes

HANDS OFF TIME
30 minutes

FOR 4–6
500g baby carrots
    (preferably rainbow),
    trimmed
2 tbsp sherry vinegar
2 tbsp honey
    (preferably chestnut)
2 tbsp extra virgin
    olive oil, plus extra
    to reheat (if needed)
A small bunch of thyme
Sea salt flakes
Freshly ground
    black pepper

These carrots are deceptive: as buttery as they taste, there is actually no butter in the recipe, just a splash of olive oil and sweet sherry vinegar. Any pot of good, runny honey will do, but I especially love the molasses colour and deep flavour of the chestnut variety. My preference is to make this with baby carrots (no chopping involved, beyond slicing off their little tops), but you can just as well slice regular carrots into batons. I never bother peeling them. When in season, I like the rainbow-coloured carrots, which look wonderfully theatrical on the table: the only thing to be mindful of is that you need to cook each shade in a different pan, as otherwise the colours run together.

Put the carrots in a large, deep pan. Add 1 tbsp of the sherry vinegar and a generous pinch of salt, then cover by just over half with cold water. Set over a high heat and bring to the boil. Reduce the heat to medium and cook, stirring now and again, for 20–25 minutes. If they look likely to dry out while they're cooking, just add a splash more water.

Once the carrots are just cooked (a knife should go through with no resistance), the water should be nearly evaporated. If not, just pour it off. Now add the remaining vinegar with the honey, oil and thyme. Cook for 3–4 minutes, stirring, to get a nice glaze on the carrots, and season.

———

Serve warm and straight away, or store in the fridge for up to 2 days, then serve at room temperature, or reheat in the pan with a dash more oil.

SERVE WITH...
I love these alongside CONFIT DUCK PIE (p.98): the tender crunch of the carrots is the perfect contrast to the buttery, creamy mash and tender, rich duck. This works well for a crowd, as both dishes scale up very nicely, and this menu has become one that we greedily wheel out every year to celebrate with friends. I throw together A REALLY GOOD CHICORY SALAD WITH CREAMY MUSTARD DRESSING (p.110) and serve with a tray (or two) of CREAMY BAKED LEEKS WITH MUSTARD & PARMESAN (p.164). The carrots also make a good, sweet side dish to ALLEGRA'S POT-ROAST BEEF (p.68).

AND FOR PUDDING...
CHOCOLATE CHESTNUT MERINGUE CAKE (p.242): three tiers of meringue filled with whipped cream, chocolate and sugared chestnuts, topped with a sea of candles, if the occasion demands.

CARROT, CUMIN & MINT SALAD

ON THE HOB

HANDS ON TIME
10 minutes

HANDS OFF TIME
At least 1 hour
    marinating,
    if you can

FOR 4–6
600g baby carrots
2¼ tsp cumin seeds
1 tsp ground
    mixed spice
Juice of 1 lemon
120ml extra virgin
    olive oil
2 tsp caster sugar
A small bunch of mint,
    leaves picked
Sea salt flakes

When I can get my hands on baby carrots – the tiny, spindly ones – my preference is for those. They are so small and skinny that grating them seems redundant, so I cut them top to toe into fine, crunchy slivers, then blanch in hot water for just over a minute to take away that crunchy edge, while leaving the crisp texture. I find that the carrots, when ever-so-slightly cooked in this way, soak up more of the aromatic dressing. In fact, the longer you can leave the carrots to swim in olive oil, lemon juice and spices (a few hours at least is ideal), the deeper and more fragrant their flavour. With regular carrots from the corner shop, however, I simply grate them, then douse liberally with the dressing.

Bring a pan of generously salted water to the boil. Trim the tops off the carrots and discard, then finely slice them, from top to tail, into long strips. I usually get 3–4 slices out of each one; just halve any really tiny carrots. Throw them in the boiling water and simmer for 1–1½ minutes, just to take the crunch off. Drain, then pile into a large bowl.

Very lightly bash the cumin seeds with a mortar and pestle, just enough to release the flavour of the spice, but retaining the crunch of the seeds. Pour into a small bowl, then add the mixed spice, lemon juice, oil, sugar and ½ tsp salt, and whisk with a fork. Pour the dressing over the still-warm carrots and toss until they're all covered in spice and oil.

Coarsely chop half the mint. Once the carrots have cooled, add the mint. Toss again, cover and put in the fridge for at least 1 hour, if you can.

—

Before serving, transfer the carrots to a serving dish – I use a shallow oval one and pile them high – tear up the last of the mint and scatter it over.

SERVE WITH...
This works in both summer or winter and is so quick to make. I like it in summer with plump baby HONEY-ROAST POUSSINS (p.94), in their spiced glaze. Then, continuing the miniature theme, try ROAST NEW POTATOES WITH BAY LEAVES (p.152). In winter, I love their crunchy, sweet freshness with something rich such as CONFIT DUCK PIE (p.98).

AND FOR PUDDING...
A delectable cloud of sharp lemon curd, soft whipped cream and chewy meringue sandwiched in the form of LEMON MERINGUE CAKE (p.244).

AN EMBARRASSMENT OF SPRING VEGETABLES

HANDS ON TIME
40 minutes

FOR 4-6
10-12 baby artichokes
Juice of 1 lemon
2 tbsp extra virgin
    olive oil, plus extra
    (optional) to dress
2 spring onions,
    finely chopped
2 garlic cloves,
    finely chopped
150g chopped pancetta
100ml white wine
400g frozen petits pois
400g frozen broad beans
A handful of mint
    leaves
40g pecorino cheese,
    shaved

In Italy we call this *vignarola*. It's a classic Roman dish where you gently simmer spring greens — whatever you have to hand — in white wine with a little crisp, salty pancetta. The result is an embarrassment of verdant, flavoursome veggies. I like mine topped with shavings of pecorino cheese, melting ever so slightly at the edges. Traditionally, you make this with baby artichokes. These can sometimes be tricky to get your hands on in the UK, though you can buy them online. If you have no joy, skip the artichokes and just increase the quantities of peas and broad beans.

Clean the artichokes by tearing away their outer, tough leaves until the leaves begin to feel tender to touch and are a soft shade of pink and pale green. Trim the top 1cm or so off the tips of the leaves and pare the stem to remove hard or knobbly bits. Halve the artichokes and toss them in a bowl of cold water with a squeeze of lemon juice to stop them browning.

In a large frying pan, heat the oil over a medium heat and add the spring onions, garlic and pancetta. Cook for 5 minutes or so, until the onions soften and the pancetta colours. Now add the drained artichokes and the wine. Cook for 5–10 minutes until coloured and tender, then add the peas and broad beans (I do this straight from frozen) and mint leaves. Cook for a further 5–10 minutes until warmed through and a bright spring green. Take off the heat and leave, covered, on the hob for a few hours if you like.

—

Before serving, warm gently on the hob, dress with a little more olive oil if you like, and top with shavings of pecorino before bringing to the table. This can be cooked a good few hours in advance, but it loses its vibrancy the longer it sits around.

SERVE WITH...
This is one of those dishes that goes wonderfully with everything: chicken, pork, beef... Recently, I made a large dish of it to have with ALLEGRA'S POT-ROAST BEEF (p.68), A REALLY GOOD TOMATO SALAD (p.114) and a light watercress salad, drenched in OLGA'S PEPPERY VINAIGRETTE (p.260).

AND FOR PUDDING...
PISTACHIO BUTTER CAKE (p.232), without the marzipan icing, just dusted with a cloud of icing sugar.

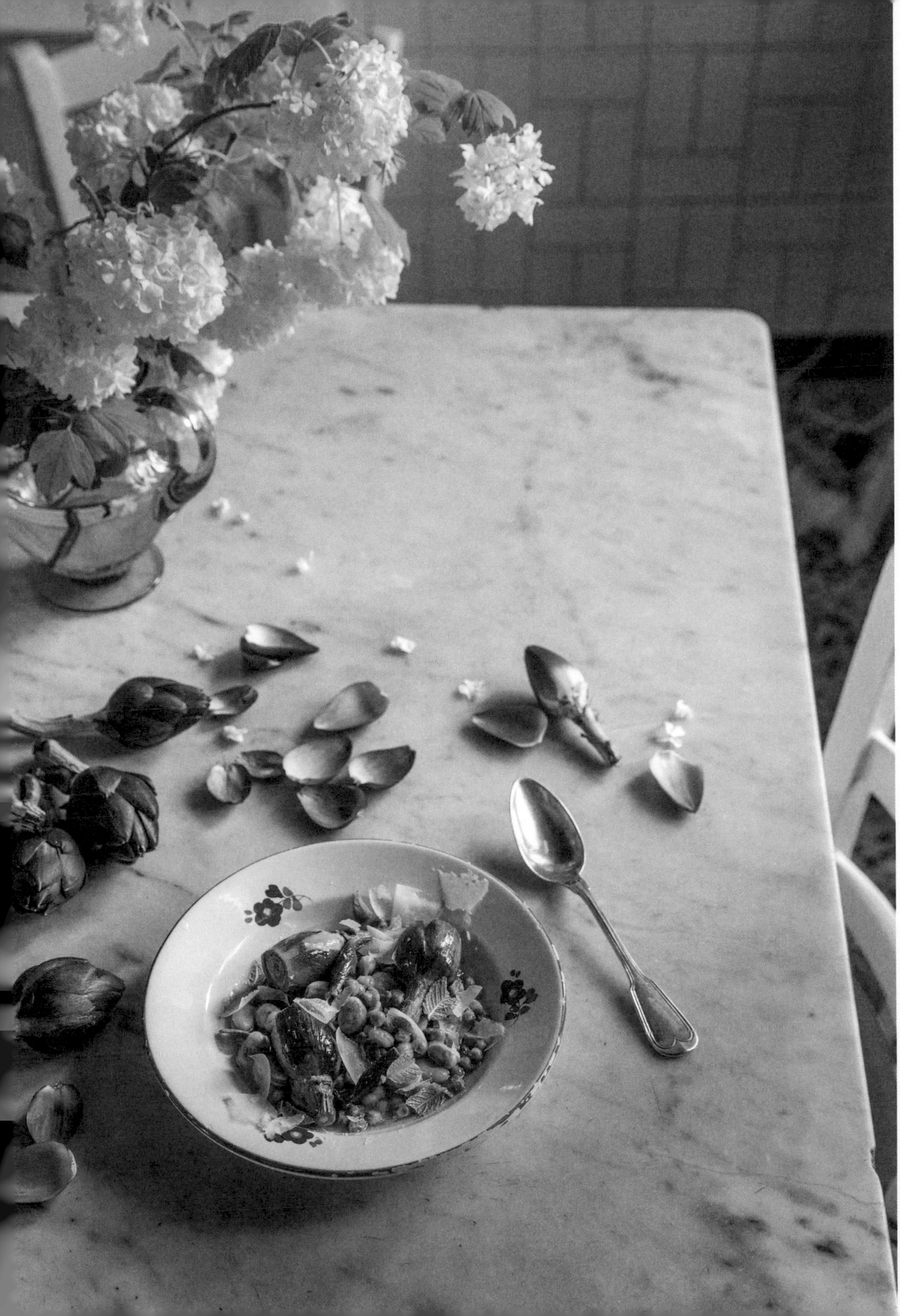

THE SIMPLEST ROAST POTATOES

HANDS ON TIME
5 minutes

HANDS OFF TIME
1¾ hours

FOR 4–6
1kg potatoes
  (preferably
  Maris Piper)
100ml extra virgin
  olive oil, plus
  extra if needed
A small bunch of thyme
A small bunch of
  rosemary
Sea salt flakes

For a long time this was pretty much the only way I cooked potatoes: no peeling, no par-boiling, no fuss and very little washing up. If you douse the potatoes in enough olive oil and leave them to cook for longer than seems sensible, they come out exquisitely golden and crisp.

Heat the oven to 200°C/fan 180°C/Gas 6.

Roughly cut each potato into 3 pieces (roughly 5cm each), cutting off each end at a slant so that you are left with a triangle-shaped wedge in the middle. There is no exact science to doing this, but conventional wisdom suggests you want equal-sized pieces so they cook evenly. However, the really crispy ones – those smaller bits that are almost burnt at the edges – are everyone's favourites, so I don't think you need be too pedantic about it. Toss the pieces into a roasting tray. If you don't want to roast the potatoes straight away, cover with a clean tea towel and set aside somewhere cool. They will keep for up to 1 day before roasting.

—

Drizzle the oil over the potatoes: it will look more than seems entirely sensible, but don't panic. Throw in the thyme and rosemary and set in the oven to cook for 1½–2 hours. Every now and then, take the tray out of the oven and shake it around to make sure the potatoes are all coated in glistening oil. If the pan starts to look a little dry, don't be afraid to drizzle in some more, and if any of the potatoes stick to the bottom or edges of the pan, just loosen them gently with a wooden spatula or a knife. Before serving, sprinkle generously with salt.

SERVE WITH...
I happily eat roast potatoes with anything, even on their own, but these work particularly well with ALLEGRA'S POT-ROAST BEEF (p.68) which is cooked on the hob, allowing plenty of space in the oven for twice as many potatoes as you think you're going to eat. To go with it, some ROAST RED ONIONS (p.166), a crisp green salad with OLGA'S PEPPERY VINAIGRETTE (p.260) and some baby BUTTERY CARROTS WITH CHESTNUT HONEY (p.142)

AND FOR PUDDING...
A tower of cocoa-dusted MERINGUES (p.238), crisp on the outside and almost marshmallow-like within.

ESPECIALLY GOOD ROAST POTATOES

HANDS ON TIME
10–15 minutes

HANDS OFF TIME
1¼ hours

FOR 4–6
1kg baby new potatoes
    (preferably Ratte)
100ml extra virgin
    olive oil
A small bunch of thyme
    or rosemary (optional)
Sea salt flakes
Freshly ground
    black pepper

My husband's cooking tends to be more involved than my own *laissez-faire* toss-in-a-pan way of doing things, and this is his recipe, which has you par-boiling the potatoes, then crushing each one individually with a fork so it drinks up the flavoursome cooking oil. However, these are so indescribably good that even I believe they're worth the extra effort.

You can prepare the dish largely in advance: par-boil the potatoes the day before and leave them somewhere cool in the kitchen (but not in the fridge). When it comes to the cooking, they need 2–3 roasting dishes. This puts oven space at a premium, so, if needs be, I par-roast them, then finish them off in the last 15 minutes before eating, while my roast or what-have-you is resting.

Heat the oven to 200°C/fan 180°C/Gas 6. Bring a large, generously salted saucepan of water to the boil. As the water begins to gallop, add the potatoes. Cook for 10–15 minutes, until tender when pricked with a fork. Drain the potatoes and arrange across 2–3 roasting trays; it's imperative not to crowd them, as it is the space between each little spud that allows it to crisp so gloriously. Drizzle generously with the oil and roast for 50 minutes, every now and then giving the trays a good shake.

When the potatoes are crisp, take the trays out of the oven, then use a fork or spoon to roughly squash each potato a little, to crack their crisp skins open so they soak up the salty, flavoursome oil. The potatoes will sit happily like this for 2–3 hours, so you can roast your meat in the oven, then pop the potatoes back in for a last blast while the roast is resting.

—

Season generously, toss in a few herbs, if you like, and set the trays back in the oven to crisp for a further 15 minutes, or until you're ready to eat.

SERVE WITH…
Because of the required oven space jiggery-pokery, if you're going to serve these with a roast, they work best with one that needs to rest for a while, such as ROAST PORK WITH HONEY-ROAST PERSIMMONS (p.96). You could also leave out the persimmons and instead try ROAST GRAPES (p.168), which you can blister in the oven alongside the potatoes.

AND FOR PUDDING…
Soft, crumbly PISTACHIO BUTTER CAKE WITH MARZIPAN ICING (p.232).

ROAST NEW POTATOES WITH BAY LEAVES

HANDS ON TIME
5–10 minutes

HANDS OFF TIME
1 hour or so

FOR 4–6
20 new potatoes
20 bay leaves
4–5 tbsp extra virgin
    olive oil
Sea salt flakes
Freshly ground
    black pepper

I first came across this way of cooking potatoes – each one stuffed with an aromatic bay leaf, then roasted until seductively golden – in Lorenza De Medici's magnificent book *The Renaissance of Italian Cooking*, and became instantly infatuated. There is indeed a wonderfully renaissant quality about these potatoes, which are like something out of an extravagant painting. Not only do they look and taste spectacular, but they're deliciously simple to prepare. I eat the bay leaves, but you can pick them out if you prefer.

Heat the oven to 180°C/fan 160°C/Gas 4.

Make a lengthways slit across the middle of each potato. Insert a bay leaf into the slit, then arrange in a roasting tray, allowing ample space between them. Drizzle over the oil, then season generously.

—

Roast in the oven for 1 hour or so (depending on the size of the potatoes), until golden brown and easily pierced.

SERVE WITH...
Like any other kind of roast potatoes, these are a wonderful addition to pretty much any menu. I like them with roast chicken - especially the exquisitely BUTTERY LEMON ROAST CHICKEN (p.92) - and perhaps a tray of roasted fruits too, such as richly hued ROAST PLUMS (p.170), alongside BUTTER-&-SAGE ROAST PUMPKIN (p.158). A REALLY GOOD GREEN SALAD (p.112), with fine slices of sweet fennel and tossed in a simple lemon dressing, and you're done.

AND FOR PUDDING...
An indulgent EASY-PEASY LEMON MERINGUE PIE (p.182) that I can make either the day before, or comfortably in the time it takes for the chicken to roast.

POMMES DAUPHINOISE

HANDS ON TIME
15 minutes

HANDS OFF TIME
35–45 minutes

FOR 4–6
900g potatoes
450ml double cream
50ml whole milk
2 garlic cloves,
    finely chopped
3 bay leaves
90g Parmesan cheese,
    grated
15g salted butter
Sea salt flakes
Freshly ground
    black pepper

It is an undisputed fact of life that everyone loves pommes dauphinoise. You might feel that I have given a recipe to feed a small army here; but when I'm catering for large numbers, this is my potato of choice. And when I'm cooking for a more intimate group of four or six, I still make this much, because there is little extra effort involved and it reheats beautifully. All leftovers are chilled (or frozen) and reheated when needed.

Heat the oven to 220°C/fan 200°C/Gas 7.

Finely slice the potatoes into 3mm rounds (I don't bother peeling them, though you could, of course, if you like). If you have a mandolin, it makes this a lot simpler.

Bring the sliced potatoes, cream, milk, garlic and bay leaves to a gentle simmer in a large, heavy-based saucepan and cook, partially covered, for 15 minutes, turning gently every now and then to stop the potatoes from sticking. Season to taste with salt and heaps of freshly ground pepper.

Tip the potatoes and their heady juices into a shallow ovenproof dish. Smooth out the top, sprinkle over the Parmesan and dot small pieces of butter here and there. You can keep this in the fridge for a few hours, if that's convenient.

———

Cook (if straight from the pan) for 15–20 minutes, or (if from the fridge) for 25–30 minutes, checking the top isn't burning after 20 minutes (if it's browning too much, cover with foil). It should be golden and bubbling.

SERVE WITH...
Pommes dauphinoise - outrageously rich and creamy - are divine with most things, but best with a roast. You can't beat the BUTTERY LEMON ROAST CHICKEN (p.92); if you're cooking for six or more, roast a couple of birds and pile them on a serving dish on a bed of thyme and rosemary. Add a tray of sweet ROAST APPLES (p.172) and something green, such as GREEN BEANS WITH BABY TOMATOES (p.140).

AND FOR PUDDING...
I love a CHOCOLATE CHESTNUT MERINGUE PIE (p.178) with its crumbly, chocolatey base and heaps of soft, swirly meringue on top.

ROAST STUFFED TOMATOES

HANDS ON TIME
20 minutes

HANDS OFF TIME
45 minutes roasting

FOR 6
6 firm medium tomatoes
125g stale crusty bread
4 parsley sprigs
4 basil sprigs
8-10 black olives,
    pitted and chopped
100g pecorino cheese,
    finely grated
140ml vegetable stock
Sea salt flakes
Freshly ground
    black pepper

I've always loved tomatoes cooked this way, the sweet flesh filled with a comforting concoction of bread, cheese and herbs imbued with umami-some tomato juice, perfectly mushy inside and golden-crisp on top. I happily eat them by the dozen. They take a little time to bring together, but they're not in any way difficult and can be made a day ahead, then reheated in the oven.

Heat the oven to 160°C/fan 140°C/Gas 3. Halve the tomatoes across their middles and scoop the seeds and most of the flesh into a small bowl, leaving a thick layer of skin. Sprinkle the insides of the tomatoes with a little salt, then lay upside down on kitchen paper to drain excess juices.

Tear the bread into chunks, put it in a food processor and blitz to rough crumbs, then tip them into a mixing bowl. Spoon the reserved tomato pulp into a sieve over the bowl and use a spoon to press it down, so all the lovely juices spill over the crumbs, giving a delicious flavour. Tear the herb leaves off their stalks and roughly chop, then add them to the bowl with the crumbs. Add the olives and just more than three-quarters of the cheese, then mix with your hands until well combined. Season to taste.

Take a sheet of baking parchment, crumple it up and run it under a gentle stream of water for a second. Stretch it out and use it to line a roasting dish, then arrange the tomato halves snugly, hollows up, in the dish. Fill generously with stuffing, so it bulges over the top, then sprinkle with the last of the cheese. Pour in the stock and seal the dish with foil. Bake for 30 minutes, then uncover and bake for 10–15 minutes, until golden.

———

Reheat in a medium oven for 15 minutes to serve warm, if you like.

SERVE WITH...
These look rather spectacular: a burst of tomato-red and enticing golden crumb. They're just as good at room temperature as warm from the oven, so are the kind of food I associate with al fresco eating, when it's awfully nice not to have to worry about timings. Serve with COLD ROAST TOPSIDE OF BEEF (p.104), SALSA VERDE (p.266) and a generous dish of NEW POTATOES WITH LEMON & SAMPHIRE (p.126).

AND FOR PUDDING...
Wobbly, chilled PINK RHUBARB & PROSECCO JELLY (p.222) with thick, runny double cream and a large bowl of ruby-red raspberries.

BUTTER-&-SAGE ROAST PUMPKIN

HANDS ON TIME
5 minutes

HANDS OFF TIME
50 minutes

FOR 3–4
380g pumpkin,
    peeled, deseeded
    and cut in 1cm-thick
    slices
50g salted butter
A small bunch of
    sage, leaves picked
Sea salt flakes
Freshly ground
    black pepper

Buttery pumpkin with a generous handful of crisped sage leaves is a classic Italian combination and an all-time favourite with the greedier members of my family (among whom I count myself). For the sake of ease, I buy bags of peeled and sliced pumpkin from the supermarket – this is sometimes a mix of squash and pumpkin, which is equally good – then just toss it in the oven with the butter and herbs.

Heat the oven to 190°C/fan 170°C/Gas 5.

Toss the sliced pumpkin into a roasting tray in a single layer. Dot the butter in among and on top of the slices, scatter the sage leaves over, then season with salt and pepper. You can do this 5–6 hours in advance.

———

Roast for 45–50 minutes until the pumpkin is tender and the edges have caramelised nicely. If you want it crisper still, then just leave it in the oven for a little while longer.

SERVE WITH...
This dish's sheer simplicity means it's one I make often, especially to stretch out a roast in the chillier months when pumpkin is in season. It is proper autumnal fare, to go with HONEY-ROAST POUSSINS (p.94), buttery SAFFRON FENNEL (p.134) and A REALLY GOOD CHICORY SALAD WITH CREAMY MUSTARD DRESSING (p.110).

AND FOR PUDDING...
A variation on WINTER FRUIT & MASCARPONE TART (p.180), made with a chocolatey biscuit base and topped with whatever fruit is in season, the more colourful the better.

COURGETTE BLOSSOM
& TALEGGIO GALETTE

HANDS ON TIME
15 minutes

HANDS OFF TIME
25 minutes

FOR 6
1 × 375g sheet ready
   rolled, all-butter
   puff pastry
1 egg, lightly beaten
250g ricotta
2 tbsp grated
   Parmesan cheese
Finely grated zest
   of 1 lemon
100g Taleggio cheese,
   finely sliced
1 small courgette,
   finely sliced
6 courgette flowers
   (optional), or another
   courgette
2 tbsp extra virgin
   olive oil
Sea salt flakes
Freshly ground
   black pepper

This is essentially just a sheet of buttery, golden puff pastry topped with whatever you fancy, or have to hand or, indeed, left over. I have a soft spot for saffron-hued courgette blossoms, but you could just as well omit them and use more sliced courgettes instead. Otherwise baby tomatoes, black olives and basil, or a more wintry combination of Gorgonzola, walnuts and a few slices of apple are both delectable variations.

Heat the oven to 200°C/fan 180°C/Gas 6. Line a baking tray with baking parchment. Unroll the sheet of pastry, score a border of 2–3cm around the edge with a sharp knife and prick all over the centre part with a fork. Brush the pastry edges with egg. Bake for 10 minutes, until dry to the touch and lightly coloured at the edges. If the pastry puffs up in the middle, just press it down with the back of a spoon or your hands.

Meanwhile, in a small bowl, combine the ricotta, Parmesan and lemon zest, stir, then set aside.

——

When you're ready to bake it, spread the ricotta over the fork-docked part of the par-baked pastry. Arrange the Taleggio over the ricotta, then the courgette slices. Season, then bake for 15 minutes, until the Taleggio has mostly melted. Carefully prise open the petals of the courgette flowers, remove the pistils and discard. Take the pastry out of the oven, arrange the flowers on top, drizzle with the oil and bake for a further 5–10 minutes until golden all over and the flowers are ever-so-slightly wilted.

Serve warm or at room temperature.

SERVE WITH...
This is the kind of recipe that seamlessly stretches a meal out. It's the kind you throw together when you're cooking roast chicken (p.90 and p.92), but you realise one of your guests is vegetarian and, as much as they say they'll happily just eat the sides, you want to make sure those constitute something that resembles a decent meal. It also lends itself well to picnics: pack it up in a basket with a chunk of cheese.

AND FOR PUDDING...
For picnics, a bag of cherries and a tin of MERINGUES (p.238) or LAVENDER HONEY PANNACOTTA (p.208). I save jars, fill three-quarters full with pannacotta and put the lids on: perfectly portable puddings.

TIMBALLO OF BAKED COURGETTES

HANDS ON TIME
15 minutes

HANDS OFF TIME
30 minutes

FOR 6
800g courgettes
3 tbsp extra virgin
  olive oil
2 garlic cloves, peeled
A small bunch of
  parsley, leaves
  picked and roughly
  chopped
Sea salt flakes
Freshly ground
  black pepper

Inspiration for this comes from a scrumptious dish they make and sell by the slice at our local delicatessen in Venice. The melting courgette comes topped with a lid of more courgette, sliced and woven into the prettiest lattice, which is why it's called *timballo* ('pie'). I'm proud to say I've found a simple trick for recreating the lattice, which you'll find below. The rest couldn't be easier: roughly chopped courgette, lightly fried with garlic, then baked. If you want something more indulgent, add grated Parmesan before baking.

Use a mandolin, or a potato peeler, to finely slice the courgettes lengthways from top to toe. You want enough slices to cover the surface of your baking dish. Arrange the strips next to each other on a sheet of greaseproof paper, side by side; if they aren't long enough for the dish, lay a second strip on top of the tail-end of the first, to extend it. Now lay perpendicular strips across the first set and weave them together. You want no visible gaps.

Roughly chop the rest of the courgettes into pieces and rounds, 2–3mm thick. Heat 2 tbsp of the oil and the garlic in a large frying pan over a medium heat. After 5 minutes or so, when the garlic has browned, discard it and toss in the courgettes. Cover and cook for 5–10 minutes, giving it a good shake now and again. Heat the oven to 180°C/fan 160°C/Gas 4.

When the courgettes are just cooked, take them off the heat and spoon them into an ovenproof baking dish, mix in the parsley, season with salt and pepper and toss through. Top with the lattice, quickly upending it over the dish on its sheet of greaseproof paper, then brush with the final 1 tbsp of olive oil. You can pop the timballo in the fridge at this point for a few hours.

—

Bake for 30 minutes, until the jade-green lattice is cooked through and it is piping hot at its centre (check by inserting a knife, then feeling its tip).

SERVE WITH...
The kind of side dish that really works well with everything: try it with thin slices of ruby-red COLD ROAST TOPSIDE OF BEEF (p.104), A REALLY GOOD TOMATO SALAD (p.114) and FRIED BROCCOLI WITH BLACK OLIVES (p.128), with its hint of anchovy, for a light summery feast.

AND FOR PUDDING...
A devilishly rich CHOCOLATE & RUM PUDDING (p.226), served with a healthy smattering of sharp berries.

CREAMY BAKED LEEKS WITH MUSTARD & PARMESAN

FOR 4–6
6–7 leeks
170ml vegetable stock
1 tbsp Dijon mustard
2 tbsp wholegrain
   mustard
250ml double cream
60g Parmesan cheese,
   grated
20g salted butter,
   in pieces

At that point in the winter when spring still feels like a distant mirage and there is so little that is exciting and fresh to cook with, this concoction – in its shamelessly decadent creamy, cheesy, mustardy sauce – is a bona fide godsend. It's warm, rich and devilishly good.

Heat the oven to 180°C/fan 160°C/Gas 4.

Trim the leeks and chop into pieces about 5cm long. Arrange the chunks of leek, standing straight up like little soldiers, in a 24cm ovenproof frying pan, or equivalent flameproof oven dish. Bring the stock to the boil in a saucepan, then whisk in both the mustards and pour over the leeks.

Set the pan over a medium heat and bring to the boil. Cover (either with an ovenproof lid, if you have one the right size, or a sheet of foil), reduce the heat a little and simmer for 10 minutes, until tender. They can sit like this, covered, for up to a day.

—

Take the pan off the heat, pour in the cream, then sprinkle a thick layer of Parmesan over the top. Dot small amounts of butter here and there and bake for 30 minutes, until almost indecently bubbling and golden on top.

SERVE WITH...
For a simple meal, I love this with APHRODITE'S ROAST CHICKEN (p.90) and A REALLY GOOD GREEN SALAD (p.112). When I'm cooking for a larger crowd, I have a soft spot for the mustardy-ness of the leeks alongside ALLEGRA'S POT-ROAST BEEF (p.68). Then I'll add a tray of ROAST NEW POTATOES WITH BAY LEAVES (p.152) and a crisp salad.

AND FOR PUDDING...
APPLE & WALNUT CRUMBLE PIE (p.246), or, if rushed, then something quick to pull together but showy nonetheless, such as FROZEN BERRIES WITH SAFFRON WHITE CHOCOLATE SAUCE (p.204), that - because it's made with frozen fruit - is so good year-round.

IN THE OVEN

ROAST RED ONIONS

HANDS ON TIME
5 minutes

HANDS OFF TIME
45 minutes

FOR 6
3 medium red onions,
    peeled
3 tbsp extra virgin
    olive oil
A small bunch of thyme
Sea salt flakes
Freshly ground
    black pepper

To call this a recipe is a little pretentious; it's just a matter of popping onions in the oven, then waiting for them to become tender and irresistibly sweet. The colour – like a deep, sumptuous glass of red wine – is little short of glorious. It may be a simple dish, but it is a spectacular addition to any table.

The timings given below – much like the proportions – are purely indicative. As a rule of thumb, I just pop the tray in the oven with the meat and leave it at that. You can't really go wrong.

Heat the oven to 220°C/fan 200°C/Gas 7.

Halve each onion and cut each half into 4 wedges, to get 8 wedges from each onion. Arrange them in a roasting tray. You can do this a good few hours in advance.

—

Now, drizzle with the olive oil. Season generously with salt and pepper and throw in the thyme sprigs.

Roast for 40–45 minutes, until deliciously sweet and tender.

SERVE WITH...
As these go with anything, this is the kind of 'filler' dish I often make when I'm worried about not having enough food. Try alongside a WINTRY SAFFRON COUSCOUS (p.48), a BEETROOT & MINT SALAD (p.118) and baby, rainbow-hued BUTTERY CARROTS WITH CHESTNUT HONEY (p.142).

AND FOR PUDDING...
A dramatic dish of RED WINE POACHED PEARS (p.212), either served simply as is, or with a dollop of SALTED HONEY ICE CREAM (p.186) and MERINGUES (p.238).

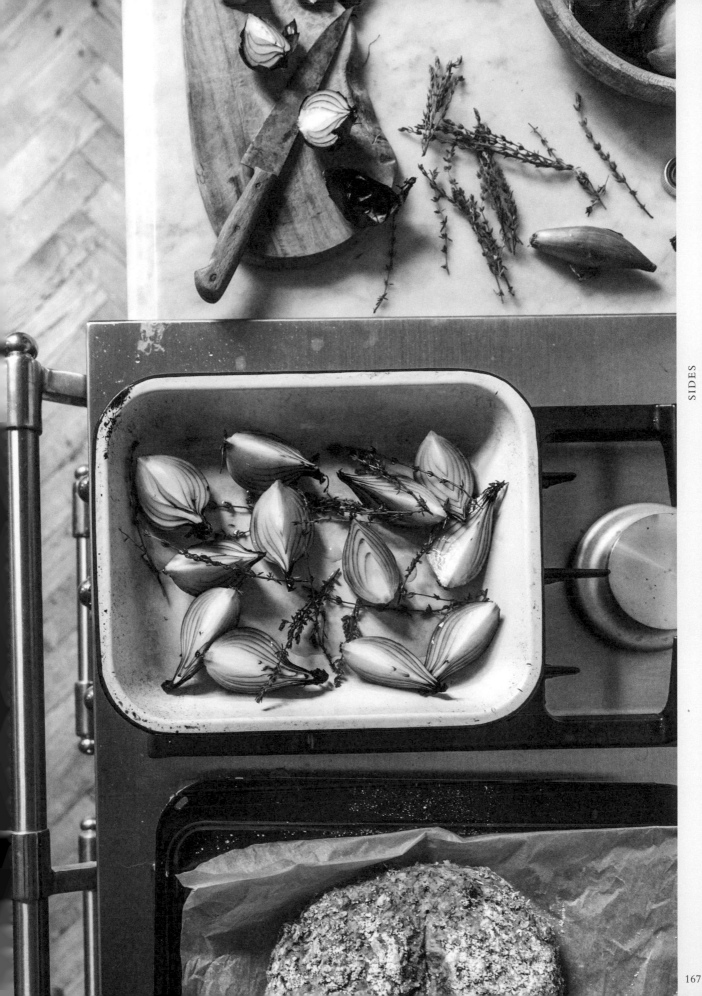

ROAST GRAPES

HANDS ON TIME
1 minute

HANDS OFF TIME
30 minutes

FOR 6–8
1kg red grapes,
   ideally seedless

Barely a recipe. You pile the grapes into a tray and roast them until their skins split and their regal-hued juices run everywhere. They taste wonderful with all meats and this is one of those dishes that – because it's so very low effort and so very high impact – I always just add on if I have a modicum of space left in the oven, while the joint rests before carving. Much like the recipes for Roast Plums (p.170) and Roast Apples (p.172) that follow, you can eat these with anything from cold cuts to warm, buttery roast chicken.

I wouldn't make these in advance; there is so little hassle involved that there's not much point. But if you can't fit a whole roasting tray in the oven, then break the grapes up into smaller bunches and tuck them around the meat you want to serve them with.

Heat the oven to 220°C/fan 200°C/Gas 7.

Arrange the grapes, still in whole bunches, in a roasting tray. Roast for 20–30 minutes, until the skins begin to split, the fruit is softened and the scarlet juices are running.

SERVE WITH...
While, strictly speaking, grapes come into season in late summer or early autumn, they're easy enough to find in the shops all year round and this is certainly a dish that I make across the seasons. Try them with HONEY-ROAST POUSSINS (p.94), or APHRODITE'S ROAST CHICKEN (p.90), a dish of creamy POMMES DAUPHINOISE (p.154) and – to gild the lily – some ROAST PLUMS (p.170), too.

AND FOR PUDDING...
My EASY-PEASY LEMON MERINGUE PIE (p.182), which involves no baking as such, but has an exquisitely buttery shortbread pie crust and a rich lemon curd filling laced with condensed milk.

ROAST PLUMS

HANDS ON TIME
5 minutes

HANDS OFF TIME
30 minutes

FOR 6
6 plums
½ tbsp caster sugar
1 tbsp extra virgin
   olive oil
Sea salt flakes
Freshly ground
   black pepper

There is something undoubtedly majestic about these: their deep colours with all the drama of a tropical sunset, and that tangy sharpness of their soft flesh. If oven space is at a premium, you could cook these up to a day in advance, then reheat for 10 minutes before serving.

Heat the oven to 180°C/fan 160°C/Gas 4.

Halve the plums, then scoop out and discard their stones. Arrange the blushing fruits, cut sides up, in a roasting tray. You can do this a few hours ahead of when you cook them: just cover and set in the fridge.

——

Sprinkle over the sugar and drizzle with the olive oil. Season generously with salt and a good grinding of pepper. Roast for 25–30 minutes, until soft and tender.

SERVE WITH...
I have a soft spot for these with roast chicken: APHRODITE'S ROAST CHICKEN (p.90), where you cook the bird and the potatoes together in the same tray, I find, works particularly well in terms of juggling oven space and so forth. Then A REALLY GOOD GREEN SALAD (p.112) drenched in OLGA'S PEPPERY VINAIGRETTE (p.260) to round it all off.

AND FOR PUDDING...
Something rich and chocolatey: either FLOURLESS CHOCOLATE, CHESTNUT & ROSEMARY CAKE (p.234) - fabulously dense - or CHOCOLATE & RUM PUDDING (p.226).

ROAST APPLES

HANDS ON TIME
1 minute

HANDS OFF TIME
1 hour 20 minutes

FOR 6
6 Pink Lady apples

This fulfils the same function at the table as apple sauce: it pays a sweet compliment to chicken, poussins, or, of course, fatty pork. But, happily, roasted apples are simpler to make than sauce: no need here for peeling, coring or slicing, nor running through a blender (and then washing the blender). I love the ceremonial feel of bringing the fruit to the table whole: the apples are such a pleasing sight nestled in their roasting tray, sweet honey-toned flesh bursting out of tender ruddy skin. I usually offer one for each person, to enjoy with their roast.

When it comes to choosing what kind of apples to roast, my preference is for Pink Lady. This is partly because those are the variety of apple that I tend to have lying around in the kitchen, and partly because I love how sweet they taste, most especially when cooked this way, as the process of roasting only intensifies their flavour.

Heat the oven to 220°C/fan 200°C/Gas 7.

Arrange the apples snugly in a roasting tray and add roughly 2.5cm of water, then cover with foil, sealing it around the edges.

Bake for 1 hour, until the apples feel soft but still firm enough to hold their shape.

Remove and discard the foil and roast for a further 20 minutes, until very tender and the fruits are bursting out of their skins.

SERVE WITH...
My recipe for PORK WELLINGTON WITH APPLE & SAGE (p.100) already comes with a buttery apple filling, but I always like to serve it with extra, sweet roast fruit, so I invariably make a tray of these too. For the rest of the meal, a dish (or two) of ROAST NEW POTATOES WITH BAY LEAVES (p.152) and a big, crunchy REALLY GOOD CHICORY SALAD WITH CREAMY MUSTARD DRESSING (p.110), perhaps with a handful of walnuts tossed in.

AND FOR PUDDING...
SALTED CARAMEL PANNACOTTA (p.210), jiggly, just set and swimming in a pool of nearly burnt, brown, perfectly salted caramel sauce.

SWEETS

I have a sweet tooth. Cakes, puddings, ice cream, jellies and elaborate meringues laced with whipped cream are the stuff of my dreams. But the real joy of pudding is about more than greed: it's an important moment in the rhythm of the meal, a moment to breathe. It's an invitation to linger at the table: to help yourself to seconds, to sip your coffee, to chatter, to relax into that delicious 'full' feeling that comes after a good meal well enjoyed, as well as into the company of those gathered with you. Pudding is tacit acknowledgement that we are not simply gathered here to feed ourselves, but for pleasure. It's an extravagant treat, and therein lies its charm. And while I will skip a starter happily (and as you know, mostly do), I believe you should never skip the sweet.

Given my love of all things sweet, it is no surprise that I like to bake more than I like to cook. Baking involves a different kind of magic: it feels like you start with next to nothing - a bag of flour, a box of eggs, a little sugar - yet somehow you end up with a cake. It's immensely satisfying. I'm not a gardener myself, but I imagine the act of baking to be a pleasure rather like planting seeds and watching them grow into a field of sugary peonies, only the gratification is rather more instant. Baking is the closest I get to quiet meditation in the kitchen. You will, therefore, find in this chapter a number of recipes that call for a little more time: cakes, sweet tarts and more. But I urge you not to be put off; if I can make them, you definitely can. They are also the kind of recipes where all the effort is ahead of time, and then, when it comes to your lunch or supper party, all you have to do is bring the dessert out and enjoy the gratifying oooh-ing and aaah-ing that it evokes.

Of course, there are many days when I don't have time to indulge in baking, but I still want to eat something sweet. For those occasions, I have included a number of dishes that involve mere assembly: there are few things more beautiful than strawberries swimming in sweet red wine syrup, for instance, or more delectable than ricotta whipped into a light frenzy with dark chocolate and sugared citrus. That they take mere moments to throw together is just the cherry on top of the proverbial cake.

CHOCOLATE CHESTNUT MERINGUE PIE

HANDS ON TIME
30 minutes

FOR 8–10
FOR THE BASE
80g dark chocolate,
  chopped
450g chocolate bourbon
  biscuits
100g salted butter,
  softened

FOR THE FILLING
350g unsweetened
  chestnut purée
75g dark muscovado
  sugar, plus extra
  to taste
30ml double cream
1 tbsp brandy

FOR THE MERINGUE
4 egg whites, at
  room temperature
¼ tsp cream of tartar
150g caster sugar

This is a Mont Blanc of sorts, in beautiful pie form. The base is made from a mix of chocolate biscuits (any old chocolate biscuit will do, but chocolate bourbons work particularly well – a tip picked up from my much-loved and worn copy of Nigella Lawson's *Kitchen*). You'll need a blowtorch to burnish the meringue. I use mine a lot: it's a small, easy-to-store and relatively inexpensive piece of kitchen equipment that I think is well worth the investment for the dramatic gilding effect it gives.

Put the chocolate in a food processor with the biscuits. Blitz until they form a crumb, then add the butter and blitz again until it starts to clump together. Press evenly into a deep 28cm fluted pie dish with a removable base and put in the freezer for 10–15 minutes to harden.

Meanwhile, spoon the chestnut purée into a bowl, add the muscovado and beat with an electric mixer or wooden spoon until the sugar has dissolved. Keep on beating as you slowly pour in the cream and brandy. Pause and taste: add a little more sugar, if you like. Pour into the chilled case, cover and store in the fridge. You can make it up to this stage 3 days before.

———

Place the egg whites in a clean, grease-free bowl and whisk on a low speed (if you have an electric whisk) until frothy. Add the cream of tartar and increase the speed to medium–high. Beat until soft peaks form, then gradually add the caster sugar and beat until firm peaks form. Dollop the meringue on to the pie and spread it out with the back of a spoon so all the deep brown filling is covered in a snowy blanket. Use the spoon to make small peaks in the meringue and caramelise with a blowtorch.

SERVE WITH...
Because it's chestnut, I gravitate towards this pie in autumn and winter. I make it for Sunday lunch, to follow on from APHRODITE'S ROAST CHICKEN (p.90) on its bed of slivers of crisp-like golden potatoes, perhaps with a warming dish of BRAISED LENTILS WITH PANCETTA (p.130) and a tray of sweet ROAST RED ONIONS (p.166).

Otherwise, my dream comfort meal – and heaven all year round – is TAGLIATELLE GRATIN (p.86), baked in a sumptuously creamy sauce and served with a green salad, drenched in my godmother OLGA'S PEPPERY VINAIGRETTE (p.260). Incidentally, this menu also works particularly well for big dinner parties.

WINTER FRUIT & MASCARPONE TART

HANDS ON TIME
30 minutes

FOR 8–10
FOR THE BASE
80g dark chocolate,
    chopped
450g chocolate bourbon
    biscuits
100g salted butter,
    softened

FOR THE FILLING
    AND TOPPING
1 egg, separated
80g caster sugar
500g mascarpone, at
    room temperature
400g redcurrants
4-5 plums, quartered
    and pitted

The recipe given here is for a winter tart, but there is no reason why you can't make it year round. Blood oranges for late winter, peeled and cut into thick rounds, then sprinkled with a smattering of demerara sugar; strawberries at the first sign of warm weather, raspberries later in the season; peaches, cut into juicy chunks, towards high summer, then figs, torn open to reveal their jewel-like insides and topped with a handful of soft green pistachios, come September. It's a blank canvas for you to play with.

This is the same base as for the Chocolate Chestnut Meringue Pie (p.178). Put the chocolate in a food processor with the biscuits. Blitz until they form a crumb mixture, then add the butter and blitz again until the mix starts to clump together. Press evenly into a deep 28cm fluted pie dish with a removable base and put in the freezer for 10–15 minutes to harden. You could put it in the fridge if you prefer, just leave it in there a little longer.

Whisk the egg white until stiff, adding half the sugar a little at a time. In a second bowl, beat the yolk with the remaining sugar until thick and lemony pale. Beat the mascarpone into the egg yolk mixture until smooth, then gently fold in the egg white.

Spoon the mascarpone cream into the case and smooth it out with the back of a spoon. Store in the fridge for up to 1 day.

—

Top with the redcurrants and plums just a few hours before serving, so the plums don't turn brown.

SERVE WITH...
You can't really go wrong with this. When the weather starts to turn cold and bitter, it makes for a welcome follow-on from a warming, buttery OSSOBUCO WITH SAGE & LEMON (p.70), served with BUTTER-&-SAGE ROAST PUMPKIN (p.158) and a richly coloured BEETROOT & MINT SALAD (p.118).

EASY-PEASY LEMON MERINGUE PIE

HANDS ON TIME
30 minutes

FOR 8–10
FOR THE BASE
500g Scottish
   shortbread biscuits
100g salted butter,
   softened

FOR THE LEMON CURD
1 × 2g gelatine sheet
2 tbsp boiling water
3 egg yolks
1 × 397g tin of
   condensed milk
100ml lemon juice
   (from a bottle is fine)
Finely grated zest
   of 1 lemon
¼ tsp salt

FOR THE MERINGUE
3 egg whites
100g caster sugar
2 tbsp lemon juice
½ tsp vanilla extract

Everything about this is joyful, from the clouds of soft meringue to the rich yellow curd and the crumbly, buttery base. You could, of course, buy a good lemon curd, but this recipe, adapted from the brilliant 1950s book *Artistry in Cold Food Preparation*, tastes so above and beyond anything you can buy that it is worth that marginal – and trust me, it really is marginal – extra effort.

Throw the biscuits into a food processor and blitz to crumbs. Add the butter and blitz again until the mix looks like wet sand. Press the buttery rubble evenly into a 25cm fluted pie dish with a removable base. Put in the freezer for 10–15 minutes to harden.

Cover the sheet of gelatine with cold water in a small bowl and set aside for 5 minutes. Lift the gelatine out of the bowl, tip away the water, then return the gelatine to the bowl, cover with the measured boiling water and stir until dissolved. Put the egg yolks in a mixing bowl and add the condensed milk, lemon juice, zest and salt. Whisk vigorously until slightly thickened. Pour in the gelatine and mix again. Pour the creamy lemon custard into the crust, levelling it out with the back of a spoon, and set in the fridge to chill. It will keep happily for 1–2 days.

———

Lift the pie crust out of its tin; if cold from the fridge, it should come out easily. Put the egg whites in a spotlessly clean mixing bowl and beat until frothy. Gradually add the sugar, spoonful by spoonful, beating all the while. Keep whisking the meringue until it becomes thick and glossy, then add the lemon juice and vanilla extract. Whisk until well combined. Dollop the meringue on to the pie and spread it out so all the glossy, sunny filling is completely covered. Use a spoon to make small peaks in the meringue, then use a blowtorch to caramelise it, so the tips are lightly golden and burnished. The pie, in its fully assembled glorious form, will happily sit in the fridge for up to 1 day. Best served chilled.

SERVE WITH...
Because this can be made so far in advance, you can afford to give a little more effort to the rest of the meal. Fine slices of COLD ROAST TOPSIDE OF BEEF (p.104) with peppery SALSA VERDE (p.266), a TOMATO, RED ONION & MINT SALAD (p.116) and NEW POTATOES WITH LEMON & SAMPHIRE (p.126), swimming in oil and with heaps of verdant parsley. One of those blissful meals you prepare almost entirely a day ahead.

RUM, RAISIN & WALNUT ICE CREAM

HANDS ON TIME
30 minutes

HANDS OFF TIME
30 minutes (and ideally
   overnight) soaking
6–8 hours freezing

FOR 6
80g raisins
100ml rum
2 egg whites
¼ tsp cream of tartar
85g caster sugar
30g walnuts, coarsely
   chopped
225g double cream

Since discovering that you can buy plain white paper ice-cream containers – the disposable variety, such as you get in proper gelato shops – online, I've been very taken with home-made ice cream for pudding. Put the tub on the table with a scoop and some cones so all can help themselves, and it makes for just about the easiest pudding you can think of.

This, like the two recipes that follow, is a no-churn ice cream, so there's no need for a machine. The rum – here in generous quantities – stops the cream from freezing fully and crystallising, so you get a cloud-like concoction laced with chunks of walnuts and plump, sweet, booze-soaked raisins.

Put the raisins in a small bowl, pour over the rum and set aside for at least 30 minutes, or ideally overnight.

In a spotlessly clean mixing bowl, whisk the egg whites and cream of tartar until frothy. Slowly add the sugar, a spoonful at a time, until you have a soft, glossy meringue. Fold in the walnuts.

Now drain the raisins, reserving the liquid, and gently fold them into the egg whites.

In a second mixing bowl, whip the cream until it forms stiff peaks. As you whip, slowly pour in the reserved rum in a steady trickle. Now fold the cream into the egg white mixture and spoon into a freezer-safe container with an airtight lid. Freeze for 6–8 hours, or overnight.

—

The ice cream will keep in the freezer for up to 3 months.

SERVE WITH...
Ice cream, most especially the home-made variety, makes for a dreamy end to any meal, served either in coupes or waffle cones. Despite this being a strictly-for-grown-ups recipe, it's nonetheless a child-like pudding that everyone delights in; though, because it's such a boozy flavour, I can't help but feel that this version suits a supper party more than a family lunch. A real treat to follow on from CONFIT DUCK PIE (p.98) with rainbow-toned BUTTERY CARROTS WITH CHESTNUT HONEY (p.142) and a crisp REALLY GOOD CHICORY SALAD WITH CREAMY MUSTARD DRESSING (p.110).

SALTED HONEY ICE CREAM

HANDS ON TIME
10 minutes

HANDS OFF TIME
6–8 hours freezing

FOR 6
600g double cream
1 × 397g tin of
   condensed milk
80g runny honey
¼ tsp sea salt flakes
100g dark chocolate,
   coarsely chopped

This salted honey flavour is a favourite of mine, but you can play with it: add chunks of dark chocolate, whole salted almonds, crystallised ginger or roughly chopped figs. Top the ice cream with a few crushed pistachios and a little more honey, for a baklava-like effect. Best of all, it's another simple no-churn recipe.

Pour the cream into a large mixing bowl and whip until stiff peaks begin to form. Take care not to over-whip, as you want the texture to be smooth and lusciously soft.

Gently pour in the condensed milk and fold it into the cream, then drizzle in the honey, sprinkle with the salt and fold all the ingredients evenly through. Toss the chocolate into the bowl and gently give the mixture a stir so it is peppered throughout with chocolate pieces.

Pour the mixture into a freezer-safe container with an airtight lid and freeze for 6–8 hours, or overnight.

—

The ice cream will keep in the freezer for up to 3 months.

SERVE WITH...
My son Aeneas absolutely loves this. His dream meal is: PORK WELLINGTON WITH APPLE & SAGE (p.100) in all its quasi-sausage roll-like glory, and a big dish of ESPECIALLY GOOD ROAST POTATOES (p.150). I would suggest also adding a tray of sweet, slightly caramelised ROAST RED ONIONS (p.166) and A REALLY GOOD GREEN SALAD (p.112) with slices of fennel (wonderful with the pork) for good measure. And then this ice cream for pudding, of course.

PINE NUT ICE CREAM 'AFFOGATO'

HANDS ON TIME
10 minutes

HANDS OFF TIME
6-8 hours freezing

FOR 6
FOR THE ICE CREAM
100g pine nuts
600g double cream
1 × 397g tin of
    condensed milk
Shortbread biscuits,
    to serve (optional)

FOR THE AFFOGATO
1 large Moka pot of
    strong, hot coffee

This is an acquired taste, but one I have long since been seduced by. My first encounter with pine nut ice cream was at the Gelateria Mela Verde in Venice, renowned for its wild and wonderful flavours, and it is their *gelato ai pinoli* that is the inspiration for the recipe here. The pine nut is oddly subtle: it doesn't taste nutty, as you'd expect, but instead incredibly rich, creamy and not too sweet. Buy the best-quality pine nuts you can get your hands on – ideally Italian – for this.

Toss the pine nuts into a food processor and blitz to a thick, creamy paste.

In a large mixing bowl, whip the cream until it forms stiff peaks. Pour in the condensed milk and keep whipping until well combined. Now gently fold in the pine nut paste and freeze for 6–8 hours, or overnight.

—

The ice cream will keep for up to 3 months in the freezer. When ready to serve, brew a Moka of hot coffee, scoop the ice cream into bowls or cups, then pour over the coffee and eat immediately, as the cold ice cream melts into the hot bitter espresso, with shortbread biscuits, if you like.

SERVE WITH...
I tend to keep a tub or so of home-made ice cream for spontaneous last-minute supper parties. For the rest of the meal, keeping things equally low-maintenance, try a comforting plate of RIGATONI WITH MASCARPONE & PANCETTA (p.64) and a crisp, peppery green salad.

COFFEE MASCARPONE BISCUIT CAKE

HANDS ON TIME
20 minutes

HANDS OFF TIME
4 hours setting

FOR 6
3 × 2g gelatine sheets
4 tbsp caster sugar
6 egg yolks
375g mascarpone, at
    room temperature
1 tsp instant coffee
3 tbsp boiling water
250g chocolate chip or
    chocolate bourbon
    biscuits, plus
    optional extra for
    the top
Cocoa powder,
    for dusting

There is something of the *tiramisù* about this cake. As it sets in the fridge, the cream soaks into the biscuits, imbuing them with flavour and softening them at the edges, so, rather like the biscuit you dunk into your morning coffee, they are soft as you bite into them but crisp at the very core. Stick a candle or two in this and it doubles up as a rather sophisticated birthday cake. The only caveat is that you need to allow a few hours for it to set.

Put the gelatine sheets in a bowl of cold water and set aside for 5 minutes until soft. Line a 20cm cake tin with cling film.

In a mixing bowl, beat the sugar and the egg yolks with an electric mixer until pale and creamy. You want as much air in them as possible and they should double in size. Slowly beat in the mascarpone 1 tbsp at a time until you have a thick, smooth cream.

In a small heatproof bowl, dissolve the coffee in the measured boiling water. Drain the gelatine and squeeze out the water, then add to the hot coffee and stir to dissolve. Gently stir the mix into the mascarpone cream.

Spoon one-third of the cream into the prepared cake tin and use the back of a spoon to spread it out evenly, then arrange half the biscuits over in a single layer. Spoon one-third more of the cream over the biscuits, and arrange a second layer of biscuits over that. Then spoon the last of the cream over everything and smooth it out. Set the tin in the fridge and chill for at least 4 hours (or up to 2 days – it will keep nicely) until set.

—

Turn the cake out on to a cake stand or plate and peel away the cling film. Dust liberally with bitter cocoa powder and crumble over a few biscuits for decoration, if you like, then serve chilled.

SERVE WITH...
When the days are at their hottest, this is the perfect halfway house between ice cream and a cake, in the baked-in-the-oven sense of the word. To go with it, stick to light food: CARPACCIO OF FIGS WITH LARDO, HONEY & ROSEMARY (p.42), and perhaps a dish of ambrosial, creamy CHILLED ALMOND SOUP (p.38), good bread (from the bakery, don't even think of baking your own in the summer heat) and a nice selection of cheeses. If you felt like spoiling your guests, you could add a dish of BURRATA WITH PRESERVED LEMONS, MINT & CHILLI (p.34).

STRAWBERRIES IN LEMONY SYRUP

HANDS ON TIME
10 minutes

HANDS OFF TIME
At least 30 minutes
     macerating

FOR 6
600g strawberries,
     hulled and halved
4 tbsp caster sugar
Juice of 1 lemon

You don't need a recipe for strawberries. When in peak season, they should be served as they are, piled high in a pretty dish with a dollop of mascarpone, clotted cream or thick double cream on the side.

But if, like me, you're too impatient to wait for strawberry season proper and find yourself with punnets of the too-early, slightly wooden-tasting ones as soon as they appear in the shops, then this recipe is the best way to give them a little oomph. As the strawberries macerate in the sugar and lemon juice, a delectable pink syrup slowly forms, coating them in a shimmering, seductive gloss.

Pile the fruit into a serving bowl, sprinkle with the sugar and squeeze in the lemon juice. Toss the strawberries so they are all well coated and set to rest in the fridge for at least 30 minutes, while you get on with the rest of dinner.

—

You can prepare the strawberries up to 1 day in advance. When you serve them, the fruit should be swimming in a sweet pink syrup.

SERVE WITH...
This is late spring fare, so you want ASPARAGUS WITH LEMON & TOASTED ALMOND GRATIN (p.138), green and tender, and at its very best at this time of year. You also want baby NEW POTATOES WITH LEMON & SAMPHIRE (p.126) and some kind of cold, light dish you can easily eat outside in the first summer sunshine: POULET ANGLAIS (p.72) with its yogurty, tarragon-scented sauce is ideal. Then a few scoops of SALTED HONEY ICE CREAM (p.186), or A VERY GOOD VANILLA PANNACOTTA (p.206), to go with these berries.

DRUNKEN STRAWBERRIES

FOR 6
600g strawberries,
    hulled and halved
Zest of 1 lemon,
    pared off in long
    thick strips
100g caster sugar
1 bottle of fruity
    red wine

Another favourite, if rather more extravagant, way to jazz up slightly bland strawberries. You can throw this together at the last minute, but the longer you leave the fruit to macerate, the more it drinks up the rich flavour of the wine. Ideally you would make these a good few hours ahead – that morning, or the day before – but if time doesn't allow that, then just toss everything together before sitting down to dinner, let it rest in the fridge while you eat, and by the time you come to dessert it should be nigh-on perfect.

Pile the strawberries into a serving bowl. Add the strips of lemon zest, sprinkle over the sugar and pour in the wine. Chill in the fridge for at least 1 hour, if possible, to allow the fruit to macerate and the flavours to develop.

——

Serve chilled, with clotted cream or a dollop of mascarpone.

SERVE WITH...
If the lemony strawberries on the previous page conjure up visions of al fresco lunches, these - drenched in red wine syrup - feel to me better suited to an elegant, grown-up supper. Heaven with a plate of BRESAOLA E GRANA (p.44), served alongside a big dish of WILD RICE & LENTIL SALAD (p.132) and a juicy TOMATO, RED ONION & MINT SALAD (p.116). The strawberries are pudding enough on their own, but if you're catering for a large crowd, add a second dish of sweet MELON IN GRAPPA SYRUP (p.196).

MELON IN GRAPPA SYRUP

HANDS ON TIME
20 minutes

HANDS OFF TIME
At least 2 hours
   chilling

FOR 6
60ml boiling water
4 tbsp caster sugar
2 lemons, zest pared
   off in strips
2 small melons
120ml grappa
A handful of mint
   leaves

Italian grappa comes in all manner of unexpected, exotic flavours, from liquorice to cinnamon, and is always packaged in the most intriguing and flamboyant bottles, as only the Italians know how. This pudding is inspired by the melon-flavoured grappa that we sometimes drink after dinner in summer. It is a classic Venetian recipe that has somewhat fallen out of fashion, though just because it is no longer in vogue doesn't mean it's not a delight to eat. Be warned: the grappa, even in sweet syrup form, is punchy; this is a pudding that could just as well pass as a cocktail.

Combine the measured boiling water, sugar and strips of lemon zest in a small, heatproof bowl. Stir until the sugar has dissolved. Squeeze in the juice of 1 of the lemons, then set aside to cool.

Halve the melons, spoon out and discard the seeds, then use a melon baller to scoop out small balls. Set them in a serving dish.

Scoop the zest pieces out of the syrup, add the grappa, stir, then pour it over the melon. Chill in the fridge for at least 2 hours.

—

Tear the mint leaves and sprinkle them over the melon. Serve chilled.

SERVE WITH...
Because this is quite boozy, it lends itself well to a supper party. It works beautifully after TORTA DI MACCHERONI (p.82), a puff pastry pie filled with creamy saffron-scented pasta, crisp pancetta and oozing melted cheese. And to serve with that, a tray of ROAST RED ONIONS (p.166), A REALLY GOOD GREEN SALAD (p.112) and a deep-coloured BEETROOT & MINT SALAD (p.118). Or, if you prefer to make everything in advance: a cheesy SPINACH, MINT & MELTED CHEESE SYRIAN FRITTATA (p.80), a big bowl of green salad and a lovely dish of GREEN BEANS WITH BABY TOMATOES (p.140).

PISTACHIO PANETTONE CAKE

HANDS ON TIME
30 minutes

FOR 8-10
FOR THE PISTACHIO
    BUTTER
120g unsalted roasted
    pistachios
60g white chocolate,
    coarsely chopped
1 tbsp caster sugar
1 tsp vanilla extract

FOR THE CAKE
450ml chilled double
    cream
2 tbsp icing sugar
750g panettone
6 egg whites
300g caster sugar
2 tsp vanilla extract

The idea to use pistachio butter here, between each layer of sweet panettone and whipped cream, comes from Lisa Markwell, my editor at *The Sunday Times* and a brilliant cook. It is inspired. Otherwise, the recipe – for all its wonderfully extravagant appearance – is simply a matter of assembly: shop-bought panettone, soft whipped cream and a cloud of caramelised meringue.

These days, panettone comes in many incarnations. If you can get your hands on a chocolate-studded cake, it works particularly well, but I also love the more traditional sweet raisins and candied peel with the pistachio cream here. And you will need a blowtorch, if you don't already have one (this is my favourite piece of kitchen kit). It's not expensive, it's easy to store and is transformative for burnished, marshmallowy meringue, as here, or in the two meringue pies on p.178 and p.182.

First make the pistachio butter: combine all the ingredients in a food processor and blitz until smooth and creamy. This will take 10 minutes or thereabouts, so be patient and bear with it.

In a mixing bowl, whip the cream until it begins to stiffen, sift in the icing sugar and whip again until stiff peaks form, taking care not to over-whip. You want the cream soft and pillowy, rather than clumpy.

Discard the paper wrapping around the panettone, then cut it horizontally into 3 layers. Arrange the bottom tier on a serving dish or cake stand, spread with half the pistachio butter, spoon over half the whipped cream and top with the second tier of panettone. Repeat this process a second time with the last of the pistachio butter and cream, then crown it with the top of the panettone.

In a large, spotlessly clean mixing bowl, whisk the egg whites with an electric mixer until they begin to froth. Add the caster sugar 1 tbsp at a time, still whisking, until you have a white, glossy meringue with stiff peaks. Whisk in the vanilla extract.

Spoon the meringue over the tower of pistachio-and-cream-laden panettone, using the back of a spoon or a butter knife to spread it out evenly, covering the entire cake. Create swirls and peaks with the spoon, then use a blowtorch to gently brown the surface, so it caramelises.

———

Store in the fridge: the cake can be made up to 1 day in advance.

SERVE WITH…
The panettone makes this an innately Christmas-y cake. Seduced by its ease, it's a recipe I turn to often in the build-up to the holidays… and in the immediate aftermath, to make good use of uneaten (and slightly stale) panettone. A wonderfully festive, easy supper to come before it is HONEY-ROAST POUSSINS (p.94) served with a large dish of BEETROOT & MINT SALAD (p.118) and a second of burrata, topped with shimmering pomegranate seeds.

Pictured overleaf →

SWEETS

SVERGOGNATA

HANDS ON TIME
10 minutes

FOR 6
750g ricotta
300g caster sugar
60g dark chocolate,
    coarsely chopped,
    plus extra for
    decoration
120g candied peel,
    coarsely chopped,
    plus extra for
    decoration
45g shelled pistachios,
    coarsely chopped,
    plus extra for
    decoration
18 biscotti

This literally translates as 'shameless', though I've never got to the bottom of whether that is because it's shamelessly easy to make or shamelessly indulgent to eat. Perhaps both. The recipe is Sicilian and is a quick riff on a cannolo. You make the ricotta filling which is, frankly, the best bit of a cannolo: silky smooth, layered with chocolate, thick candied peel and pastel-green pistachios. Then, instead of fiddling around with fried pastry cones, you serve the cream in small bowls or cups, with biscotti for dipping.

Combine the ricotta and sugar in a mixing bowl and beat with a wooden spoon until smooth. Add the chocolate, candied peel and pistachios, then stir until well combined.

Scoop a generous amount of the ricotta cream into teacups or small serving bowls and top with more pistachios, chocolate and a few slivers of glistening candied peel. You can make this up to a day in advance of serving, just cover and store in the fridge.

——

Serve with biscotti (almond or pistachio varieties are particularly good here), for dipping.

SERVE WITH...
The temptation to make a Sicilian extravaganza to go with this is too great to resist: a summery SICILIAN COUSCOUS SALAD (p.46) with oily tuna, flaked almonds and salty caper berries; a big plate of juicy TOMATO, RED ONION & MINT SALAD (p.116), drenched in olive oil; and a TIMBALLO OF BAKED COURGETTES (p.162). The kind of meal that makes you feel like you're on a sunny, southern Italian holiday, even on a weeknight.

FROZEN BERRIES WITH SAFFRON WHITE CHOCOLATE SAUCE

HANDS ON TIME
15 minutes

FOR 6
1 tsp saffron strands
A pinch of caster sugar
160ml double cream
200g white chocolate,
    chopped
800g mixed frozen
    berries, such
    as raspberries,
    blackberries,
    blueberries and
    redcurrants (not
    strawberries)

This is pure 1990s nostalgia, inspired by the iconic frozen berries in white chocolate sauce at The Ivy restaurant. I serve them family-style, the glistening frozen berries heaped on a cake stand (ideally the kind with a lip round the edge to catch the sweet, dripping sauce) for everyone to dig in. Then, at the table, I ceremoniously pour the vibrant yellow hot chocolate sauce over: it cools instantly and turns to a fudgy, thick caramel. The saffron is by no means compulsory and, if you prefer something more pure in spirit, can be omitted, but I love the warmth – both of colour and taste – that it gives.

Because I loathe fussing in the kitchen when I want to be sitting at the table enjoying dinner with my guests, I make the sauce well ahead of time, even the morning before, and leave it to rest on the hob, still in its saucepan, but covered. Then I reheat it for a few minutes while I dish out the berries.

Combine the saffron and sugar in a mortar and pestle and grind it to a terracotta-coloured powder.

Bring the cream to just under the boil in a small saucepan, but don't boil it. There is a point at which you will see the tiniest bubbles coming to the surface round the edge of the pan. Sprinkle in the chocolate at that moment, and stir vigorously until it has melted. Add the ground saffron mixture and stir until you have a vibrant yellow, thick sauce. Cover and set aside until you are ready to use.

—

Arrange the fruit on a lipped serving plate or cake stand.

Gently warm the sauce on the hob, then pour it over the icy fruit at the table.

SERVE WITH...
For full nostalgic effect, try this with PORK WELLINGTON WITH APPLE & SAGE (p.100): filled with sweet, buttery slices of apple, it's basically a glorified sausage roll. To go with that, a light salad – A REALLY GOOD CHICORY SALAD WITH CREAMY MUSTARD DRESSING (p.110) would be particularly nice here – and, as we're indulging in all things retro and comfort, add a fragrant pan of POMMES DAUPHINOISE (p.154) topped with golden, bubbly melted Parmesan.

A VERY GOOD VANILLA PANNACOTTA

HANDS ON TIME
15 minutes

HANDS OFF TIME
4–6 hours setting

FOR 6
3 × 2g gelatine sheets
500ml double cream
250ml whole milk
150g icing sugar
1 vanilla pod

There are three variations on the theme of pannacotta in this book, which you might call excessive; but then, I love pannacotta. Its beauty lies in its utter simplicity, both to make (just warm the ingredients gently, then leave to set), and in the virginal simplicity of its flavour and silky texture. You want it with the right amount of wobble: just set, so it holds its shape when you turn it out of its mould, but still tastes like velvety cream on your tongue, barely thickened and sweetened. This can be happily served as is, or you can dress it up and serve with poached fruit such as Red Wine Poached Pears (p.212), or Ambrosial Apricots (p.224), a handful of berries, or even a spoonful of jam.

I've set the pannacotta in a single large mould, to bring to the table whole, like a wobbly jelly. But you could, of course, set it in individual moulds or glasses instead. The ceremonial un-moulding of pannacotta is a task I always approach with a degree of trepidation. The technique I've settled on below, however, is nigh-on infallible.

Fill a small bowl with cold water and soak the sheets of gelatine in it for 5 minutes, until soft. In a saucepan, warm the cream, milk and sugar over a gentle heat. Slice open the vanilla pod and scrape the seeds into the pan.

Bring the cream mixture to the point just before boiling: when you see the tiniest bubbles at the edges, take it off the heat. Squeeze the gelatine to wring out the water, add it to the cream and stir until dissolved. Pour the cream into a jelly mould (or individual moulds) and leave to cool. Put in the fridge for at least 4 hours, or until set.

———

To serve, plunge the mould up to about two-thirds into a deep dish of hot water. Hold down for a few seconds, then gently loosen the edges of the pannacotta with a warm butter knife if it needs the encouragement. Place a serving dish over the top and invert both to turn it out.

SERVE WITH…
Pannacotta works particularly well for weeknights, because it's quick and simple enough to make in the morning before work, then leave to set in the fridge and serve for dinner, perhaps with something a little sharp, such as a large bowl of blackberries. To go with it, something equally low-effort but delicious, such as a big dish of RIGATONI WITH MASCARPONE & PANCETTA (p.64), accompanied by a crisp green salad and a good bottle of wine.

LAVENDER HONEY PANNACOTTA

HANDS ON TIME
10 minutes

HANDS OFF TIME
4-6 hours setting

FOR 8
3 × 2g gelatine sheets
30ml good runny honey,
    plus extra (optional)
    to decorate
2 tbsp water
1 tsp lavender
500ml double cream
250ml whole milk
A few fresh lavender
    sprigs, to decorate
    (optional)

This is a milder, more delicate version of pannacotta, sweetened with just a dollop of runny honey rather than sugar. If lavender is out of season, you can buy dried lavender in the spice aisles of most supermarkets.

I often make this for summer picnics, in individual jam jars, sealed either with their lids or a sheet of greaseproof paper tied on with string. But there is no reason why you shouldn't serve it at home in a single large mould (as with A Very Good Vanilla Pannacotta, p.206), or in glasses.

Fill a small bowl with cold water and soak the sheets of gelatine in it for 5 minutes, until soft.

In a small saucepan, warm the honey, measured water and lavender for 5 minutes or so, to infuse the honey with the scent of the flowers. Then add the cream and milk and bring to the point just before boiling: when you see the tiniest bubbles floating to the surface at the edges, take it off the heat. Squeeze the sheets of gelatine in your hands to wring off the water, then add to the warm cream and stir until dissolved.

Strain the scented cream into jam jars, or glasses (or a jelly mould, if you prefer) and leave to cool to room temperature. Put in the fridge to chill for at least 4 hours, or until set.

———

If you would like to turn these out of their moulds, warm a knife in hot water and carefully release the edges, then tip on to a plate. Serve with a drizzle more honey and with fresh lavender sprigs, if you like.

SERVE WITH...
For summer picnics, I will happily pack my bag or basket with sandwiches (egg mayonnaise - on baguette and made with a proper HOME-MADE MAYONNAISE, p.262 - is a particular favourite) and some hard cheeses. If feeling extravagant, then I might bring a flask of ice-cold GAZPACHO (p.40) or creamy CHILLED ALMOND SOUP (p.38) as well. For pudding, jars of this pannacotta, of course.

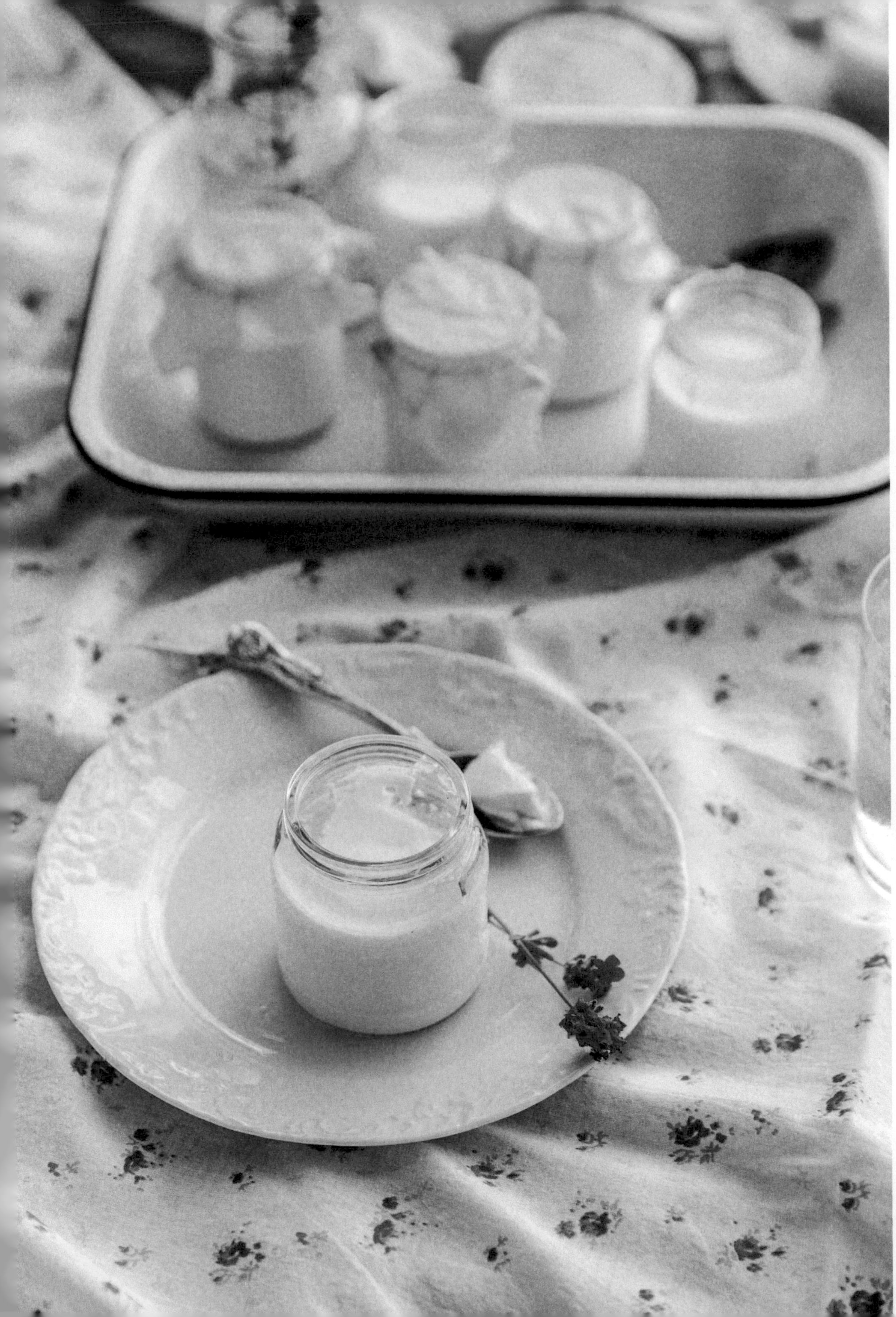

SALTED CARAMEL PANNACOTTA

HANDS ON TIME
20 minutes

HANDS OFF TIME
4–6 hours setting

FOR 8
3 × 2g gelatine sheets
500ml double cream
250ml whole milk
150g icing sugar
100g caster sugar
A generous pinch
    of sea salt flakes
4 tbsp water

Halfway between a pannacotta and a French crème caramel. As with the French dessert, you line the moulds with dark, bitter caramel before pouring in the thick custard, so when you turn each pudding out, it comes topped with a halo of delectable, syrupy burnt sugar. The only difference is that, instead of gently baking the custard in a bain-marie in the oven (as you would with crème caramel), you chill it in the fridge. This, I find, gives a lighter, silkier texture and is also – frankly – less of a faff.

Fill a small bowl with cold water and soak the sheets of gelatine in it for 5 minutes, until soft.

In a small saucepan, warm the cream, milk and icing sugar. When the sugar has dissolved, squeeze the gelatine in your hands to wring off the water, then add to the warm cream and stir to dissolve. Remove from the heat.

Now make the salted caramel: over a low heat and in a small, heavy-based saucepan, melt the caster sugar, salt and measured water. Once the sugar has dissolved, bring to the boil. Do not stir the mixture; it will simmer for 6 minutes until it starts to turn golden. At this point, shake the pan vigorously until it begins to turn golden brown, another 1–2 minutes. Take the pan off the heat and carefully pour the burning-hot caramel into 8 individual heatproof moulds (or 1 large mould). Swirl to coat.

Now pour in the thickened cream, leave to cool to room temperature, then put in the fridge for at least 4 hours, until set. You can happily make this the day before and leave it to rest in the fridge.

———

To turn out of the moulds, plunge them up to about two-thirds into a deep dish of hot water for a few seconds, then turn out on to plates or a serving dish. If you need to, use a warm butter knife to gently release the edges of the pannacotta.

SERVE WITH...
There is something wonderfully comforting about this pannacotta: the velvety cream, the slightly salted caramel, its pudding-like quality. I don't think you can improve on a meal of CONFIT DUCK PIE (p.98) – layers of melting duck with creamy mashed potato – a dish of vibrant yellow SAFFRON FENNEL (p.134) and a rainbow-hued baby CARROT, CUMIN & MINT SALAD (p.144), followed by this pannacotta.

RED WINE POACHED PEARS

HANDS ON TIME
15 minutes

HANDS OFF TIME
55 minutes

FOR 8
4 cinnamon sticks
4 cloves
2 star anise
200g caster sugar
1 litre full-bodied,
    fruity red wine
8 pears, peeled

These are not only easy to make, but can be prepared days in advance. Just keep them covered in the fridge, swimming in their own syrupy juices, as they taste best when chilled.

For effect, I tend to poach more pears than we need to eat, partly because it is little extra effort to double the quantities, and partly because I enjoy eating the leftovers for breakfast the next morning, sitting on a bowl of thick, white Greek yogurt. I love how they look, arranged upright like little soldiers sitting in a pool of scarlet winey juices, on a footed fruit bowl or cake stand (the kind with a little lip is best to catch the syrup). Like something out of a Caravaggio painting. I plonk the dish at the centre of the table for all to help themselves, and serve with a gargantuan chunk of Gorgonzola cheese, or ice cream.

Put the cinnamon, cloves, star anise and sugar in a large saucepan, then pour over the wine and stir to mix. Lower in the pears and, if need be, top up with a little water so they are just covered with deep red cooking liquid. Set over a high heat and bring to the boil.

Reduce the heat, cover the pan and simmer gently for 20 minutes or so. To test if the pears are done, gently insert a butter knife into the base of a fruit: it should slide in with no resistance. Leave to cool.

Gently lift the pears out of the pan, slice roughly 1cm off their bases so they can stand up straight, then place in a large bowl. Increase the heat to medium-high and bring the wine to a gentle boil. Let it bubble away for 30–35 minutes, until reduced by three-quarters to a syrup. Pour this over the pears and cover, then chill in the fridge until ready to serve.

———

Up to a few hours ahead, stand the pears on a cake stand with a lip, pour over some of the juice (serve the rest in a jug) and bring to the table.

SERVE WITH...
Though you can buy pears all year round, they are innately a winter –
or at least an autumnal – fruit. This is a cold-weather pudding that
follows on very nicely as a sharp burst of colour from something rich,
creamy and largely brown, such as TAGLIATELLE GRATIN (p.86). Serve
the pasta with a big, crisp, scarlet-hued REALLY GOOD CHICORY
SALAD WITH CREAMY MUSTARD DRESSING (p.110) and nothing else.

PISTACHIO, MASCARPONE & SALTED CARAMEL CHEESECAKE

HANDS ON TIME
40 minutes

HANDS OFF TIME
4 hours chilling

FOR 8–10
FOR THE BASE
200g malted milk
   biscuits
240g pistachios
110g salted butter

FOR THE FILLING
500g mascarpone
150g caster sugar
200g cream cheese
6 × 2g gelatine sheets
200ml double cream

FOR THE TOPPING
25g light brown sugar
1 tsp salted butter
1 tbsp double cream
A generous pinch
   of sea salt flakes
A handful of pistachios,
   coarsely chopped

This is so wonderfully, unbelievably rich that you almost just want to eat it on its own with nothing to precede it and nothing – but for a short, intense cup of espresso, or perhaps a nap – to follow. Thick mascarpone and pistachio cream, barely set, on a base of buttery biscuits and topped with trickles of salted caramel. Divine.

Line the base of a 23cm springform cake tin with greaseproof paper. Blitz the biscuits and 40g of the pistachios together until you have a rubble of sandy crumbs. In a small saucepan over a gentle heat, melt the butter, then pour it into the crumbled biscuits and mix until you have something that resembles wet sand. Press the biscuit crumble together in the base of the cake tin and set in the fridge while you get on with making the rest of the pudding.

Throw the rest of the pistachios into a food processor, then blitz until you have a thick nut butter; this will take 8–10 minutes.

Meanwhile, in a mixing bowl, combine the mascarpone and sugar for the filling and whisk together until smooth, then add the cream cheese and whisk again until well combined. Spoon in the pistachio butter and whisk until you have a smooth, soft green cream.

Put the gelatine sheets in a small bowl and cover with cold water, then leave to soak for 5 minutes until soft. Warm the cream in a small saucepan, drain the gelatine and squeeze out the excess water, then add it to the cream and stir until melted. Whisk the cream mixture into the cheese mixture, then pour over the biscuit base. Even out with the back of a spoon and put in the fridge to set for 4 hours. This could be made the day before.

For the topping, heat the sugar, butter and cream together slowly in a small saucepan until the sugar has dissolved, then bring it to boiling point. As soon as the first bubbles start to appear, take the pan off the heat. Add the salt and stir well, then set aside to cool for at least 15 minutes.

———

Take the cheesecake out of its tin – when you release the springform, the sides come away easily – and arrange on a serving plate. Pour the lightly cooled caramel into a piping bag with a very fine nozzle (I use a disposable piping bag or freezer bag and cut off the very tip of the corner) and drizzle over the chilled cheesecake. Sprinkle over the pistachios.

The cheesecake will keep like this, decorated, for up to a day in the fridge. Any longer and the caramel might start to bleed a little into the smooth pistachio filling. It will still taste good, it just won't look quite so pretty.

SERVE WITH...
When pudding is this rich, the rest of your menu should be light and simple: perhaps a bowl of brothy, flavoursome TUSCAN SPRING VEGETABLE SOUP (p.58) with good bread, either from the shops or - should it take your fancy - a loaf of WALNUT SODA BREAD (p.254), still warm from the oven. I wouldn't bother with much else, except a good bottle of wine and perhaps a nice plate of cheeses or charcuterie.

Pictured overleaf $\longrightarrow$

HONEY, FIG & WALNUT SEMIFREDDO

HANDS ON TIME
20 minutes

HANDS OFF TIME
3 hours freezing

FOR 10
600ml double cream
2 eggs, plus 8 egg yolks
200g runny honey,
   ideally wildflower
   honey, plus extra
   (optional) to decorate
10 figs, plus extra
   (optional) to decorate
75g walnuts, plus extra
   (optional) to decorate

As much as I delight in eating ice cream and fantasise about making it, I also suffer from a phobia of cumbersome kitchen gadgets. So we don't have an ice-cream maker at home. The joy of semifreddo, of course, is that you don't need a machine or any laborious churning to make it: what you get is something that, much as the name suggests, is 'semi-chilled', like half-melted gelato. Better still: you can shape it in a tin and serve it like a cake. Top it with fresh figs, drizzle with shimmering honey, if you like, and it is every bit as beautiful to bring to the table as it is good to eat.

A note on seasonality: you really want to eat this in the late summer, when figs are at their plumpest. Though should you want to make it in autumn, try this recipe with roasted plums and a few almonds instead, or chunks of honeycomb and shavings of dark chocolate at any time of year.

Line a 23cm round cake tin with cling film, leaving a generous overhang. Pour the cream into a mixing bowl and whip until thick and stiff.

Now, find a heatproof bowl that will fit over a saucepan of simmering water, but without the bowl touching the water. Bring the water to simmering point, then beat the eggs, egg yolks and honey in the bowl over the water, until the mixture is thick and pale. Gently fold the egg custard into the whipped cream. Roughly chop the figs and walnuts and mix them in. Pour the mixture into the cake tin, cover with the overhanging cling film and set in the freezer for 3 hours, until solid.

———

When you're ready to serve the semifreddo, turn it out on to a plate and drizzle with golden honey, if you want. Then decorate with more figs (sliced, or just tear them open) and a handful of walnuts, if you like.

SERVE WITH...
Given that the pudding is so extravagant, I feel confident keeping the rest of the menu simple: a big dish of SPAGHETTI WITH CREAMY LEMON SAUCE (p.60) and perhaps A REALLY GOOD TOMATO SALAD (p.114), made with a mix of variegated tomatoes.

If I'm feeding a larger crowd (and the semifreddo lends itself well to that), then I'll add BURRATA WITH PRESERVED LEMONS, MINT & CHILLI (p.34), a big dish of nutty WILD RICE & LENTIL SALAD (p.132) and a COURGETTE BLOSSOM & TALEGGIO GALETTE (p.160).

LIMONCELLO SEMIFREDDO

HANDS ON TIME
40 minutes

HANDS OFF TIME
15 minutes simmering
10 hours freezing

FOR 12
12 large Amalfi lemons,
    or large unwaxed
    lemons
Finely grated zest
    of 1 lemon
5 tbsp caster sugar
4 tbsp limoncello
3 eggs, separated
1 tbsp icing sugar
200ml double cream

My mother's garden at the house where I grew up in Venice is full of lemon trees. Their fruit is unevenly shaped with thick, hardy skins and bright green leaves, just perfect for this pudding. When I make this at home in London, I buy Amalfi lemons – the big, gnarly ones you see at Italian delicatessens – which are a close approximation of those I can pick in my mother's garden. Otherwise you can use regular unwaxed lemons, which don't have quite the same leafy flourish, but are colourful and pretty nonetheless. If you can't find the right lemons – or just can't be bothered to hollow them out – you can freeze the semifreddo in a cake or loaf tin (just remember to line it with cling film before pouring in the thick lemon custard, as with the recipe on the previous page). When you are ready to serve, turn it out of the tin on to a serving dish or cake stand, top with a few mint sprigs, if you like, or some flowers, then serve slices at the table.

Slice the top of the lemons off and set aside, then slice the bases off so they can sit up straight. Use a teaspoon to scoop out the flesh, digging in around the segments. Set the pulp of 3 lemons aside. Slot the base slices inside the shells, to hold the semifreddo so none runs out of the bottom.

Squeeze the pulp of the 3 lemons to extract 100ml juice. Pour into a saucepan with the zest and 3 tbsp of the caster sugar. Set over a low heat and simmer for 10 minutes. Take off the heat and add the limoncello.

In a heatproof bowl, whisk the yolks and remaining 2 tbsp of caster sugar until pale and frothy. Set over a pan of simmering water and whisk until it thickens; this takes about 5 minutes. Slowly pour in the syrup, whisking until you have a thick custard; this takes about 10 minutes. Leave to cool.

In a spotlessly clean mixing bowl, whisk 2 egg whites until frothy (you don't need the third egg white here). Sift in the icing sugar and keep whisking until a soft, glossy meringue forms. Fold the snowy white peaks into the thick yellow custard. In a second bowl, whip the cream until soft peaks form, then fold into the lemon concoction. Spoon the semifreddo into the lemon shells, top with their (ideally) green-leafed hats and put in the freezer to set for 10 hours. Serve straight from the freezer.

SERVE WITH...
This delicate pudding is dreamy to follow a light dinner of CHILLED ALMOND SOUP (p.38), served with ROASTED FENNEL FOCACCIA (p.256) and a big dish of BABY ARTICHOKE, FENNEL & PECORINO SALAD (p.122).

PINK RHUBARB & PROSECCO JELLY

HANDS ON TIME
30 minutes

HANDS OFF TIME
10 minutes straining
6 hours setting

FOR 6
800g forced pink
    rhubarb
280g caster sugar
600ml water
9 × 2g gelatine sheets
200ml Prosecco

This is a fantasy of frivolous pastel pink: the bubbles of the prosecco give a sharpness to the sweet rhubarb syrup, taking what could otherwise be a rather childish pudding into the realms of sophistication. Use forced rhubarb – the really pink kind – if you can find it. Once you've poached the stems to make the syrup, don't discard the fruit: I blitz it in a blender until smooth, then warm it and serve with roast or cold meats as you would apple sauce.

You need to allow time for the jelly to set, so make it the morning – or even the day before – you plan to eat it. The challenge is, of course, the unmoulding in a single intact piece. I do this before my guests arrive and leave the jelly, quivering, in the fridge; if it's chilled it will hold its shape easily for up to a day.

Roughly cut the rhubarb into 2–3cm long pieces. Put it into a large pan, add the sugar and pour over the measured water. Set over a medium heat and bring to the boil, stirring. When it bubbles, reduce the heat and leave to simmer for 15 minutes, until tender. Carefully pour the rhubarb into a sieve over a large measuring jug. Don't push down on it, just let it sit for 10 minutes and allow the juices to drip down little by little. You should have 600ml of pastel-pink syrup. If you have less, make it up with water. (If you have more, it makes a delightful cordial, or cocktail mixer.)

Soak the gelatine in a bowl of cold water for 5 minutes, to soften. Pour the syrup back into the pan, set over a medium heat and bring to a gentle boil. Then remove from the heat, squeeze the water out of the gelatine and whisk into the syrup to dissolve. Add the Prosecco slowly, then pour the whole concoction into your jelly mould. Chill for 6 hours, until set.

———

To un-mould, fill a large dish with hot water, immerse the jelly mould in it (up to roughly two-thirds) and hold there firmly for a few seconds. Cover the mould with a serving dish and tip the jelly upside down, so it slips out in a single piece. Store in the fridge until ready to serve.

SERVE WITH...
There is something wonderfully, gratifyingly retro - nostalgic even - about a good wobbly jelly. And so you need a suitably retro menu to go with it: BUTTERY LEMON ROAST CHICKEN (p.92) and a tray of ESPECIALLY GOOD ROAST POTATOES (p.150). To serve with the meat, blushing pink rhubarb sauce (made with the pulp left over from the jelly), and CREAMY BAKED LEEKS WITH MUSTARD & PARMESAN (p.164).

AMBROSIAL APRICOTS

HANDS ON TIME
10 minutes

HANDS OFF TIME
15 minutes

FOR 6
250ml mild runny
    honey, preferably
    acacia or wildflower
120ml water
2 lemons
12 apricots, halved
    and pitted
40g pistachios,
    coarsely chopped

This is a sunny day in a bowl: sweet and fragrant and gloriously colourful. The recipe is taken – barely adapted – from Colman Andrews's *Country Cooking of Italy* and I make it often through the summer months. Though it will keep happily in the fridge for up to three days, the fruits will discolour.

Combine the honey and measured water in a saucepan and set over a medium heat. Pare off the zest of 1 lemon in thick strips, add to the pan, then squeeze in the juice of both lemons. Bring to the boil and, when the syrup begins to bubble, reduce the heat.

Add the apricot halves and poach for 5–6 minutes until soft (you may need to cook them in batches). You can tell if the fruit is done by piercing the hollow where the stone once was with a fork or knife; there should be little or no resistance. Once cooked, lift the apricots out of the syrup with a slotted spoon and put them into a large bowl.

Pour the honey syrup over the fruit, allow to cool, then cover and chill in the fridge for up to 3 days.

—

Before serving, sprinkle the pistachios over the fruit.

SERVE WITH...
Eat as is, chilled and the apricots swimming in their honeyed syrup, or pair with a dollop of SALTED HONEY ICE CREAM (p.186). For the rest of the meal, keep it simple: a big bowl of SICILIAN COUSCOUS SALAD (p.46) laced with oily tuna and salty caper berries, some good MOZZARELLA WITH CELERY, OLIVES & PINE NUTS (p.36), and a dish of BABY ARTICHOKE, FENNEL & PECORINO SALAD (p.122).

CHOCOLATE & RUM PUDDING

HANDS ON TIME
20 minutes

HANDS OFF TIME
4 hours setting

FOR 8
800ml whole milk
150g salted butter
160g caster sugar
180g dark chocolate,
    coarsely chopped
80g plain flour,
    preferably type '00'
2 tbsp rum
Sugared raspberries
    and redcurrants,
    to serve

In Italian we call this *buddino* (pronounced 'boo-dee-noh'). I love that name, it has an onomatopoeic quality that means you can almost hear the wiggle of the custard as you say it out loud. I grew up with *buddino* and it was always a treat. Ornella, a family friend and wonderful cook, would make it in a large mixing bowl, topped with crumbled biscuits, so you just dug in by the spoonful. The version here is a grown-up interpretation and is how I like to serve it now, at supper parties for friends.

The pudding has a rather majestic quality: a tower or a mound – depending on what sort of mould you go for – of decadently dark chocolate. A few spoonfuls are enough. I like to serve it with sharp berries, or, in the winter months, finely sliced oranges topped with a smattering of demerara sugar, to cut through the richness of the custard. The rum is entirely optional, you could simply leave it out, or substitute ½ tsp ground cinnamon, a splash of orange flower water and some chopped candied orange peel, or throw in a handful of dark (or white) chocolate chips, if you prefer.

In a small saucepan, set the milk over a gentle heat and bring to just before the boil. In a second saucepan, melt the butter over a very gentle heat, then stir in the sugar. Add the chocolate and whisk vigorously until smooth and melted. Sift in the flour, little by little and keep whisking until you have a smooth, chocolatey custard.

Pour the hot milk into the chocolate cream and keep whisking over a very low heat until the mixture thickens; this should take 2–3 minutes. Stir in the rum and pour the chocolate custard into a large jelly mould. Leave to cool for 30 minutes, then set in the fridge for 4 hours, or until set. You can keep the pudding like that, covered, for up to 4 days.

—

When you are ready to serve it, plunge the mould (up to roughly two-thirds) into a dish of hot water for a few seconds, then turn it out on to a plate. Serve with the berries.

SERVE WITH...
With such a rich pudding, you want to keep the rest of the meal relatively light and simple, such as a bowl of chilled GAZPACHO (p.40) served with thick slices of WALNUT SODA BREAD (p.254) - better still if slightly warm - and perhaps a WATERMELON, FETA & PISTACHIO CARPACCIO (p.120) on the side.

CHRISTMAS CAKE WITH MARZIPAN AND GLACÉ FRUITS

HANDS ON TIME
30 minutes

HANDS OFF TIME
24–48 hours soaking
4¼ hours baking
4 hours cooling

FOR 8–10
FOR THE CAKE
100g glacé cherries,
 halved
100g mixed peel
225g currants
225g raisins
225g sultanas
300ml brandy
250g salted butter, plus
 extra for the tin
250g dark muscovado
 sugar
2 tbsp black treacle
5 eggs
1 tsp mixed spice
2 tsp ground nutmeg
250g self-raising flour
A large pinch of fine
 sea salt

FOR THE DECORATION
200g marzipan
100g apricot jam
1 tbsp water
A selection of glacé
 fruits and nuts,
 such as glacé pears,
 plums, orange slices,
 cherries, pecans
 and walnuts

This is my mother's recipe and I've made it every year for the better part of my life, first with my mother as a child, now with my elder son Aeneas. It is a rich cake, and while the brandy, fruit, nuts and glacé fruits on top mean it can work out as rather costly, Christmas feels like the one time of year when extravagance is *de rigueur*. Each winter, I make several of these to give as gifts: you can bake them a couple of months before Christmas, then wrap, uniced and undecorated, in foil until you are ready to gift (or eat) them. Just add the marzipan and fruits before boxing the cake up; it will then keep for a couple of weeks.

A note on glacé fruits: these can be tricky (and expensive) to buy in the UK. I've found online is the best bet: I've been buying a selection of baby pears, figs, peaches, apricots and orange slices from a small producer called Country Products for years and have found them to be excellent. In the absence of whole glacé fruits, decorate the cakes with a mix of dried apricots, figs, nuts and glacé cherries (all of which you can easily buy in supermarkets), then paint with a thick glaze of shimmering apricot jam for a simpler, more rustic-looking – but still charming and festive – cake.

Put the glacé cherries, peel, currants, raisins and sultanas in a large bowl, pour over the brandy, cover and leave to steep for 24–48 hours. The longer you leave the fruit, the more flavour and moisture it will give to the cake.

When you are ready to make the cake, heat the oven to 140°C/fan 120°C/Gas 1. Butter and double-line a 23cm round cake tin, then cut a circle of greaseproof paper the same size as the base of the tin and set aside.

Beat together the butter and sugar until they become paler and fluffy, then add the treacle and beat until smooth. Crack each egg at a time into a small bowl, beat lightly with a fork, then add to the mixture, little by little, and beat until well combined. Now sift in the spices, flour and salt and mix with a wooden spoon until well combined. Finally, add the fruit and any remaining soaking liquid and mix well together.

Spoon the batter into the prepared tin and gently even out the top with the back of the spoon. Cover with the circle of greaseproof paper and set it on the bottom shelf of the oven to bake for 4½ hours. The cake is cooked when a skewer inserted into the centre comes out clean. Cover with a clean tea towel and leave to cool in its tin. You can make the cake up to this point months in advance if you like, and store wrapped in foil.

To decorate the cake, roll the marzipan out into a sheet roughly as thick as a £1 coin. Cut out a circle of marzipan the same diameter as the cake.

Spoon the jam into a small saucepan, add the measured water and set over a medium heat until it begins to bubble lightly. Use a pastry brush to glaze the top of the cake, then carefully lay the circle of marzipan over. Brush the glaze over the marzipan and, while it is still tacky, stick on glacé fruits and nuts, arranging them as you like. I usually do this in concentric circles, with nuts on the outside and a collection of cherries, whole orange slices and a couple of tiny sugared pears and a plum half or so at the centre. Finally, use what is left of the apricot jam to glaze the nuts and fruits, to give them a lovely shine. The cake will keep happily like this for 2–3 weeks.

SERVE WITH…
During the festive season, I find myself hosting friends for lunch and for dinner with such merry frequency that I often run out of ideas as to what to cook (not to mention the time to do it). Assuming you have made a few of these cakes earlier in the year, it's easy to unwrap one and decorate it (and if you haven't, buy a plain fruit cake and decorate it with the marzipan and sugared fruits, as in the recipe). For the rest of the meal, try HONEY-ROAST POUSSINS (p.94), a tray of decadently creamy, cheesy POMMES DAUPHINOISE (p.154), then a plate of shimmering red beetroot salad, with blue cheese and walnuts crumbled over.

Pictured overleaf →

SWEETS

PISTACHIO BUTTER CAKE WITH MARZIPAN ICING

HANDS ON TIME
20 minutes

HANDS OFF TIME
1¼ hours baking
2 hours cooling

FOR 8–10
FOR THE CAKE
200g salted butter,
    softened, plus extra
    for the tin
120g unsalted roasted
    pistachios
60g white chocolate,
    broken up or chopped
200g caster sugar, plus
    1 tbsp
1 tsp vanilla extract
120g plain yogurt
3 large eggs
200g self-raising flour
Fine sea salt

FOR THE ICING
2 tbsp boiling water
75g marzipan, grated
300g icing sugar
150g salted butter,
    softened
Juice of ¼ lemon
A handful of pistachios,
    coarsely chopped

I dream about this cake. The recipe is one that I first developed as a picnic loaf for my column in *The Sunday Times*: sponge, unbelievably soft and light, but fabulously rich. I make it year round, however, even once summer picnics are but a distant memory. The icing, sweet almondy marzipan melted into whipped butter and sugar, is light and airy – and by no means necessary, as the cake works very well plain – but makes it even more extravagant.

Heat the oven to 180°C/fan 160°C/Gas 4. Butter a 20cm springform cake tin and line the base and sides with baking parchment.

In a food processor, combine the pistachios, chocolate, the 1 tbsp of caster sugar and the vanilla extract. Blend for 10 minutes or so until very creamy, occasionally stopping the machine to scrape down the sides with a spatula.

In a large bowl, use an electric mixer to cream the remaining 200g of caster sugar with the butter, then add the pistachio cream and a generous pinch of salt and beat until smooth. Slowly beat in the yogurt and eggs. Sift in the flour and beat until you have a smooth batter. Pour into the tin and bake for 40 minutes, then cover with a sheet of foil and bake for a further 35 minutes, until lightly golden and a knife comes out clean when inserted into the middle. Turn the cake out of the tin and cool on a rack. The cold cake will keep in an airtight container for up to 24 hours.

—

To make the icing, add the measured boiling water to the marzipan and mix it with a fork to melt it slightly (this stops it going clumpy when mixed with the buttercream). Use an electric beater to mix the icing sugar and butter until pale and fluffy, then add the marzipan. Beat at high speed for several minutes to fluff up. Squeeze in the lemon juice and beat until smooth. Smother the cake in the icing and decorate with pistachios.

SERVE WITH...
One of my great pleasures in life is afternoon tea, and this works particularly well for that. Alongside, I make egg sandwiches on soft white bread with proper HOME-MADE MAYONNAISE (p.262), or TRUFFLE MAYONNAISE (p.264), if feeling indulgent. I add a plate of biscuits, usually shop-bought, as I find them fiddly to bake, STRAWBERRIES IN LEMONY SYRUP (p.192) and MERINGUES (p.238), baked slightly smaller than usual (so more manageable to eat) and piled extravagantly high on a cake stand.

FLOURLESS CHOCOLATE, CHESTNUT & ROSEMARY CAKE

HANDS ON TIME
10 minutes

HANDS OFF TIME
45 minutes baking
2 hours cooling

FOR 8–10
Salted butter,
    for the tin
500g sweetened
    chestnut purée
4 eggs
75g ground almonds
40g cocoa powder
Leaves from 4 rosemary
    sprigs, plus extra
    sprigs for the top
Icing sugar, to dust

A few years ago, I made this for a bake sale at my elder son Aeneas's school, and found myself swamped with requests for the recipe, which is adapted from the old Venetian cookbook, *A Tola Coi Nostri Veci* by Mariù Salvatori. Chocolate cake is often dry and, in spite of its dark, sumptuous appearance, rather disappointing to eat. This, however, chic-ly dusted in a cloud of icing sugar, is the ideal balance of velvety chestnut and rich, fudgey chocolate. The rosemary is entirely optional, but gives it a soft grown-up-ness.

I use the cans of sweetened chestnut purée here, for ease and convenience. An import from France, it can be tricky to find, so I stock up whenever I see tins at the supermarket or in delicatessens, as it always comes in handy, even to serve over vanilla ice cream with a little chopped dark chocolate and crumbled meringue. But if you can't find it easily, feel free to use the unsweetened variety readily available in British supermarkets: use 400g, whisking it lightly with 100g icing sugar, until smooth, before you begin.

Heat the oven to 180°C/fan 160°C/Gas 4. Butter a 20cm round cake tin and line with baking parchment.

Pour the chestnut purée into a large mixing bowl. Separate the eggs and lightly beat the yolks with a fork, then add them to the purée. Pour in the ground almonds, add the cocoa and mix well. Roughly chop the rosemary leaves and add them to the batter, then stir until well combined.

In a second bowl, whisk the egg whites until stiff, then fold into the chocolate mix. Pour into the tin and sprinkle on a few rosemary sprigs. Bake for 40–45 minutes until a skewer comes out clean. Leave to cool in the tin, then turn out. The cake will keep nicely for 2–3 days.

—

Dust with icing sugar before serving.

SERVE WITH...
Because of the chestnut (albeit canned), this feels like a cold weather pudding and it works well with wintry, autumnal flavours; moreover, because it's a cake, it will make up for an otherwise simple meal. For dinner on a weeknight, I love TAGLIATELLE WITH GORGONZOLA, PEAR & WALNUT (p.62), which takes moments to throw together, alongside A REALLY GOOD CHICORY SALAD WITH CREAMY MUSTARD DRESSING (p.110), then this cake, prepared a day (or more) ahead.

COFFEE & WALNUT CAKE

HANDS ON TIME
30 minutes

HANDS OFF TIME
45 minutes baking
2 hours cooling

FOR 8–10
FOR THE CAKE
350g salted butter,
   at room temperature,
   plus extra for the tin
350g dark muscovado
   sugar
140g walnuts, roughly
   chopped
6 eggs
250g self-raising flour
1¼ tsp baking powder
100g ground almonds
3 tsp instant coffee
1 tbsp boiling water

FOR THE ICING
400g mascarpone, at
   room temperature
200g icing sugar

This cake, smothered in thick mascarpone icing, is one I wheel out regularly. It is adapted from one of food writer Rose Prince's recipes, which I return to time and again. It's laced with buttery nuts, the seductive aroma of strong coffee and – for me – joyful, celebratory family memories. As to decoration, I'm hopeless with a piping bag, so heaps of fresh flowers – pretty much whatever is in season at the time (as long as it's not noxious) – plonked casually on top and, if the occasion demands, candles are all you need.

Heat the oven to 160°C/fan 140°C/Gas 3. Butter and line two 23cm round cake tins.

In a large mixing bowl, cream the butter and sugar together with an electric whisk until smooth. Stir in the walnuts, then add the eggs one by one, beating after each addition until well combined into the batter. Sift in the flour, baking powder and ground almonds and fold through. Mix the coffee with the measured boiling water to form a strong syrup-like liquid, then pour it into the batter and mix well.

Spoon the batter into the prepared tins, dividing it equally, and bake in the middle of the oven for 45 minutes, or until the cakes feel firm to touch and a knife comes out clean when inserted into the middle.

Leave to cool for 5 minutes in the tins before turning out and setting on a wire rack to cool completely.

——

Beat the mascarpone until slightly softened, then sift in the icing sugar and beat until smooth. Spread half over the first cake, then sandwich the second on top and layer on the rest of the icing. Decorate with flowers.

SERVE WITH...
I sometimes make this as a birthday cake, and I love to mark a birthday with dinner in our kitchen - with a few more people than we would otherwise sensibly squeeze round the table. I've learned to keep the menu simple; one that can be prepared in advance. For my birthday, in early spring, I choose TAGLIATELLE GRATIN (p.86), swimming in thick, cheesy sauce, followed by a green salad. And because birthdays are all about excess, I might put out a large dish of COLD ROAST TOPSIDE OF BEEF (p.104), cooked the day before, sliced tissue-thin and smothered in SALSA VERDE (p.266).

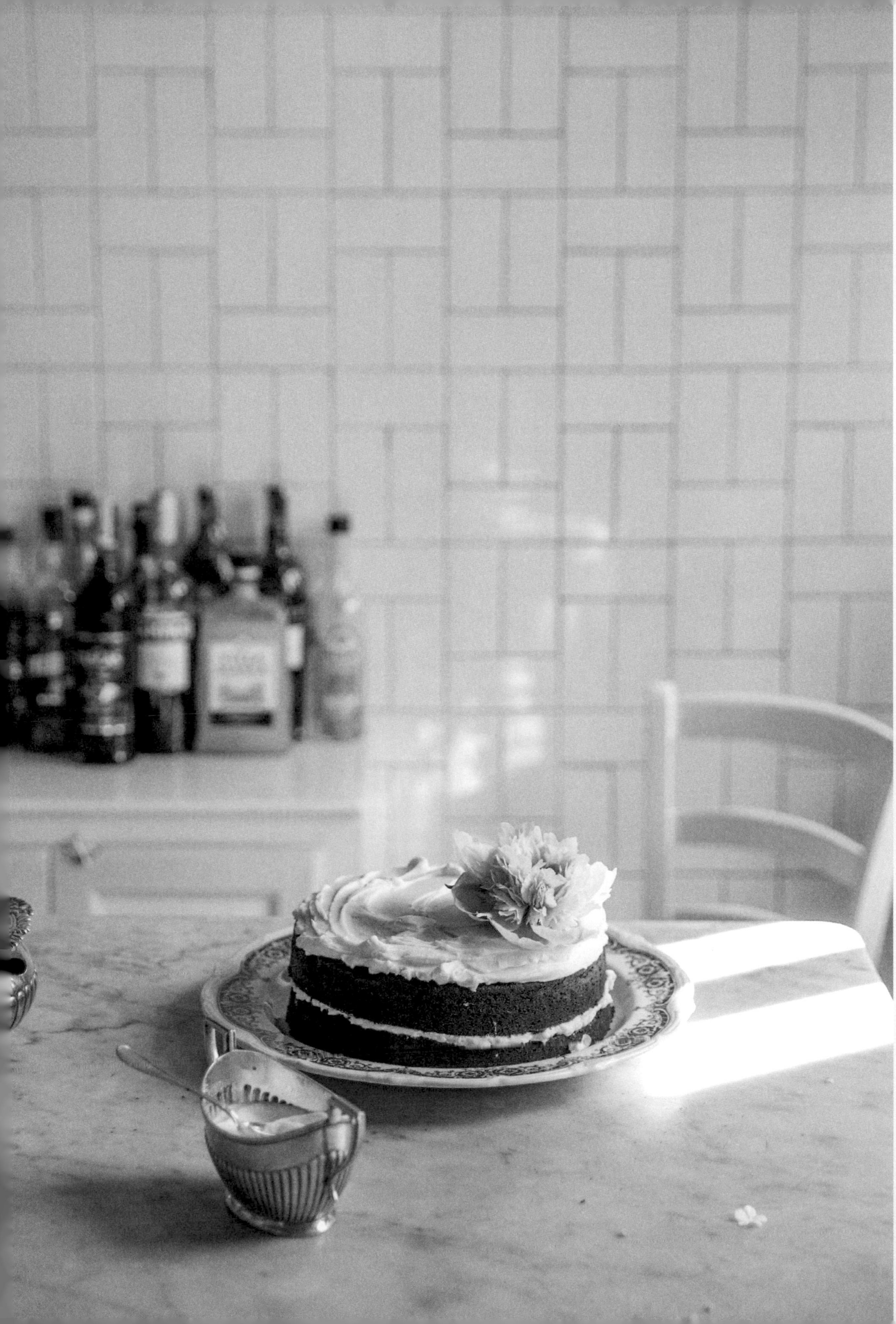

MERINGUES

HANDS ON TIME
15 minutes

HANDS OFF TIME
1 hour baking
1 hour cooling

**MAKES 8 LARGE
MERINGUES**
4 egg whites
200g caster sugar
Cocoa powder, to dust

Two things in life I feel strongly about: first, meringues should be extravagantly, overwhelmingly big, like white clouds of sugary goodness; second, everyone needs a good recipe for them. Meringues are my go-to pudding when I'm at a loss about what to cook. They look showy, they can be made a good few days ahead and stored in a tin, and everyone likes them (gluten-free, dairy-free, nut-free and so forth).

You can make the meringues plain, or dust with a cloud of bitter cocoa powder as I've done here, but you can also flavour them. Try adding 1 tsp orange flower water, rose water or vanilla extract to the raw meringue as you whisk it. Then, for an extra something, trickle a couple of drops of food colouring on top of each shaped meringue before baking and use a toothpick to create spirals in the glossy white mass. When baked, they will sport flamboyant, colourful swirls.

Heat the oven to 140°C/fan 120°C/Gas 1.

Pour the egg whites into an immaculately clean bowl, as even a spot of grease will stop them from peaking. Using an electric whisk, beat on a medium-low speed until the whites begin to froth, then add the sugar a spoonful at a time, whisking on a high speed until the whites become glossy and begin to form stiff peaks.

Line 2 baking trays with baking parchment and spoon the mixture on to the trays. Set in the middle of the oven and bake for 1 hour. Switch the oven off and leave the meringues in there, without opening the door, for another hour, until cooled.

———

Pile the meringues on a plate and dust lightly with cocoa before serving.

SERVE WITH...
Serve as is, or with whipped cream and - in the summer - a luscious bowl of STRAWBERRIES IN LEMONY SYRUP (p.192). They go with absolutely everything.

SUMMER BERRY CLOUD CAKE

HANDS ON TIME
25 minutes

HANDS OFF TIME
1 hour baking
1 hour cooling

FOR 8–10
Flavourless oil,
   for the trays
6 egg whites
300g caster sugar,
   plus 2 tbsp
2 tsp cornflour
1 tsp white wine
   vinegar
850ml double cream
150g blackberries
300g raspberries
300g blueberries
30g flaked almonds
Thyme sprigs,
   redcurrants
   and flowers, for
   decoration (optional)

An ode to the fruits of British summer. If you are catering for friends with dairy intolerance, you can also make this with whipped chilled coconut cream, which is every bit as good.

Heat the oven to 150°C/fan 130°C/Gas 2. Oil 3 baking trays and line with baking parchment. Draw a circle on each roughly 23cm in diameter (I trace around a cake tin).

In a clean mixing bowl, whisk the egg whites until they begin to peak, then add the sugar a spoonful at a time, whisking all the while. When all the sugar has been added and the mixture is glossy, gently fold in the cornflour and the vinegar. Spoon the meringue on to the baking trays, spreading it out to make 3 discs. Bake for 1 hour, then switch the oven off and leave the meringues in there to harden for another hour. You want the meringue to be crisp so that it can support the weight of the cream.

You can make the meringue up to 3 days in advance and store it in an airtight container.

——

To make the filling, whip the cream with an electric whisk until peaks form, but take care not to over-whip it, or it will lose that silky quality.

Take the first meringue disc and spoon roughly one-third of the cream on top, then sprinkle with one-third of the berries, half the flaked almonds and 1 tbsp caster sugar. Top with the second layer of meringue and repeat. Top with the third meringue, spoon on the last one-third of the cream and decorate with berries, thyme sprigs and flowers (just make sure they're not noxious), if you like.

SERVE WITH...
Everyone loves BUTTERY LEMON ROAST CHICKEN (p.92), cooked so the skin is golden and crisp and the meat succulent, almost sweet. To go with it, THE SIMPLEST ROAST POTATOES (p.148), A REALLY GOOD GREEN SALAD (p.112) and plenty of good bread (I love WALNUT SODA BREAD, p.254, but good bread from the bakery will do just as well). You literally can't go wrong. Follow with this dreamy, creamy concoction and strong espresso or mint tea (just mint leaves in a pot of boiling water). If you're cooking for a crowd, this works every bit as well: just scale up to two (or three) birds and perhaps make a second cake.

CHOCOLATE CHESTNUT MERINGUE CAKE

HANDS ON TIME
25 minutes

HANDS OFF TIME
1 hour baking
1 hour cooling

FOR 8–10
Redcurrant sprigs,
    to decorate
300g caster sugar,
    plus extra to frost
    the redcurrants
Flavourless oil,
    for the trays
6 egg whites
2 tsp cornflour
1 tsp white wine
    vinegar
4 tbsp icing sugar
600ml double cream
300g marrons glacés
100g dark chocolate
Thyme sprigs, plus
    other herb sprigs
    if you like, to
    decorate

Think of this as a winter variation of the Lemon Meringue Cake on the next page. In place of sharp citrus curd, you fold crumbled sugared chestnuts and dark chocolate into the cream. Though you could add chunks of sugared orange peel, pistachios or almonds, chopped crystallised ginger, or even coarsely chopped Toblerone. I go wild with decoration here, particularly as this is a recipe I tend to wheel out around the festive season: redcurrants dipped in sugar so they shimmer like jewels; rosemary sprigs, thyme and dark green bay leaves to create a wreath encircling the meringue tower.

Heat the oven to 150°C/fan 130°C/Gas 2. Dip the redcurrant sprigs in water, then gently roll them in caster sugar and set aside to dry out. Oil 3 baking trays and line with baking parchment. Draw a circle on each roughly 23cm in diameter (I trace around a cake tin).

Whisk the egg whites until soft peaks begin to form, then add the caster sugar spoonful by spoonful. Once the eggs become stiff, gently fold in the cornflour and vinegar. Spoon the meringue on to the baking trays, spreading it out evenly to make 3 discs. Bake for 1 hour, then switch the oven off and leave the meringues in there to harden for another hour. You want the meringue to be crisp so it can support the weight of the cream. Sift the icing sugar into the cream and whip until firm, but still silky.

—

Set the first meringue on a serving dish and top with one-third of the cream and one-third of the marrons, crumbling them over. Roughly chop the chocolate and sprinkle half of it over. Top with the second meringue and repeat. Top with the third meringue and cover with whipped cream.

Decorate with herb sprigs, the sugared redcurrants and the last of the crumbled marrons. Chill in the fridge until you are ready to serve. It will keep for up to 12 hours.

SERVE WITH...
There is a distinct festive quality to this, so, for the dinner itself, serve a good ROAST PORK (p.96), without the honey-roast persimmons, but with whole ROAST APPLES (p.172). To go with the meat, a tray of CREAMY BAKED LEEKS (p.164), topped with a layer of golden, melted cheese. And for good measure, if feeding a crowd, I might make a pot of BRAISED LENTILS WITH PANCETTA (p.130) too, slow-cooked with fennel until buttery, soft and almost sweet.

LEMON MERINGUE CAKE

HANDS ON TIME
25 minutes

HANDS OFF TIME
1 hour baking
1 hour cooling

FOR 8–10
Flavourless oil,
   for the trays
6 egg whites
300g caster sugar
2 tsp cornflour
1 tsp white wine
   vinegar
600ml double cream
1 × 320g jar lemon curd

This most blissfully extravagant confection is rather like a pavlova, but with bells and whistles: three tiers of meringue layered with whipped cream and sharp citrus curd, towering high like a cake.

You can make it in stages, if you like, though the only actual 'making' bit is baking the meringue; the rest is merely assembly. You can do this at the last minute, or a few hours in advance of when you plan on eating it, though if it's a warm day it's best to store it in the fridge to ensure it holds its shape.

Heat the oven to 150°C/fan 130°C/Gas 2. Oil 3 baking trays and line with baking parchment. Draw a circle on each roughly 23cm in diameter (I trace around a cake tin).

Whisk the egg whites until soft peaks begin to form, then add the sugar spoonful by spoonful. Once you have added all the sugar and the eggs become stiff, gently fold in the cornflour and vinegar. Spoon the meringue on to the baking trays, spreading it out evenly to make 3 discs.

Bake in the oven for 1 hour, then switch the oven off and leave the meringues in there to harden for another hour. You want it to be crisp so that it can support the weight of the cream.

———

In a large mixing bowl, whip the cream until it folds in peaks: stiff enough to ripple nicely, but billowing rather than over-whipped.

Set the first meringue disc on a serving dish, spoon over half the lemon curd and spread it out, then top with one-third of the whipped cream. Sandwich on the second meringue disc and repeat. Top with the third meringue disc and cover with cream. Decorate as you like with flowers (make sure they're not noxious). Chill in the fridge until ready to serve.

SERVE WITH…
Last summer I made this for a special dinner for twenty-odd people, so I baked two, both of which were devoured to the last crumb, along with a large glass trifle dish of DRUNKEN STRAWBERRIES (p.194), swimming in sweet wine syrup. For the rest of the menu: HONEY-ROAST POUSSINS (p.94), ASPARAGUS WITH LEMON & TOASTED ALMOND GRATIN (p.138), BURRATA WITH PRESERVED LEMONS, MINT & CHILLI (p.34) and A REALLY GOOD GREEN SALAD (p.112).

APPLE & WALNUT CRUMBLE PIE

HANDS ON TIME
25 minutes

HANDS OFF TIME
30 minutes chilling
65 minutes cooking

FOR 8–10
FOR THE CRUST
220g cold salted butter,
    cut into cubes, plus
    extra for the tin
250g plain flour
180g cream cheese

FOR THE FILLING
5 small or medium
    apples, preferably
    Pink Lady
400ml crème fraîche
200g caster sugar
¼ tsp fine sea salt
50g plain flour
1 egg

FOR THE TOPPING
100g walnuts
50g plain flour
110g salted butter,
    softened
50g caster sugar
50g demerara sugar
1 tsp ground cinnamon

I cannot overstate how unbelievably good this is, and I speak as someone who has spent a lifetime feeling deeply underwhelmed by apple pie. The pastry – and you must categorically here make it from scratch, rather than use (as I normally would) shop-bought – is just-as-you-want-it crumbly. The filling is rich and custard-like and the topping – a sort of crumble of sugar, butter and walnuts – while not the most majestic looking, is exactly the kind of stuff I could happily devour on its own by the spoonful. Ideally this is best served warm, but it is also perfectly good at room temperature; just warm a little cream to go with it, or serve with a scoop of ice cream.

Butter and line a cake tin (I use a springform that is 24cm in diameter). Combine the crust ingredients in a food processor and pulse until a soft dough forms. Roll it out into a large circle and line the tin, pressing it up the sides. Set in the fridge for 30 minutes or so.

Meanwhile, heat the oven to 230°C/fan 210°C/Gas 8, then core and finely slice the apples. Combine the crème fraîche, sugar, salt and flour in a mixing bowl. Crack the egg into a smaller bowl, lightly beat with a fork and stir into the mixture. Add the apple slices and stir well. Spoon the filling into the pie crust and bake in the oven for 10 minutes, then reduce the oven temperature to 175°C/fan 155°C/not-quite Gas 4 and bake for a further 35 minutes.

Roughly chop the nuts and toss them into a mixing bowl. Add the rest of the ingredients for the topping and mix well, rubbing in the butter so you have a lumpy crumble. Spoon over the pie and bake for 20 minutes, or until golden brown. Leave to cool in the tin before serving, slightly warm.

—

Bake this up to a day in advance, if you like, then cover with foil and reheat in an oven heated to 150°C/fan 130°C/Gas 2 for 25 minutes.

SERVE WITH...
One of the most comforting meals I can think of is CARROT & CINNAMON SOUP (p.56), slightly spiced and ridiculously creamy, served with a warm loaf of home-made DAMPER BREAD (p.252), smothered in salted butter, then this pie, ideally still warm, with or without a dollop of RUM, RAISIN & WALNUT ICE CREAM (p.184) or SALTED HONEY ICE CREAM (p.186). There is, in my view, no greater manifestation of domestic eutopia.

EXTRAS

There are many ways to lay a table: with linens, crisp white cloths and a sea of flickering candles to set a celebratory mood. You might keep the table bare, but layer it with bowls of gleaming cherries and soft pink peaches, to create the illusion of an al fresco lunch even when indoors. But one constant is bread: a table should always have bread. Bread sets the scene for a feast, it makes the table feel abundant and plentiful.

Mostly I buy bread from a good bakery: crunchy baguettes, a nice ciabatta that looks as delectable as it tastes. I cut into it before we sit down, to encourage others to help themselves, and always err on the side of more rather than less. What doesn't get eaten then and there gives me an excuse to make panzanella (p.50-55), which, selfishly put, I love. Sometimes, however, when I have time and feel in the mood, I make my own bread. This is hugely rewarding; few things speak as profoundly of domestic prowess as the scent of bread in the oven. The recipes for bread in this chapter are simple: either made without yeast, so no more temperamental than any baking; or like focaccia, where you need a little patience and elbow grease (or a sturdy mixer), but is nonetheless a very forgiving loaf.

The recipes here are all those sorts of recipes. They're salad dressings that will transform the saddest bag of supermarket leaves into something peppery and moreish; salsa verde to dress up cold cuts; or cocktails that make supper feel like a party. Think of these as extras: you can make a lovely meal without home-made sticky caramel sauce or your own salsa verde, but sometimes you're in the mood to go that extra mile. These extras also allow you the luxury to be relaxed with the rest of the meal; if you bake your own bread, you can serve it with nothing but scrambled eggs; if you make a rich, eggy truffle mayonnaise, you can happily serve yesterday's leftover cold chicken with it; and so on.

Only one caveat: once you have tasted home-made mayonnaise, thick and custardy yellow, rich with grassy olive oil, you will find you'll never again eat the stuff from the jar. On that, there is no turning back.

DAMPER BREAD

HANDS ON TIME
10 minutes

HANDS OFF TIME
45 minutes

MAKES 1 SMALL LOAF
450g self-raising flour
2 tsp sea salt flakes
30g salted butter
1 tbsp caster sugar
300ml water
1 egg yolk
1 tbsp milk

As a child I spent a lot of time in Australia and it was there that I first discovered the pleasure of damper bread, eaten warm with lashings of salted butter. Damper is a campsite bread that you can make with basic ingredients in a single bowl, then wrap in foil and cook in the embers of an open fire. I have since found that it translates wonderfully to a home kitchen: no floury surfaces, very little mess (handy when you're expecting company), and so quick and simple that it fits in seamlessly with the busy-ness of day-to-day life. It's best eaten straight from the oven, slathered in butter or dipped in olive oil.

Heat the oven to 190°C/fan 170°C/Gas 5.

Combine the flour and salt in a mixing bowl – sifted if you like, though it doesn't seem to affect the bread greatly if you don't bother – and rub in the butter. Once you have obtained a mixture with a crumb-like consistency, stir in the sugar and create a well in the centre. Pour in the measured water and, using your hands – this is the fun bit – mix to a soft dough. Knead until smooth(ish).

Loosely line the base of a round ovenproof dish with greaseproof paper (mine is 15cm in diameter and 9cm high) and place in the dough, rounded side up. Trace a cross on the top with a sharp knife. Lightly beat the egg yolk with the milk and brush the loaf lightly with this to glaze.

Cover loosely with foil and bake in the oven for about 45 minutes. After 20 minutes, remove the foil and return the loaf to the oven for the remaining cooking time, so the top becomes golden and crusty. Rest for a few minutes before turning out of its serving dish, then cut into generous chunks and eat warm, with plenty of butter.

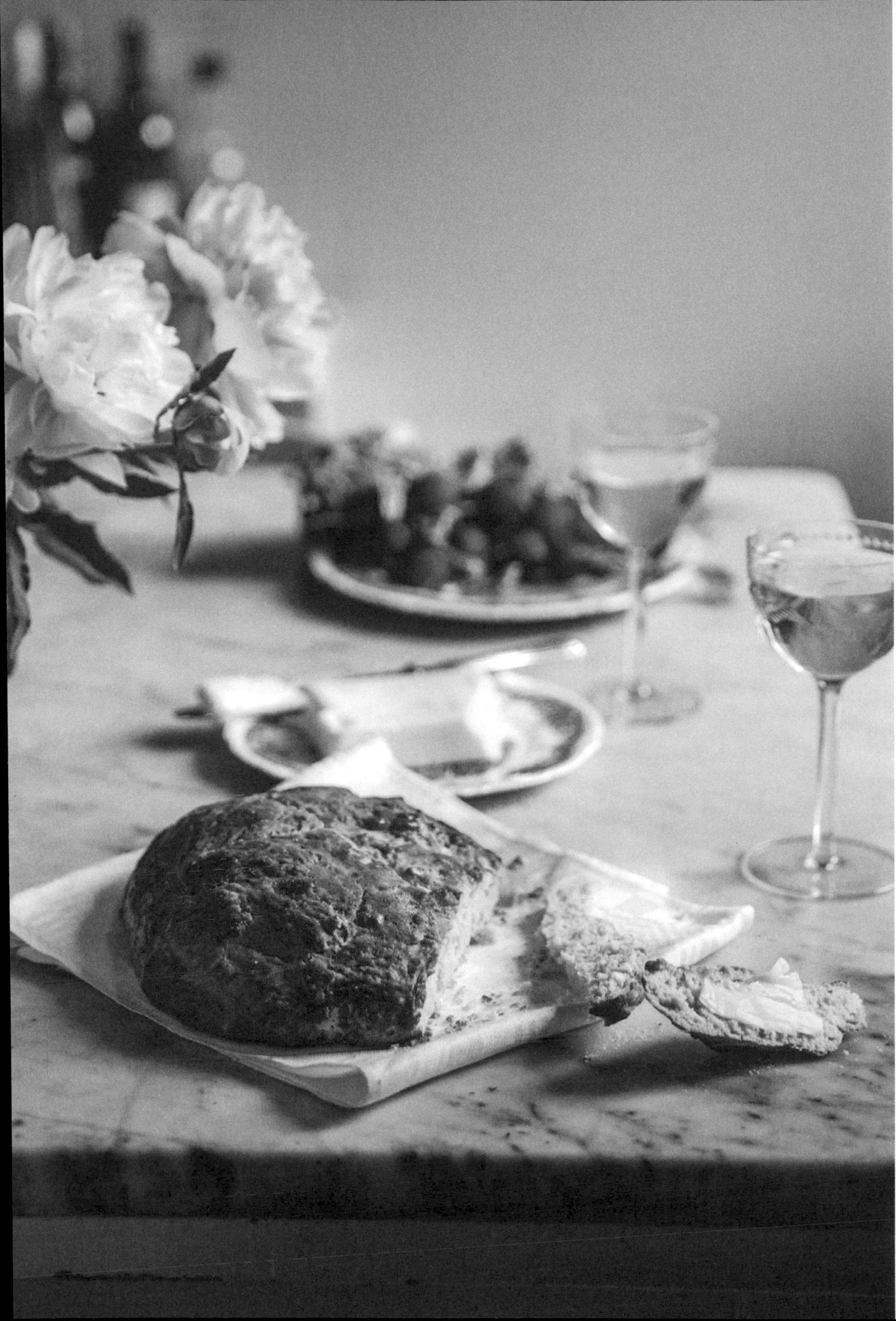

WALNUT SODA BREAD

HANDS ON TIME
10 minutes

HANDS OFF TIME
50 minutes

MAKES 1 SMALL LOAF
450g wholemeal spelt
    flour, plus extra
    for dusting
50g porridge oats
1 tsp fine sea salt
1 tsp bicarbonate
    of soda
250ml buttermilk
200ml plain yogurt
1 tbsp runny honey
100g walnuts, coarsely
    chopped

The recipe for this comes via my friend Sarah Standing, who is one of the best cooks I know. We went for supper at her house and, with the artfulness of a true domestic goddess, she produced a loaf of this bread – still warm – with a slab of butter. I've been badgering her for the recipe ever since, and have reproduced it for you below just as she passed it on to me. Sarah uses spelt flour, which gives the bread a subtle nutty texture and a delicious brown colour, but you could just as well make it with plain flour, if that is what you have, or even a mix of plain and wholemeal. I like it with walnuts, but you could throw in a handful of sticky dates as well (or instead), or use rosemary, or pistachios. Any which way, it's a dream.

Heat the oven to 180°C/fan 160°C/Gas 4 and line a baking tray with baking parchment. Combine the flour, oats, salt, bicarbonate of soda, buttermilk, yogurt and honey together in a large mixing bowl, stir, then add the walnuts.

Tip the dough out on to a floured surface and shape into a large ball. Set it on the prepared tray and use a sharp knife to score deep slits in the loaf, marking it in quarters. Dust generously with more flour.

Bake for 50 minutes, until golden brown and a hard crust has formed. It should sound hollow when you tap the bottom of the loaf. Best eaten warm with – and this is imperative – lashings of butter embedded with salt flakes.

ROASTED FENNEL FOCACCIA

HANDS ON TIME
30 minutes

HANDS OFF TIME
1 hour proving
1 hour rising
20 minutes baking

MAKES 1 LARGE LOAF
500g strong white
    flour, plus extra
    if needed and
    for dusting
2 tsp fine sea salt
1 x 7g sachet easy-bake
    yeast
6 tbsp extra virgin
    olive oil, plus extra
    for greasing
320ml cold water, plus
    extra if needed
2 medium fennel bulbs
20g salted butter
1 tbsp caster sugar
1 tsp fennel seeds
A small bunch of thyme
Freshly ground
    black pepper
Sea salt flakes, for
    sprinkling

All bread when freshly baked is a treat, but focaccia particularly so: it is soft and pillowy and – if made properly – should be dripping with olive oil. Feel free to make the recipe below without any topping, just scattered generously with sea salt flakes or a few rosemary sprigs, but the variation I give here – studded with lightly caramelised fennel wedges and aromatic fennel seeds – is at once exquisitely sweet and savoury. It also looks mighty fine on the table.

As far as breads go, focaccia is simple and – you will find – foolproof to make. It does take some time, to allow for proving and resting, but little of that is hands on, beyond the kneading. And if you have a free-standing mixer with a dough hook, don't hesitate to use it.

Mix the flour, salt and yeast in a bowl, then add 2 tbsp of the olive oil and the measured water and stir until well combined. Transfer to a lightly floured surface and knead for 10 minutes or so, until you have a lovely smooth and elastic dough. You should be able to poke it with your finger and see it bounce back. If the dough feels too sticky, add a little more flour. Equally, if it feels too dry, add a splash more water.

Wash the bowl, lightly oil it and return the dough. Cover with a damp tea towel and leave in a warm place for 1 hour or until doubled in size.

Now turn out of the bowl, knock it down with your knuckles and knead for a couple of minutes. Lightly oil a large baking tray and put the dough in it, stretching it out into a piece 4–5cm thick. Cover with tea towels and once again set in a warm place for an hour, until doubled in size.

Meanwhile, cook the fennel. Cut off and discard the fronds, then slice off some of the root and remove any outer layers that look tough or brown. Slice lengthways 1–2cm thick. In a large frying pan, melt the butter and 2 tbsp more olive oil over a high heat. When the mixture starts to foam, add a layer of fennel. You don't want to overcrowd the pan, so you may need to do this in batches. Cook for roughly 2 minutes, without turning or stirring, until lightly golden on one side. Flip the slices over and cook on the second side for a further 1–2 minutes. Remove from the pan and repeat to cook the other fennel slices. Once all the fennel has been seared, toss it back in the pan, add the sugar and fennel seeds, season generously, then fry for a further 2–3 minutes, just long enough to coat the fennel in the sugar and seeds and allow it to caramelise slightly. Remove.

—

When you are ready to bake the loaf, heat the oven to 220°C/fan 200°C/ Gas 7.

Use your fingers to make hollows in the dough and drizzle generously with the last 2 tbsp of olive oil, letting it flood into the indentations. Gently press the fennel slices into the indentations, so almost all the dough is covered in caramelised veg. Sprinkle generously with sea salt flakes and thyme.

Bake for 20 minutes or until lightly golden. To test if the bread is done, lift it up and tap the underside with a knife or your fingers: it should sound hollow. Best eaten warm from the oven – of course – but ideally within a day of baking.

Pictured overleaf →

OLGA'S PEPPERY VINAIGRETTE

HANDS ON TIME
5 minutes

FOR A LARGE SALAD
2 heaped tbsp
   English mustard
2 tbsp white
   wine vinegar
4 tbsp extra virgin
   olive oil

The difference between undressed salad – which is bitter and a little bland – and greens that come dripping in a sharp, salty dressing is quite simply so great that I hesitate to call the two by the same name. This, my godmother Olga's recipe, cannot be improved upon, so I have replicated it exactly as she gave it to me: more eye-wateringly peppery English mustard than seems sensible, a dash of white wine vinegar and lashings of good olive oil. No other seasoning needed. It's the most moreish vinaigrette I've ever tasted and, incidentally, is unbelievably good poured over plain boiled new potatoes to make a mustardy potato salad of sorts.

Combine the mustard and vinegar in a small bowl or jug and whisk together until smooth with a fork. Pour in the olive oil and whisk again until you have a runny yellow dressing. This can be made days in advance and stored in a jar.

—

Use it to dress a salad just before serving, and set a jug containing the remainder on the table for all to help themselves to more if they like. They will.

HOME-MADE MAYONNAISE

HANDS ON TIME
10 minutes

MAKES A BIG BOWL
(ROUGHLY 330g)
3 egg yolks
2 tsp Dijon mustard
3 tsp white wine
    vinegar
200ml sunflower oil
100ml extra virgin
    olive oil
Sea salt flakes
Freshly ground
    black pepper

This tastes completely different to its shop-bought counterpart and infinitely, undoubtedly superior. What few will tell you is that it's also far simpler to make than you think it's going to be: the trick is to add the olive oil to the eggs in a very slow, almost imperceptibly fine trickle to begin with, then build up towards a great glug. It helps if you have a free-standing electric mixer. Or strong arms. I sometimes add a handful of finely chopped tarragon leaves, which give the rich sauce an almost sweet flavour, and is particularly nice with cold leftover chicken.

Place the yolks in a mixing bowl, add the mustard, 1 tsp of the vinegar and a generous pinch of salt, then whisk vigorously for 30 seconds or so, until they are blended and the yolks begin to thicken a little.

Slowly add the sunflower oil, a few drops at a time to begin with, beating all the time. As the mixture becomes well blended, add a little more. You will see the mayonnaise begin to grow in volume and, as the mass grows, you can pour in the oil with more confidence. Add another 1 tsp of the vinegar, and, if it looks too thick, 1 tbsp of cold water. Now pour in the olive oil, in a constant trickle.

Every now and then, pause the trickle and whisk, until the most recent splash of oil is well combined into the mixture. Keep going until you have used up the last of the oil and have a thick, eggy mayonnaise. Mix in a little more salt and pepper to taste, then the last of the vinegar.

If the mayonnaise splits and begins to look like scrambled eggs, add 1–2 tsp of cold water to help the oil and egg re-emulsify. If it doesn't come together, add another 1 tsp of water and keep whisking.

—

Cover and store in the fridge for up to 3 days, until you are ready to serve.

TRUFFLE MAYONNAISE

HANDS ON TIME
10 minutes

MAKES A BIG BOWL
(ROUGHLY 330g)
3 egg yolks
Juice of 1 lemon
130ml extra virgin
  olive oil
100ml sunflower oil
70ml truffle oil
Sea salt flakes
Freshly ground
  black pepper

While Home-Made Mayonnaise (p.262) is just fine on almost all occasions, this version, laced with truffle oil, is a particularly special treat. Bliss with Cold Roast Topside of Beef (p.104), to perk up leftover roast chicken the next day, or – my favourite – in egg sandwiches.

Place the yolks in a mixing bowl, add half the lemon juice, a generous pinch of salt and a good grinding of black pepper, then whisk vigorously for 30 seconds or so, until the ingredients are blended and the yolks begin to thicken a little.

Slowly add the olive oil, a few drops at a time to begin with, beating all the time. As the mixture becomes well blended, add a little more. You will see the mayonnaise begin to grow in volume and, as the mass grows, you can pour in the oil with more confidence, until eventually you add it in a steady trickle. Now add the sunflower oil, again in a constant trickle, and finally the truffle oil. As you go, add 1–2 tbsp of cold water if it is getting too thick.

Keep going until you have used up the last of the oil and have a thick, eggy mayonnaise. Mix in a little more salt and pepper to taste, then the last of the lemon juice.

—

Cover and store in the fridge until you are ready to serve. The mayonnaise will keep for up to 3 days.

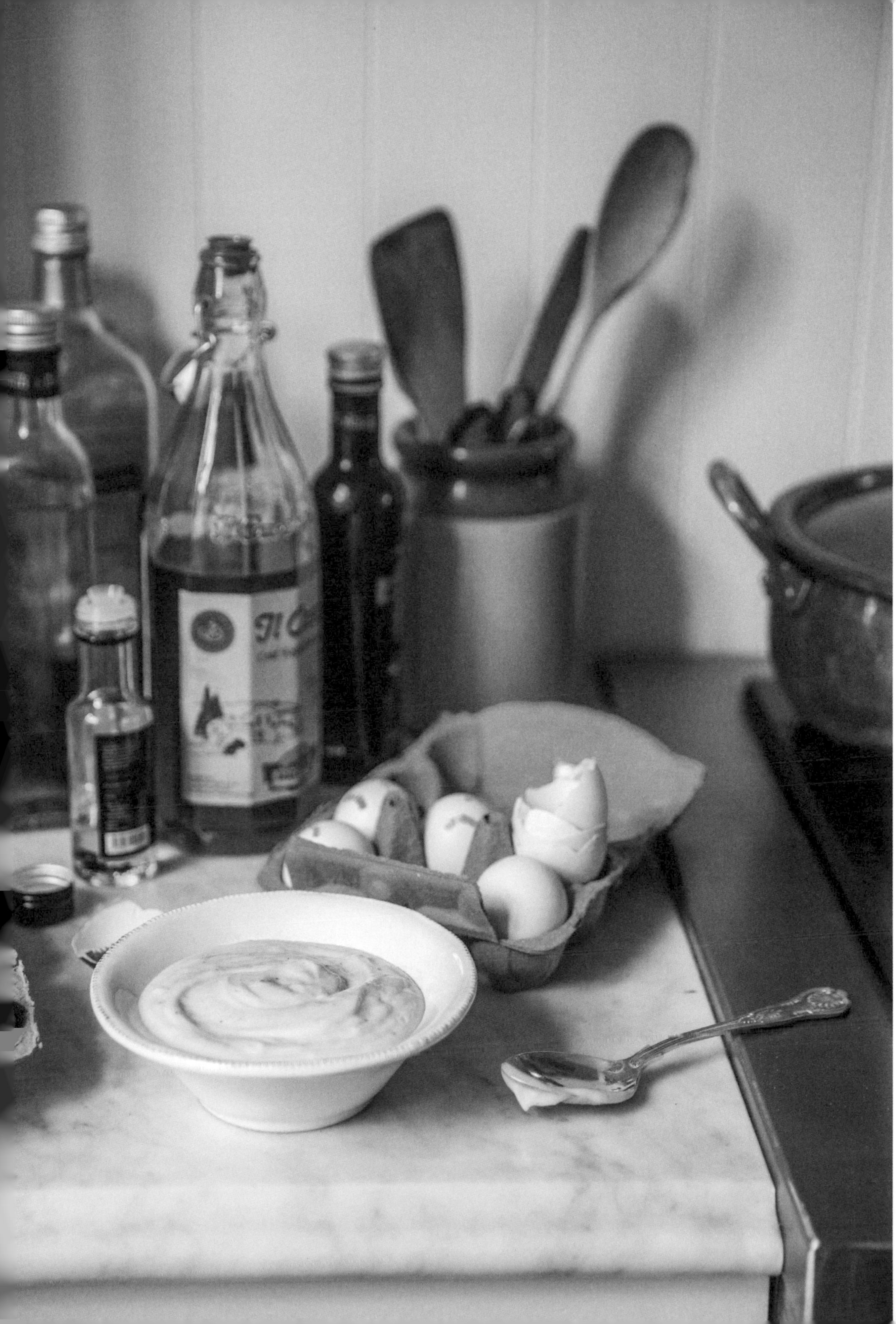

SALSA VERDE

HANDS ON TIME
10 minutes

MAKES A LARGE JARFUL
(ROUGHLY 370ml)
70g stale bread
30ml apple cider
    vinegar
A large handful of
    basil leaves
A large handful of
    parsley leaves
2 anchovy fillets
1 tbsp capers, drained
230ml extra virgin
    olive oil

A good salsa verde, peppery and verdant, is a great thing to have up your proverbial and culinary sleeve. It's ideal for lifting a plate of cold meats – I always serve it with cold roast beef (p.104) – but it is also traditional with plainer boiled meats, so works very well with plain poached chicken breasts (p.72) in place of the creamier cucumber, yogurt and poppy seed sauce given on that page.

It's one of those recipes you needn't be proscriptive about: throw in a handful of rocket, if you have it to hand, crushed garlic if you like, sweet tarragon leaves, more capers, more salt, more olive oil… really you can adapt it as you please. This is my preferred recipe, made with stale bread which gives the sauce an irresistible soft green colour and very creamy texture. I use apple cider vinegar, as I find it to be mellower than red or white wine vinegars, less raspy and less sour, but whatever you prefer and have hanging about in the kitchen cupboard will do very nicely.

Place the bread in a bowl, pour the vinegar over and leave for a few minutes to soak up all the liquid. Put the basil and parsley into a blender. Rinse the anchovies and capers under cold running water to get rid of any excess saltiness, then add them to the blender. Blitz until everything is finely chopped.

Lift the bread out of the bowl and squeeze out any excess vinegar with your hands. Add to the blender and blitz to a soft green paste. Slowly add the olive oil, trickle by trickle, blitzing all the while, until you have a thick, full-bodied sauce.

—

The salsa verde will keep nicely in the fridge for 1–2 days. After that, it turns a rather unappetising colour.

EASY SALTED CARAMEL SAUCE

HANDS ON TIME
10 minutes

HANDS OFF TIME
10 minutes cooling

MAKES A LARGE JARFUL
(ROUGHLY 370ml)
60g salted butter
90g soft brown sugar
60g golden syrup
180g condensed milk
A generous pinch of sea
    salt flakes
A little whole milk
    (optional)

Caramel – most particularly the slightly salted variety – is one of life's greatest culinary pleasures, though rather temperamental to make. You might call the recipe below a cheat's version, in that it is quick, easy and eschews that process of browning the sugar until the point it caramelises, which I always find so stressful. However, there is absolutely nothing about the rich, buttery flavour of this sauce, or its soft, luscious texture, that in any way feels like a compromise. I happily eat it by the spoonful, though it's particularly good warmed gently and drizzled over ice cream, or served in a bowl, with strawberries, Cape gooseberries, chunks of sweet peach and the like for dipping.

Place a heavy-based saucepan over a medium heat, gently melt the butter, then stir in the sugar, syrup and condensed milk.

Stir constantly over the heat with a wooden spoon until the sauce is thick and smooth and turns a rich caramel colour; this takes about 5 minutes. Add the salt and stir well.

———

You can store this in a jar in the fridge for up to a week, or, if serving straight away, leave it to cool for about 10 minutes, then stir in a few tablespoons of milk, if you would like a runnier sauce.

A GREAT ALL-ROUND COCKTAIL

HANDS ON TIME
5 minutes

HANDS OFF TIME
30 minutes chilling

FOR 12
250ml dry gin
250ml Campari
250ml sweet red
    vermouth
Ice
¼ orange, finely sliced

Negroni is a classic cocktail and my go-to for lunches, suppers and parties. The trick is to make a batch ahead of time, so when everyone arrives all you have to do is pour a glass of something, rather than fussing about mixing it. While a cocktail shaker is the rather more elegant way to do this, I have found that shaking everything together in a clean glass or plastic bottle is more practical. Store it in the freezer until you're ready to transfer your negroni into a big, ice-filled jug.

To go with drinks, I like to put out a plate of something easy (usually shop-bought) to nibble on: fennel seed *taralli*, a hunk of pecorino cheese with a small dish of runny honey for dipping, a bowl of juicy olives, salami and so forth. See p.20–21 for more ideas.

Combine the gin, Campari and vermouth in a cocktail shaker (or bottle) and shake vigorously. Store in the freezer for at least 30 minutes to chill, or as long as you like (the alcohol means it won't freeze).

—

When ready to serve, fill a large glass jug with ice and orange slices, then pour over the negroni.

A GREAT COCKTAIL FOR LUNCHTIME

HANDS ON TIME
5 minutes

FOR 12
750ml dry sherry
750ml lemonade
Ice
A handful of
    mint leaves

This recipe comes from my friend Emily Fitzroy, who more than anyone knows how to throw a great party. It's the kind of fruity, light cocktail that you happily and unabashedly knock back over lunch, especially on a sunny day. I mix it up in large jugfuls so everyone can help themselves. Not only does that make life simpler, but it feels all-round more relaxed.

Mix the sherry and lemonade together over ice in a large glass jug. Add the mint leaves. Serve immediately.

A GREAT COCKTAIL FOR DINNER

HANDS ON TIME
5 minutes

HANDS OFF TIME
30 minutes chilling

FOR 12
700ml vodka
A capful of vermouth
Big, juicy green olives,
    to serve

This is a cheat's martini, and, while there is nothing to stop you serving it for lunch, there is a sort of glamorous dress-up quality about martinis that I inevitably associate with dinner and parties. You can serve this by the jugful, as with the sherry cocktail (p.272) or pour it straight from the chilled glass bottle into individual glasses, then dress with a briny olive.

Combine a bottle of vodka with the vermouth in a large, clean glass bottle, shake and set in the freezer to chill for at least 30 minutes, or as long as you like: ready-made martini. The alcohol means it won't freeze, so you can make it days, even weeks, in advance and have the bottle ready to go whenever you need it.

—

Serve in martini glasses with a big, juicy green olive.

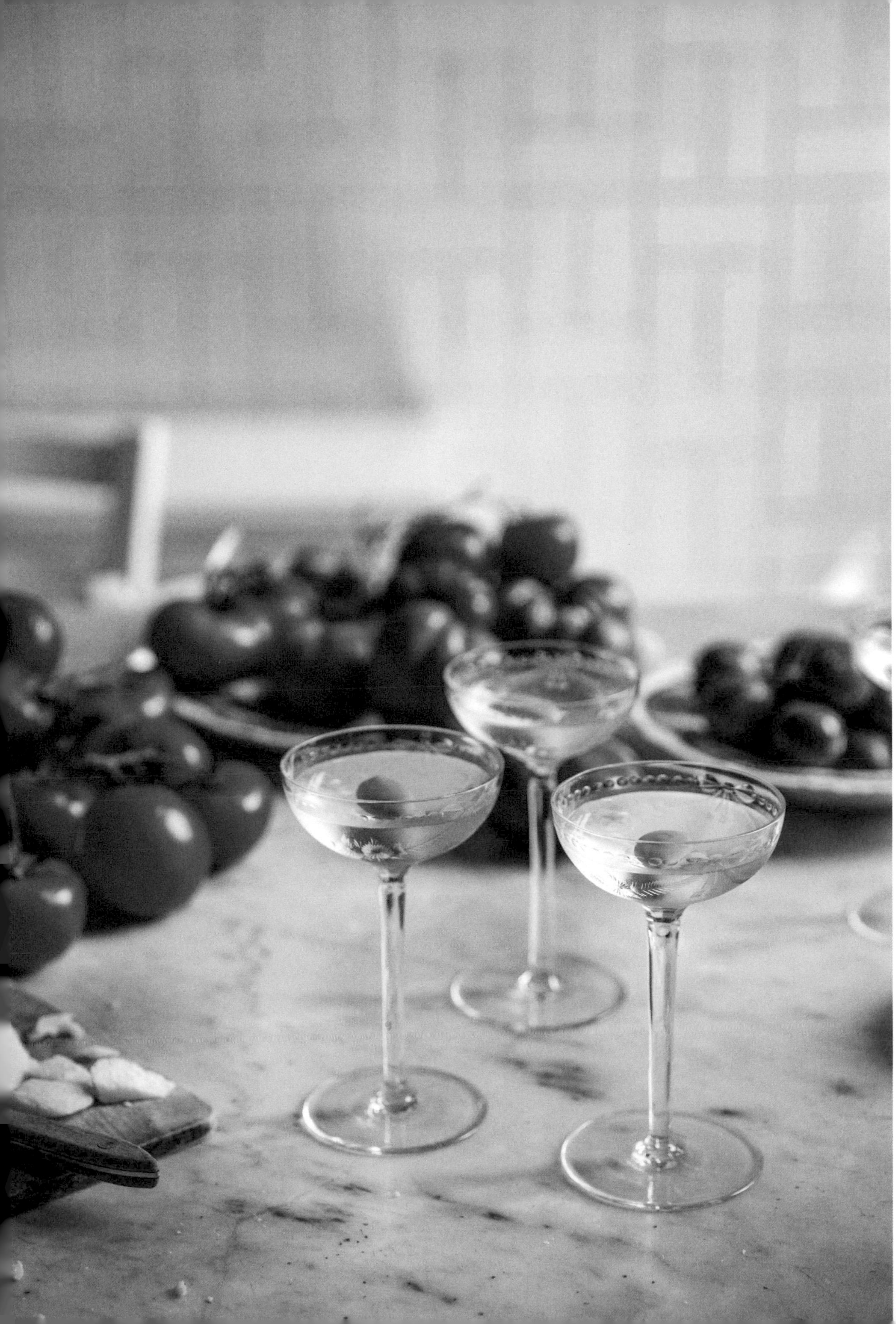

HOW TO
COOK
BY SEASON

Gathered here is a collection of menus: these are flavour combinations that work especially well together and meals that I have particularly enjoyed over the years, and which I thought you might enjoy too. Much like the 'Serve with…' notes you will find alongside each of the recipes in this book, the menus in the pages that follow are not intended as proscriptive: they are simply suggestions, a starting point. There is absolutely no reason why you should eat tagliatelle baked in a creamy gratin for your birthday; it's just that (served with slivers of cold roast beef, a big green salad and followed by a coffee and walnut cake), it is what I like to do to celebrate mine.

The menus are organised by season. This is because cooking seasonally makes life easier; what we feel like eating on a hot summer's day tends to be very different from the kind of comforting, nourishing food that we crave in the depths of winter. Just as the ingredients available in autumn are very different from what you will find in the shops in spring. All rules are, of course, made to be broken and certain dishes somehow defy the notion of seasonality: these you will see pop up again and again. A good salad, for example, is something that I serve year round and with pretty much everything. Likewise, roast chicken is a dish that I always feel like eating, though I might have it with a plate of juicy tomatoes dressed in olive oil and a large bowl of home-made mayonnaise in the summer, and with a tray of mustardy baked leeks and golden roast potatoes in winter.

SPRING

A DELICIOUSLY SIMPLE LUNCH

Mozzarella with Celery, Olives & Pine Nuts (p.36)
Baby Artichoke, Fennel & Pecorino Salad (p.122)
Tuscan Panzanella (p.50)
A big bowl of mixed berries, with a dollop of
    mascarpone on the side, and Meringues (p.238),
    if you fancy

A CASUAL LIGHT LUNCH

Tuscan Panzanella (p.50)
Carrot, Cumin & Mint Salad (p.144)
A Really Good Chicory Salad with Creamy Mustard
    Dressing (p.110)
Rose Meringues (p.238)
Drunken Strawberries (p.194)
    with mascarpone

UNBEATABLE SUNDAY LUNCH

Cold Roast Topside of Beef (p.104), with Salsa
    Verde (p.266)
Especially Good Roast Potatoes (p.150)
Green Beans with Baby Tomatoes (p.140)
Salted Caramel Pannacotta (p.210)

WARMING-BUT-LIGHT SOUP LUNCH

Tuscan Spring Vegetable Soup (p.58)
Green salad with Olga's Peppery Vinaigrette (p.260)
Damper Bread (p.252), straight from the oven
    with salted butter
Pink Rhubarb & Prosecco Jelly (p.222)

FANCY-BUT-EASY DINNER
PARTY FOOD

Bresaola e Grana (p.44)
Roast New Potatoes with Bay Leaves (p.152)
Beetroot & Mint Salad (p.118)
A Really Good Chicory Salad with Creamy Mustard
    Dressing (p.110)
Coffee Mascarpone Biscuit Cake (p.190)

A SUMPTUOUS SUPPER
OF COLD BITS

Cold Roast Topside of Beef (p.104)
Home-Made Mayonnaise (p.262), with tarragon
Panzanella with Garden Peas & Baby Artichokes (p.52)

MAKE-AHEAD WEEKNIGHT SUPPER

Spinach, Mint & Melted Cheese Syrian Frittata (p.80)
Fried Broccoli with Black Olives (p.128)
A Really Good Tomato Salad (p.114)
Pistachio Butter Cake with Marzipan Icing (p.232)

BIRTHDAY DINNER

Tagliatelle Gratin (p.86)
Cold Roast Topside of Beef (p.104), with Salsa
    Verde (p.266)
A Really Good Green Salad (p.112)
A Really Good Tomato Salad (p.114)
Coffee & Walnut Cake (p.236)

A SPOILING AFTERNOON TEA

Pistachio Butter Cake with Marzipan Icing (p.232)
Egg sandwiches with Truffle Mayonnaise (p.264)
Strawberries in Lemony Syrup (p.192)
Meringues (p.238), and good shop-bought biscuits

FIRST PICNIC OF THE YEAR

Sicilian Couscous Salad (p.46)
Good hard cheeses, cold hams and / or salami
Damper Bread (p.252) with salted butter
Pistachio Butter Cake with Marzipan Icing (p.232)
A punnet of strawberries

A SICILIAN EXTRAVAGANZA

Sicilian Couscous Salad (p.46)
Tomato, Red Onion & Mint Salad (p.116)
Timballo of Baked Courgettes (p.162)
Svergognata (p.202)

A PICNIC YOU CAN PREPARE WELL IN ADVANCE

Wild Rice & Lentil Salad (p.132)
Quail's eggs with celery salt
Crudités with Truffle Mayonnaise (p.264)
Charcuterie with bread from the bakery
Strawberries
A Very Good Vanilla Pannacotta (p.206), in small jars

EASTER PICNIC LUNCH

Torta Pasqualina (p.76)
Tomato, Red Onion & Mint Salad (p.116)
Baby Artichoke, Fennel & Pecorino Salad (p.122)
Ambrosial Apricots (p.224) with double cream
    or mascarpone

EASY KITCHEN SUPPER
(or lunch, for that matter)

Panzanella with Tuna & Anchovies (p.54)
A Really Good Green Salad (p.112) with Olga's Peppery
    Vinaigrette (p.260)
Fried Broccoli with Black Olives (p.128)
Coffee Mascarpone Biscuit Cake (p.190)

EASY-PEASY ROAST CHICKEN DINNER

Buttery Lemon Roast Chicken (p.92)
Roast New Potatoes with Bay Leaves (p.152)
Roast Apples (p.172)
A Really Good Green Salad (p.112) with finely
    sliced fennel thrown in
Easy-Peasy Lemon Meringue Pie (p.182)

AN ACCIDENTALLY VEGETARIAN FEAST

Panzanella with Garden Peas & Baby Artichokes (p.52)
A good selection of cheese
Roast Stuffed Tomatoes (p.156)
Courgette Blossom & Taleggio Galette (p.160)
Frozen Berries with Saffron White Chocolate
    Sauce (p.204)

A ROAST WITH A TINY TWIST

Honey-Roast Poussins (p.94)
Carrot, Cumin & Mint Salad (p.144)
Roast New Potatoes with Bay Leaves (p.152)
A Really Good Green Salad (p.112)
Lemon Meringue Cake (p.244)

WHEN IT'S ALMOST SUMMER...

Poulet Anglais (p.72)
Asparagus with Lemon & Toasted Almond Gratin (p.138)
New Potatoes with Lemon & Samphire (p.126)
Strawberries in Lemony Syrup (p.192)
Salted Honey Ice Cream (p.186) or A Very Good Vanilla
    Pannacotta (p.206)

A REALLY SATISFYING ROAST

Roast Pork (without Honey-Roast Persimmons) (p.96)
Roast Grapes (p.168)
Especially Good Roast Potatoes (p.150)
A Really Good Red Chicory Salad with Creamy Mustard
    Dressing (p.110)
An Embarrassment of Spring Vegetables (p.146)
Pistachio Butter Cake with Marzipan Icing (p.232)

EVERYONE'S FAVOURITE

Buttery Lemon Roast Chicken (p.92)
The Simplest Roast Potatoes (p.148)
A Really Good Green Salad (p.112)
Summer Berry Cloud Cake (p.240)

A LITTLE SOMETHING LIGHT
(followed by a fabulously rich pudding)

Tuscan Spring Vegetable Soup (p.58)
Walnut Soda Bread (p.254), or good bread from the bakery
Cheeses or charcuterie
Pistachio, Mascarpone & Salted Caramel Cheesecake (p.214)

SUMMER

NO-COOK LUNCH IN THE GARDEN

Chilled Almond Soup (p.38)
Beetroot & Mint Salad (p.118)
Watermelon, Feta & Pistachio Carpaccio (p.120)
Salted Honey Ice Cream (p.186)

MAKE-AHEAD COLD SUMMER LUNCH

Whole Poached Cold Salmon (p.74)
Saffron Fennel (p.134), served at
    room temperature
Watercress salad with Olga's Peppery
    Vinaigrette (p.260)
Tomato, Red Onion & Mint Salad (p.116)
Ambrosial Apricots (p.224)

WHEN YOU'RE IN THE MOOD FOR A TREAT

Chilled Almond Soup (p.38)
Warm Walnut Soda Bread (p.254)
Burrata with Preserved Lemons, Mint & Chilli (p.34)
Chocolate & Rum Pudding (p.226)
A bowl of raspberries

A BLISSFULLY SIMPLE LUNCH

Mozzarella with Celery, Olives & Pine Nuts (p.36)
Roast Stuffed Tomatoes (p.156)
Baby Artichoke, Fennel & Pecorino Salad (p.122)
Sicilian Couscous Salad (p.46)
Peaches with mascarpone and Meringues (p.238),
    if you fancy

SUPER-RELAXED LUNCH

Tuscan Panzanella (p.50)
Spinach, Mint & Melted Cheese Syrian Frittata (p.80)
Carrot, Cumin & Mint Salad (p.144)
Red chicory salad (p.110) with a handful of roughly torn
    parsley leaves and finely sliced radishes thrown in
Melon in Grappa Syrup (p.196)

QUICK BUT SPOILING LUNCH

Burrata with Preserved Lemons, Mint & Chilli (p.34)
A Really Good Tomato Salad (p.114)
Carpaccio of Figs with Lardo, Honey & Rosemary (p.42)
Drunken Strawberries (p.194) with mascarpone

LATE SUMMER LUNCH AL FRESCO
(for a few friends)

Spaghetti with Creamy Lemon Sauce (p.60)
A Really Good Tomato Salad (p.114)
Honey, Fig & Walnut Semifreddo (p.218)

LATE SUMMER LUNCH AL FRESCO
(for a crowd)

Burrata with Preserved Lemons, Mint & Chilli (p.34)
Wild Rice & Lentil Salad (p.132)
Courgette Blossom & Taleggio Galette (p.160)
Lemon Meringue Cake (p.244)

LUNCH IN A HURRY

Watermelon, Feta & Pistachio Carpaccio (p.120)
Wild Rice & Lentil Salad (p.132)
Mozzarella with Celery, Black Olives and Pine
    Nuts (p.36)
Svergognata (p.202)

CASUAL LUNCH FOR A CROWD
(with a dash of retro charm)

Poulet Anglais (p.72)
New Potatoes with Lemon & Samphire (p.126)
Baby Artichoke, Fennel & Pecorino Salad (p.122)
Coffee & Walnut Cake (p.236)

SUMMER SUPPER PARTY

Bresaola e Grana (p.44)
Wild Rice & Lentil Salad (p.132)
Tomato, Red Onion & Mint Salad (p.116)
Drunken Strawberries (p.194)
Melon in Grappa Syrup (p.196)

COSY SUPPER

Gazpacho (p.40)
Bresaola e Grana (p.44)
Asparagus with Lemon & Toasted Almond Gratin (p.138)
Warm Damper Bread (p.252)
Easy-Peasy Lemon Meringue Pie (p.182)
A tower of Meringues (p.238) with fresh raspberries

INDULGENT WEEKNIGHT SUPPER

Carpaccio of Figs with Lardo, Honey & Rosemary (p.42)
Courgette Blossom & Taleggio Galette (p.160)
Panzanella with Garden Peas & Baby Artichokes (p.52)
Salted Honey Ice Cream (p.186), in cones

WEEKNIGHT SUPPER OF SALAD-Y BITS

Panzanella with Tuna & Anchovies (p.54)
A Really Good Green Salad (p.112), with Olga's
    Peppery Vinaigrette (p.260)
Asparagus with Lemon & Toasted Almond Gratin (p.138)
Honey, Fig & Walnut Semifreddo (p.218)

QUICK PASTA SUPPER FOR
A FEW FRIENDS

Spaghetti with Creamy Lemon Sauce (p.60)
A crisp green salad with Olga's Peppery
    Vinaigrette (p.260)
Melon In Grappa Syrup (p.196), or Frozen Berries
    with Saffron White Chocolate Sauce (p.204)

WEEKNIGHT SUPPER OF COLD BITS

Poulet Anglais (p.72)
Asparagus with Lemon & Toasted Almond Gratin (p.138)
New Potatoes with Lemon & Samphire (p.126)
A Really Good Green Salad (p.112)
Pine Nut Ice Cream 'Affogato' (p.188)

A DELIGHTFULLY LAZY ROAST
CHICKEN SUPPER

Buttery Lemon Chicken (p.92)
The Simplest Roast Potatoes (p.148)
Fried Broccoli with Black Olives (p.128)
Svergognata (p.202)

A RELAXED DINNER ON
A BALMY SUMMER'S EVE

Honey-Roast Poussins (p.94)
Watermelon, Feta & Pistachio Carpaccio (p.120)
Timballo of Baked Courgettes (p.162)
Rum, Raisin & Walnut Ice Cream (p.184), in cones
    or as Affogato (p.188)

A VERY SPECIAL DINNER
FOR TWENTY (or more)

Honey-Roast Poussins (p.94)
Asparagus with Lemon & Toasted Almond Gratin (p.138)
Burrata with Preserved Lemons, Mint & Chilli (p.34)
A Really Good Green Salad (p.112)
Lemon Meringue Cake (p.244)
Drunken Strawberries (p.194)

FOR A SUMMER PARTY

Whole Poached Cold Salmon (p.74), with Home-Made
    Mayonnaise (p.262)
Green Beans with Baby Tomatoes (p.140)
New Potatoes with Lemon & Samphire (p.126)
Limoncello Semifreddo (p.220)

PICNIC LUNCH

Gazpacho (p.40), in a vacuum flask
Torta Pasqualina (p.76)
Cold cuts: ham, salami, prosciutto (or what have you)
Chunks of raw fennel, carrot, peppers, radishes
    and Home-Made Mayonnaise (p.262)
A punnet of strawberries with clotted cream,
    or a jar of Easy Salted Caramel Sauce (p.268)

A LIGHT & EASY SUMMER PICNIC

Courgette Blossom & Taleggio Galette (p.160)
Cheeses
Cherries with Meringues (p.238)
Lavender Honey Pannacotta (p.208)

HOLIDAY MOOD

Chilled Almond Soup (p.38)
Courgette Blossom & Taleggio Galette (p.160)
Baby Artichoke, Fennel & Pecorino Salad (p.122)
Limoncello Semifreddo (p.220)

MIDSUMMER'S FEAST

Cold Roast Topside of Beef (p.104) with Salsa
    Verde (p.266)
New Potatoes with Lemon & Samphire (p.126)
A Really Good Tomato Salad (p.114), with a handful
    of black olives thrown in
Summer Berry Cloud Cake (p.240)

A SUMMERY ROAST

Aphrodite's Roast Chicken (p.90)
Fried Broccoli with Black Olives (p.128)
A Really Good Tomato Salad (p.114)
A Really Good Green Salad (p.112)
A Very Good Vanilla Pannacotta (p.206)
Strawberries in Lemony Syrup (p.192)

WHEN IT'S TOO HOT TO COOK

Carpaccio of Figs with Lardo, Honey & Rosemary (p.42)
Chilled Almond Soup (p.38)
A nice selection of cheeses
Coffee Mascarpone Biscuit Cake (p.190)

SUMMER FEAST WITH BELLS & WHISTLES

Torta di Maccheroni (p.82)
Roast Red Onions (p.166)
A Really Good Chicory Salad with Creamy Mustard
    Dressing (p.110), with a few Baby Gem leaves
    tossed through
Beetroot & Mint Salad (p.118)
Melon in Grappa Syrup (p.196)

AN ACCIDENTALLY VEGETARIAN SUMMER MENU

Spinach, Mint & Melted Cheese Syrian Frittata (p.80)
A Really Good Green Salad (p.112)
Green Beans with Baby Tomatoes (p.140)
Melon in Grappa Syrup (p.196)

A FEAST OF COLD PLATES

Cold Roast Topside of Beef (p.104), with Salsa
    Verde (p.266)
Roast Stuffed Tomatoes (p.156)
New Potatoes with Lemon & Samphire (p.126)
Ambrosial Apricots (p.224)

AUTUMN

THE PERFECT WEEKEND LUNCH

Buttery Lemon Roast Chicken (p.92)
Beetroot & Mint Salad (p.118)
Butter-&-Sage Roast Pumpkin (p.158)
Especially Good Roast Potatoes (p.150)
Apple & Walnut Crumble Pie (p.246)

MY GO-TO FOR A LAZY SUNDAY LUNCH

Aphrodite's Roast Chicken (p.90)
Braised Lentils with Pancetta (p.130)
Roast Red Onions (p.166)
A Really Good Green Salad (p.112)
Chocolate Chestnut Meringue Pie (p.178)

AN ESPECIALLY SPOILING SUNDAY LUNCH

Allegra's Pot-Roast Beef (p.68), with Truffle
    Mayonnaise (p.264)
A Really Good Tomato Salad (p.114)
Roast New Potatoes with Bay Leaves (p.152)
Chocolate & Rum Pudding (p.226)

SUNDAY LUNCH FOR A CROWD

Cold Roast Topside of Beef (p.104), with Home-Made
    Mayonnaise (p.262)
Panzanella with Garden Peas & Baby Artichokes (p.52)
A Really Good Tomato Salad (p.114), with a handful
    of black olives thrown in
Summer Berry Cloud Cake (p.240)

A VERY RELAXED WEEKNIGHT SUPPER

Sausages with Grapes (p.66)
Roast New Potatoes with Bay Leaves (p.152)
A Really Good Chicory Salad with Creamy Mustard
    Dressing (p.110)
Salted Caramel Pannacotta (p.210)

WHEN YOU NEED SUPPER IN A HURRY

Rigatoni with Mascarpone & Pancetta (p.64)
A Really Good Green Salad (p.112)
Bresaola e Grana (p.44)
Svergognata (p.202)

A DEEPLY COMFORTING SUPPER

Burrata with Preserved Lemons, Mint & Chilli (p.34)
Carrot & Cinnamon Soup (p.56)
Wild Rice & Lentil Salad (p.132)
Red Wine Poached Pears (p.212)

FIRST BLUSH OF AUTUMN SUPPER

Honey-Roast Poussins (p.94)
Roast New Potatoes with Bay Leaves (p.152)
Roast Plums (p.170)
Baby Artichoke, Fennel & Pecorino Salad (p.122)
Frozen Berries with Saffron White Chocolate
    Sauce (p.204)

A COSY SOUP SUPPER

Carrot & Cinnamon Soup (p.56)
A warm loaf of Damper Bread (p.252), with butter
A nice plate of charcuterie
Flourless Chocolate, Chestnut & Rosemary Cake (p.234),
    with clotted cream

A WONDERFULLY SOOTHING PASTA SUPPER

Bresaola e Grana (p.44)
Tagliatelle with Gorgonzola, Pear & Walnut (p.62)
Chocolate Chestnut Meringue Cake (p.242)

ANTHONY'S BIRTHDAY PARTY DINNER

Confit Duck Pie (p.98)
Buttery Carrots with Chestnut Honey (p.142)
A Really Good Chicory Salad with Creamy Mustard
    Dressing (p.110)
Creamy Baked Leeks with Mustard & Parmesan (p.164)
Chocolate Chestnut Meringue Cake (p.242)

MAKE IN ADVANCE KITCHEN SUPPER

Spinach, Mint & Melted Cheese Syrian Frittata (p.80)
Butter-&-Sage Roast Pumpkin (p.158)
Wild Rice & Lentil Salad (p.132)
Buttery Carrots with Chestnut Honey (p.142)
Flourless Chocolate, Chestnut & Rosemary Cake (p.234)

QUICK WEEKNIGHT SUPPER

Rigatoni with Mascarpone & Pancetta (p.64)
A Really Good Green Salad (p.112)
A Very Good Vanilla Pannacotta (p.206)
    with a bowl of blackberries

AN AUTUMNAL ROAST

Roast Pork with Honey-Roast Persimmons (p.96)
Fennel & Parmesan Purée (p.136)
A Really Good Chicory Salad with Creamy Mustard
    Dressing (p.110)
Apple & Walnut Crumble Pie (p.246) with runny
    double cream

A RICH & WONDERFULLY COSY FEAST

Tagliatelle Gratin (p.86)
A Really Good Chicory Salad with Creamy Mustard
    Dressing (p.110)
Red Wine Poached Pears (p.212)
A big hunk of Gorgonzola

PARTY FOR A CROWD

Torta di Maccheroni (p.82)
Beetroot & Mint Salad (p.118)
A Really Good Chicory Salad with Creamy Mustard
    Dressing (p.110)
Some nice cheeses
Coffee & Walnut Cake (p.236)

FAILSAFE, FOOLPROOF LUNCH *(or dinner)* FOR EIGHT

Two Buttery Lemon Roast Chickens (p.92) on a bed
    of rosemary
Especially Good Roast Potatoes (p.150)
Carrot, Cumin & Mint Salad (p.144)
A Really Good Chicory Salad with Creamy Mustard
    Dressing (p.110)
Roast Grapes (p.168)
Apple & Walnut Crumble Pie (p.246) with Salted Honey
    Ice Cream (p.186) or double cream

EFFORTLESS COOKING FOR A CROWD

Honey-Roast Poussins (p.94)
Pommes Dauphinoise (p.154)
Beetroot & Mint Salad (p.118)
Buttery Carrots with Chestnut Honey (p.142)
Flourless Chocolate, Chestnut & Rosemary Cake (p.234)

A FEAST FOR THE EYES

Roast Pork with Honey-Roast Persimmons (p.96)
The Simplest Roast Potatoes (p.148)
Roast Red Onions (p.166)
Saffron Fennel (p.134)
Coffee Mascarpone Biscuit Cake (p.190)

WINTER

NOT FOR THE FAINT OF HEART...

Confit Duck Pie (p.98)
Saffron Fennel (p.134)
A Really Good Chicory Salad with Creamy Mustard
    Dressing (p.110)
Carrot, Cumin & Mint Salad (p.144)
Salted Caramel Pannacotta (p.210)

A SUPER-EASY ROAST FOR A CROWD

Honey-Roast Poussins (p.94)
Butter-&-Sage Roast Pumpkin (p.158)
Saffron Fennel (p.134)
A Really Good Chicory Salad with Creamy Mustard
    Dressing (p.110)
Winter Fruit & Mascarpone Tart (p.180)

WHEN ALL YOU CRAVE IN LIFE IS SIMPLICITY

Aphrodite's Roast Chicken (p.90)
A Really Good Chicory Salad with Creamy Mustard
    Dressing (p.110)
A Really Good Tomato Salad (p.114)
Pine Nut Ice Cream, either 'Affogato' (p.188), or with
    Easy Salted Caramel Sauce (p.268)

AENEAS'S DREAM MEAL

Pork Wellington with Apple & Sage (p.100)
Especially Good Roast Potatoes (p.150)
Roast Red Onions (p.166)
A Really Good Green Salad (p.112) with fennel
Salted Honey Ice Cream (p.186)

LOW-EFFORT BUT HIGH-REWARD WEEKEND LUNCH

Roast Pork with Honey-Roast Persimmons (p.96)
Beetroot & Mint Salad (p.118)
A Really Good Chicory Salad with Creamy Mustard
    Dressing (p.110)
The Simplest Roast Potatoes (p.148)
Salted Caramel Pannacotta (p.210)

PERFECT SUNDAY LUNCH ON A BITTER WINTER'S DAY

Pork Wellington with Apple & Sage (p.100)
Braised Lentils with Pancetta (p.130)
A Really Good Chicory Salad with Creamy Mustard
    Dressing (p.110)
Butter-&-Sage Roast Pumpkin (p.158)
Winter Fruit & Mascarpone Tart (p.180)

FOOD FOR CELEBRATION

Chilled Almond Soup (p.38)
Roast Pork with Honey-Roast Persimmons (p.96)
A Really Good Chicory Salad with Creamy Mustard
    Dressing (p.110)
Pistachio Panettone Cake (p.198)

SIMPLE DINNER PARTY FOOD

Bresaola e Grana (p.44)
Pommes Dauphinoise (p.154)
Creamy Baked Leeks with Mustard & Parmesan (p.164)
A Really Good Chicory Salad with Creamy Mustard
    Dressing (p.110)
Svergognata (p.202)

$\longrightarrow$

A FABULOUSLY COLOURFUL KITCHEN SUPPER

Wintry Saffron Couscous (p.48)
Blood Orange, Red Onion, Black Olive & Basil Salad (p.124)
Roast Red Onions (p.166)
Buttery Carrots with Chestnut Honey (p.142)
Rum, Raisin & Walnut Ice Cream (p.184) served as
    'Affogato' (p.188)

UNBELIEVABLY COMFORTING KITCHEN SUPPER

Ossobuco with Sage & Lemon (p.70)
Blood Orange, Red Onion, Black Olive & Basil Salad (p.124)
Fennel & Parmesan Purée (p.136)
A Really Good Chicory Salad with Creamy Mustard
    Dressing (p.110)
Flourless Chocolate, Chestnut & Rosemary Cake (p.234)

SUPER-EASY KITCHEN SUPPER

Bresaola e Grana (p.44)
Tagliàtelle with Gorgonzola, Pear & Walnut (p.62)
Pink Rhubarb & Prosecco Jelly (p.222)

GROWN-UP NURSERY-FOOD SUPPER

Confit Duck Pie (p.98)
Fried Broccoli with Black Olives (p.128)
Buttery Carrots with Chestnut Honey (p.142)
Red Wine Poached Pears (p.212)
Salted Honey Ice Cream (p.186)

WHEN SPRING IS NUDGING IN

Burrata with Preserved Lemons, Mint & Chilli (p.34)
Braised Lentils with Pancetta (p.130)
Blood Orange, Red Onion, Black Olive & Basil Salad (p.124)
Pink Rhubarb & Prosecco Jelly (p.222)

A CORNUCOPIA OF WINTER FRUIT

Roast Pork (without Honey-Roast Persimmons) (p.96),
    but served with Roast Grapes (p.168)
Blood Orange, Red Onion, Black Olive & Basil Salad (p.124)
Fennel & Parmesan Purée (p.136)
A Really Good Chicory Salad (p.110)
Winter Fruit & Mascarpone Tart (p.180)

WHAT EVERYONE SECRETLY WANTS TO EAT AT A PARTY

Tagliatelle Gratin (p.86)
Green salad with Olga's Peppery Vinaigrette (p.260)
Chocolate Chestnut Meringue Pie (p.178)

A DELICIOUSLY RETRO MENU

Buttery Lemon Roast Chicken (p.92) with rhubarb
    sauce (p.222)
Especially Good Roast Potatoes (p.150)
Creamy Baked Leeks with Mustard & Parmesan (p.164)
A Really Good Green Salad (p.112)
Pink Rhubarb & Prosecco Jelly (p.222)

A POP OF COLOUR *(for when it's grey outside)*

Ossobuco with Sage & Lemon (p.70)
Butter-&-Sage Roast Pumpkin (p.158)
Beetroot & Mint Salad (p.118)
Winter Fruit & Mascarpone Tart (p.180)

MAKE-AHEAD COMFORT FOOD

Tagliatelle Gratin (p.86)
A Really Good Green Salad (p.112)
Svergognata (p.202)

VERY FAST FOOD

Tagliatelle with Gorgonzola, Pear & Walnut (p.62)
A Really Good Chicory Salad with Creamy Mustard
    Dressing (p.110)
Flourless Chocolate, Chestnut & Rosemary Cake (p.234)

VEGETARIAN COMFORT FOOD

Spinach, Mint & Melted Cheese Syrian Frittata (p.80)
Wild Rice & Lentil Salad (p.132)
Buttery Carrots with Chestnut Honey (p.142)
Butter-&-Sage Roast Pumpkin (p.158)
Flourless Chocolate, Chestnut & Rosemary Cake (p.234)

WHEN IT'S COLD OUTSIDE

Ossobuco with Sage & Lemon (p.70)
Fennel & Parmesan Purée (p.136)
Blood Orange, Red Onion, Black Olive & Basil Salad (p.124)
Roast New Potatoes with Bay Leaves (p.152)
Cocoa-dusted Meringues (p.238)

A PRE-CHRISTMAS FEAST FOR FRIENDS

Honey-Roast Poussins (p.94)
Pommes Dauphinoise (p.154)
Beetroot & Mint Salad (p.118), with nuts and blue cheese
A Really Good Chicory Salad with Creamy Mustard
    Dressing (p.110)
Christmas Cake with Marzipan & Glacé Fruits (p.228)

A CHRISTMAS-Y FEAST

Pork Wellington with Apple & Sage (p.100)
Fennel & Parmesan Purée (p.136)
Roast New Potatoes with Bay Leaves (p.152)
Creamy Baked Leeks with Mustard & Parmesan (p.164)
A Really Good Chicory Salad with Creamy Mustard
    Dressing (p.110)
Christmas Cake with Marzipan & Glacé Fruits (p.228)

ANOTHER (SIMPLER) CHRISTMAS-Y FEAST

Honey-Roast Poussins (p.94)
Beetroot & Mint Salad (p.118)
Burrata topped with a smattering of pomegranate seeds
The Simplest Roast Potatoes (p.148)
A Really Good Chicory Salad (p.110)
Pistachio Panettone Cake (p.198)

A FABULOUSLY COLOURFUL VEGETARIAN SUPPER

Wintry Saffron Couscous (p.48)
Roast Red Onions (p.166)
Beetroot & Mint Salad (p.118)
Buttery Carrots with Chestnut Honey (p.142)
Red Wine Poached Pears (p.212)
Salted Honey Ice Cream (p.186)
Meringues (p.238)

A PROPER INDULGENT ROAST FOR A CROWD

Allegra's Pot-Roast Beef (p.68)
Roast New Potatoes with Bay Leaves (p.152)
Creamy Baked Leeks with Mustard & Parmesan (p.164)
A Really Good Chicory Salad with Creamy Mustard
    Dressing (p.110)
Frozen Berries with Saffron White Chocolate
    Sauce (p.204)

A SIMPLE RECIPE FOR DOMESTIC UTOPIA

Carrot & Cinnamon Soup (p.56)
Damper Bread (p.252), or Walnut Soda Bread (p.254),
    served still warm and with salted butter
Apple & Walnut Crumble Pie (p.246)
Salted Honey Ice Cream (p.186), or Rum, Raisin
    & Walnut Ice Cream (p.184)

WHEN SPRING FEELS LIKE IT'S ON ITS WAY

Allegra's Pot-Roast Beef (p.68)
An Embarrassment of Spring Vegetables (p.146)
Watercress salad with Olga's Peppery Vinaigrette (p.260)
A Really Good Tomato Salad (p.114), with a handful
    of black olives
Pistachio Butter Cake (p.232), without its icing,
    but dusted with a cloud of icing sugar

HOW TO
COOK
BY NUMBERS

More than anything, the secret to culinary success is starting with recipes that work well for the number of people you are feeding.
A dish of pasta, for instance, is something you can and should whip up at the last moment and is perfect for dinner for four, but becomes unwieldy very quickly if you're trying to cook it for a larger group.
A dish of shepherd's pie, on the other hand – or better still Confit Duck Pie (p.98) – is something sturdy that will sit happily in the oven for as long as you need it to and is just what you want for bigger parties.

You will find here, grouped together as 'stars', 'sides' and 'sweets', recipes that work best for all scenarios. There is, of course, a degree of overlap: some recipes have that magical quality of working whether you're cooking for four, twelve or twenty, but others – because they are fiddly to make, rely on sensitive timings, or the ingredients are pricey – are best made in smaller batches.

A note on quantities: as a rule of thumb (and depending, of course, on what you're cooking), for a well-balanced menu you will need a 'star', a salad (green, chicory or tomato), a second 'side', and a 'sweet' (sometimes two, for reasons of pure indulgence). When I'm feeling extravagant, I might throw in a third side, but very rarely more than that. Broadly speaking, this is a menu structure that works as well for smaller groups (often with leftovers for the next day) as for parties of twenty (simply scale up the quantities). Finally, if cooking for a crowd, it's always better to cook lots of a single recipe than to give in to the temptation of trying to cook many more different dishes.

COOKING FOR FOUR TO SIX

STARS

SOUP
Chilled Almond Soup (p.38)
Gazpacho (p.40)
Carrot & Cinnamon Soup (p.56)
Tuscan Spring Vegetable
    Soup (p.58)

SALAD
Burrata with Preserved Lemon,
    Mint & Chilli (p.34)
Mozzarella with Celery, Olives
    & Pine Nuts (p.36)
Carpaccio of Figs with Lardo,
    Honey & Rosemary (p.42)
Bresaola e Grana (p.44)
Sicilian Couscous Salad (p.46)
Wintry Saffron Couscous (p.48)
Tuscan Panzanella (p.50)
Panzanella with Garden Peas
    & Baby Artichokes (p.52)
Panzanella with Tuna & Anchovies
    (p.54)

PASTA
Spaghetti with Creamy Lemon
    Sauce (p.60)
Tagliatelle with Gorgonzola,
    Pear & Walnut (p.62)
Rigatoni with Mascarpone
    & Pancetta (p.64)
Tagliatelle Gratin (p.86), with
    leftovers – bliss reheated
    the next day

PIES & FRITTATA
Torta Pasqualina (p.76), with
    some leftovers
Spinach, Mint & Melted Cheese
    Syrian Frittata (p.80), with
    leftovers – delicious reheated
    the next day
Torta di Maccheroni (p.82),
    with leftovers

MEAT & FISH
Sausages with Grapes (p.66)
Allegra's Pot-Roast Beef (p.68)
Ossobuco with Sage & Lemon (p.70)
Poulet Anglais (p.72)
Aphrodite's Roast Chicken (p.90)
Buttery Lemon Roast Chicken (p.92)
Honey-Roast Poussins (p.94)
Roast Pork with Honey-Roast
    Persimmons (p.96)
Confit Duck Pie (p.98), with
    leftovers – very good reheated
Pork Wellington with Apple
    & Sage (p.100)
Cold Roast Topside of Beef (p.104)

SIDES

SALAD
A Really Good Chicory Salad
    with Creamy Mustard
    Dressing (p.110)
A Really Good Green Salad (p.112)
A Really Good Tomato Salad (p.114)
Tomato, Red Onion & Mint
    Salad (p.116)
Beetroot & Mint Salad (p.118)
Watermelon, Feta & Pistachio
    Carpaccio (p.120)
Baby Artichoke, Fennel & Pecorino
    Salad (p.122)
Blood Orange, Red Onion, Black
    Olive & Basil Salad (p.124)
Carrot, Cumin & Mint Salad (p.144)

POTATOES
New Potatoes with Lemon
    & Samphire (p.126)
The Simplest Roast Potatoes (p.148)
Especially Good Roast Potatoes
    (p.150)

Roast New Potatoes with Bay
    Leaves (p.152)
Pommes Dauphinoise (p.154), with
    leftovers to reheat and enjoy
    the next day

VEGETABLES
Fried Broccoli with Black
    Olives (p.128)
Saffron Fennel (p.134)
Fennel & Parmesan Purée (p.136)
Asparagus with Lemon & Toasted
    Almond Gratin (p.138)
Green Beans with Baby
    Tomatoes (p.140)
Buttery Carrots with Chestnut
    Honey (p.142)
An Embarrassment of Spring
    Vegetables (p.146)
Roast Stuffed Tomatoes (p.156)
Butter-&-Sage Roast Pumpkin (p.158)
Timballo of Baked Courgettes
    (p.162)
Creamy Baked Leeks with
    Mustard & Parmesan (p.164)

FRUIT SIDES
Roast Grapes (p.168)
Roast Plums (p.170)
Roast Apples (p.172)

MIGHT-AS-WELL-BE
MAIN DISHES
Braised Lentils with Pancetta
    (p.130)
Wild Rice & Lentil Salad (p.132)
Courgette Blossom & Taleggio
    Galette (p.160)

SWEETS

FRUIT
Winter Fruit & Mascarpone Tart
    (p.180), likely with leftovers
Strawberries in Lemony Syrup
    (p.192)
Drunken Strawberries (p.194)
Melon in Grappa Syrup (p.196)
Frozen Berries with Saffron
    White Chocolate Sauce (p.204)
Red Wine Poached Pears (p.212),
    allow for leftovers -
    particularly good with
    Greek yogurt for breakfast
    the next day
Pink Rhubarb & Prosecco Jelly
    (p.222)
Ambrosial Apricots (p.224)

ICES
Rum, Raisin & Walnut Ice Cream
    (p.184)
Salted Honey Ice Cream (p.186)
Pine Nut Ice Cream 'Affogato' (p.188)
Honey, Fig & Walnut Semifreddo
    (p.218) - allow for leftovers,
    though they keep happily in
    the freezer for three months
Limoncello Semifreddo (p.220)

CAKE
Christmas Cake with Marzipan
    & Glacé Fruits (p.228)
Pistachio Butter Cake with
    Marzipan Icing (p.232), with
    leftovers for tea the next day
Flourless Chocolate, Chestnut
    & Rosemary Cake (p.234), with
    leftovers for tea the next day
Coffee & Walnut Cake (p.236), with
    leftovers for tea the next day
Summer Berry Cloud Cake (p.240),
    with leftovers

Chocolate Chestnut Meringue Cake
    (p.242), with leftovers
Lemon Meringue Cake (p.244),
    with leftovers

NO-BAKE CAKE
Coffee Mascarpone Biscuit Cake
    (p.190), with some leftovers
Pistachio Panettone Cake (p.198),
    with some leftovers
Pistachio, Mascarpone & Salted
    Caramel Cheesecake (p.214),
    with some leftovers

PIE
Apple & Walnut Crumble Pie (p.246),
    with some leftovers -
    particularly good for
    breakfast the next day

NO-BAKE PIE
Chocolate Chestnut Meringue Pie
    (p.178), though you will likely
    have leftovers
Easy-Peasy Lemon Meringue Pie
    (p.182), likely with leftovers

OTHER SWEETS
Svergognata (p.202)
A Very Good Vanilla Pannacotta
    (p.206)
Lavender Honey Pannacotta (p.208)
Salted Caramel Pannacotta (p.210)
Chocolate & Rum Pudding (p.226),
    with plenty of leftovers
Meringues (p.238)

COOKING FOR EIGHT TO TEN

STARS

SOUP
Chilled Almond Soup (p.38),
    you may need to blitz this
    in two batches
Gazpacho (p.40), you may need
    to blitz this in two batches,
    and allow extra time to chop
    the vegetables
Carrot & Cinnamon Soup (p.56)
Tuscan Spring Vegetable
    Soup (p.58)

SALAD
Burrata with Preserved Lemon,
    Mint & Chilli (p.34)
Mozzarella with Celery, Olives
    & Pine Nuts (p.36)
Carpaccio of Figs with Lardo,
    Honey & Rosemary (p.42)
Bresaola e Grana (p.44)
Sicilian Couscous Salad (p.46)
Wintry Saffron Couscous (p.48)
Tuscan Panzanella (p.50)
Panzanella with Garden Peas & Baby
    Artichokes (p.52)
Panzanella with Tuna & Anchovies
    (p.54)

PASTA
Tagliatelle Gratin (p.86)

PIES & FRITTATA
Torta Pasqualina (p.76)
Spinach, Mint & Melted Cheese
    Syrian Frittata (p.80)
Torta di Maccheroni (p.82), make
    two pies, or just one and bulk
    it out with lots of sides

MEAT & FISH
Allegra's Pot-Roast Beef (p.68)
Ossobuco with Sage & Lemon (p.70),
    made in two pans or across
    two batches
Poulet Anglais (p.72)
Whole Cold Poached Salmon (p.74)
Aphrodite's Roast Chicken (p.90),
    roast two birds - any leftovers
    you can use to make salad or
    sandwiches the next day
Buttery Lemon Roast Chicken
    (p.92), roast two birds - any
    leftovers for salad or
    sandwiches the next day
Honey-Roast Poussins (p.94)
Roast Pork with Honey-Roast
    Persimmons (p.96)
Confit Duck Pie (p.98)
Pork Wellington with Apple
    & Sage (p.100)
Cold Roast Topside of Beef (p.104)

SIDES

SALAD
A Really Good Chicory Salad
    with Creamy Mustard
    Dressing (p.110)
A Really Good Green Salad (p.112)
A Really Good Tomato Salad (p.114)
Tomato, Red Onion & Mint
    Salad (p.116)
Beetroot & Mint Salad (p.118)
Watermelon, Feta & Pistachio
    Carpaccio (p.120)
Baby Artichoke, Fennel & Pecorino
    Salad (p.122)
Blood Orange, Red Onion, Black
    Olive & Basil Salad (p.124), but
    allow extra time to peel and
    slice the oranges
Carrot, Cumin & Mint Salad (p.144)

POTATOES
New Potatoes with Lemon
    & Samphire (p.126)
The Simplest Roast Potatoes (p.148)
Especially Good Roast Potatoes
    (p.150)
Roast New Potatoes with Bay
    Leaves (p.152)
Pommes Dauphinoise (p.154)

VEGETABLES
Fried Broccoli with Black
    Olives (p.128)
Saffron Fennel (p.134)
Fennel & Parmesan Purée (p.136)
Asparagus with Lemon & Toasted
    Almond Gratin (p.138)
Green Beans with Baby
    Tomatoes (p.140)
Buttery Carrots with Chestnut
    Honey (p.142)
An Embarrassment of Spring
    Vegetables (p.146)
Roast Stuffed Tomatoes (p.156)
Butter-&-Sage Roast Pumpkin
    (p.158)
Timballo of Baked Courgettes
    (p.162)
Creamy Baked Leeks with
    Mustard & Parmesan (p.164)
Roast Red Onions (p.166)

FRUIT SIDES
Roast Grapes (p.168)
Roast Plums (p.170)
Roast Apples (p.172)

MIGHT-AS-WELL-BE
MAIN DISHES
Braised Lentils with Pancetta
    (p.130)
Wild Rice & Lentil Salad (p.132)
Courgette Blossom & Taleggio
    Galette (p.160)

SWEETS

COOKING FOR TWELVE *(or thereabouts)*

STARS

SOUP
Chilled Almond Soup (p.38),
    you may need to blitz this
    in two or three batches
Gazpacho (p.40), you may need
    to blitz this in two or three
    batches and allow extra time
    to chop the vegetables
Carrot & Cinnamon Soup (p.56)
Tuscan Spring Vegetable
    Soup (p.58)

SALAD
Burrata with Preserved Lemon,
    Mint & Chilli (p.34), a
    little pricey for a large
    crowd, but such a time-saver
    it's worth it
Mozzarella with Celery, Olives
    & Pine Nuts (p.36), but with
    a friendly warning that
    the fine chopping can be
    a little tedious
Bresaola e Grana (p.44)
Sicilian Couscous Salad (p.46)
Wintry Saffron Couscous (p.48)
Tuscan Panzanella (p.50)
Panzanella with Garden Peas & Baby
    Artichokes (p.52)
Panzanella with Tuna & Anchovies
    (p.54)

PASTA
Tagliatelle Gratin (p.86), make
    at least two trays

PIES & FRITTATA
Torta Pasqualina (p.76), make two
    pies and bank on a few slices
    for lunch the next day
Spinach, Mint & Melted Cheese
    Syrian Frittata (p.80), make
    two dishes – leftovers are so
    good reheated the next day

Torta di Maccheroni (p.82), make
    two pies and just serve a
    simple salad with them

MEAT & FISH
Allegra's Pot-Roast Beef (p.68)
Poulet Anglais (p.72)
Whole Cold Poached Salmon (p.74)
Buttery Lemon Roast Chicken
    (p.92), roast three birds
Honey-Roast Poussins (p.94)
Roast Pork with Honey-Roast
    Persimmons (p.96)
Confit Duck Pie (p.98), make two
    trays and bank on leftovers
    to reheat the next day
Pork Wellington with Apple & Sage
    (p.100), make two
Cold Roast Topside of Beef (p.104)

SIDES

SALAD
A Really Good Chicory Salad
    with Creamy Mustard
    Dressing (p.110)
A Really Good Green Salad (p.112)
A Really Good Tomato Salad (p.114)
Tomato, Red Onion & Mint
    Salad (p.116)
Beetroot & Mint Salad (p.118)
Watermelon, Feta & Pistachio
    Carpaccio (p.120)
Blood Orange, Red Onion, Black
    Olive & Basil Salad (p.124)
Carrot, Cumin & Mint Salad (p.144),
    slightly laborious to slice
    the carrots, but you can do
    it in advance

POTATOES
New Potatoes with Lemon
    & Samphire (p.126)

The Simplest Roast Potatoes (p.148)
Especially Good Roast Potatoes
    (p.150), though you need a lot
    of oven space, so focus on
    dishes you can throw together
    or cook on the hob for the rest
    of the meal
Roast New Potatoes with Bay
    Leaves (p.152)
Pommes Dauphinoise (p.154)

VEGETABLES
Saffron Fennel (p.134)
Fennel & Parmesan Purée (p.136)
Asparagus with Lemon & Toasted
    Almond Gratin (p.138)
Green Beans with Baby
    Tomatoes (p.140)
Buttery Carrots with Chestnut
    Honey (p.142)
Roast Stuffed Tomatoes (p.156),
    a little fiddly to prepare
    en masse, but can be done well
    in advance
Butter-&-Sage Roast Pumpkin
    (p.158)
Creamy Baked Leeks with Mustard
    & Parmesan (p.164)
Roast Red Onions (p.166)

FRUIT SIDES
Roast Grapes (p.168)
Roast Plums (p.170)
Roast Apples (p.172)

MIGHT-AS-WELL-BE
MAIN DISHES
Braised Lentils with Pancetta
    (p.130)
Wild Rice & Lentil Salad (p.132)
Courgette Blossom & Taleggio
    Galette (p.160), make two
    tarts and enjoy the leftovers
    the next day

SWEETS

FRUIT

Winter Fruit & Mascarpone Tart
   (p.180), you could make two,
   or just one with extra fruit
   on the side
Strawberries in Lemony Syrup
   (p.192)
Drunken Strawberries (p.194)
Melon in Grappa Syrup (p.196)
Frozen Berries with Saffron White
   Chocolate Sauce (p.204)
Red Wine Poached Pears (p.212)
Pink Rhubarb & Prosecco Jelly
   (p.222), either make two,
   or serve with ice cream
   to stretch it out
Ambrosial Apricots (p.224)

ICES

Rum, Raisin & Walnut Ice
   Cream (p.184)
Salted Honey Ice Cream (p.186)
Pine Nut Ice Cream
   'Affogato' (p.188)
Limoncello Semifreddo (p.220)

CAKE

Christmas Cake with Marzipan &
   Glacé Fruits (p.228), one should
   be enough, as it's very rich,
   then stretch it out with a bowl
   of brandy butter
Pistachio Butter Cake with
   Marzipan Icing (p.232),
   stretched out with a bowl of
   Drunken Strawberries (p.194)
   or other fresh fruit
Flourless Chocolate, Chestnut
   & Rosemary Cake (p.234),
   stretched out with whipped
   cream or mascarpone
Coffee & Walnut Cake (p.236),
   bulked out with a bowl of
   raspberries and clotted cream

Summer Berry Cloud Cake (p.240),
   but stretch it out with berries
   and extra whipped cream
Chocolate Chestnut Meringue
   Cake (p.242)
Lemon Meringue Cake (p.244), but
   bulk it out with Drunken
   Strawberries (p.194)

NO-BAKE CAKE

Coffee Mascarpone Biscuit Cake
   (p.190), make two, or
   serve with a large dish
   of raspberries
Pistachio Panettone Cake (p.198),
   stretched out with winter
   fruit and whipped cream
Pistachio, Mascarpone & Salted
   Caramel Cheesecake (p.214)

PIE

Apple & Walnut Crumble Pie (p.246),
   stretched out with ice cream

NO-BAKE PIE

Chocolate Chestnut Meringue Pie
   (p.178), make two and count on
   a few leftovers
Easy-Peasy Lemon Meringue Pie
   (p.182), with a dish of
   strawberries to stretch it out

OTHER SWEETS

Svergognata (p.202), served in a
   large trifle dish for everyone
   to help themselves
A Very Good Vanilla Pannacotta
   (p.206)
Lavender Honey Pannacotta (p.208)
Salted Caramel Pannacotta (p.210)
Chocolate & Rum Pudding (p.226),
   stretched out with berries
   and cream
Meringues (p.238)

COOKING FOR TWENTY (or more)

STARS

SOUP
Chilled Almond Soup (p.38), you
    may need to do this in several
    batches – for ease, make it the
    day before and store in the
    fridge in plastic bottles
Carrot & Cinnamon Soup (p.56)

SALAD
Burrata with Preserved Lemon,
    Mint & Chilli (p.34),
    a little pricey for a large
    crowd, but such a time-saver
    it's worth it
Mozzarella with Celery, Olives
    & Pine Nuts (p.36), with a
    friendly warning that the fine
    chopping can be a bit tedious
Bresaola e Grana (p.44), this won't
    sit on the table for more than
    an hour, so dress it and lay it
    out last minute-ish
Sicilian Couscous Salad (p.46)
Wintry Saffron Couscous (p.48)
Tuscan Panzanella (p.50)
Panzanella with Garden Peas
    & Baby Artichokes (p.52)
Panzanella with Tuna & Anchovies
    (p.54)

PASTA
Tagliatelle Gratin (p.86),
    make two or more trays

PIES & FRITTATA
Torta Pasqualina (p.76), make
    two pies in advance
Spinach, Mint & Melted Cheese
    Syrian Frittata (p.80), make
    two in advance
Torta di Maccheroni (p.82), make
    two or more – you can make the
    pasta filling the day before and
    assemble the pies on the day

MEAT & FISH
Poulet Anglais (p.72)
Whole Cold Poached Salmon (p.74),
    cook two or more
Honey-Roast Poussins (p.94)
Roast Pork with Honey-Roast
    Persimmons (p.96), slow-cooked
    pork shoulder is a brilliant
    option for very large crowds:
    cook at 220°C/fan 200°C/Gas 7
    for 35–40 minutes, then reduce
    the heat to 100°C/fan 80°C/Gas ¼
    and roast for up to fourteen
    hours, then leave to rest for
    a couple of hours while you use
    the oven for whatever else you
    need it for
Confit Duck Pie (p.98), make two
    or more
Pork Wellington with Apple
    & Sage (p.100), make two
    or more in advance
Cold Roast Topside of Beef (p.104)

SIDES

SALAD
A Really Good Chicory Salad
    with Creamy Mustard
    Dressing (p.110)
A Really Good Green Salad (p.112)
A Really Good Tomato Salad (p.114)
Tomato, Red Onion & Mint
    Salad (p.116)
Beetroot & Mint Salad (p.118)
Watermelon, Feta & Pistachio
    Carpaccio (p.120)
Blood Orange, Red Onion, Black
    Olive & Basil Salad (p.124),
    there is a fair amount
    of slicing involved, but
    you can make it up to two
    days in advance

POTATOES
New Potatoes with Lemon
    & Samphire (p.126)
The Simplest Roast Potatoes
    (p.148), though you will need
    lots of roasting trays and
    oven space
Roast New Potatoes with Bay Leaves
    (p.152), though you will need
    lots of roasting trays and
    oven space
Pommes Dauphinoise (p.154),
    make at least two trays

VEGETABLES
Saffron Fennel (p.134), cooked
    in batches then reheated
Fennel & Parmesan Purée (p.136)
Asparagus with Lemon & Toasted
    Almond Gratin (p.138)
Green Beans with Baby
    Tomatoes (p.140)
Buttery Carrots with Chestnut
    Honey (p.142)
An Embarrassment of Spring
    Vegetables (p.146)
Butter-&-Sage Roast Pumpkin
    (p.158), though allow plenty
    of oven space
Creamy Baked Leeks with Mustard
    & Parmesan (p.164), made in
    advance and reheated at the
    last minute
Roast Red Onions (p.166)

FRUIT SIDES
Roast Plums (p.170)
Roast Apples (p.172)

MIGHT-AS-WELL-BE
MAIN DISHES
Braised Lentils with
    Pancetta (p.130)
Wild Rice & Lentil Salad (p.132)

SWEETS

FRUIT
Winter Fruit & Mascarpone Tart
(p.180), make two or more
Strawberries in Lemony Syrup
(p.192)
Drunken Strawberries (p.194)
Melon in Grappa Syrup (p.196)
Frozen Berries with Saffron White
Chocolate Sauce (p.204)
Red Wine Poached Pears (p.212), you
may need to do this in batches
Pink Rhubarb & Prosecco Jelly
(p.222), make two or more
Ambrosial Apricots (p.224)

ICES
Rum, Raisin & Walnut Ice
Cream (p.184)
Salted Honey Ice Cream (p.186)
Pine Nut Ice Cream
'Affogato' (p.188)
Limoncello Semifreddo (p.220),
allow plenty of space in your
freezer as well as time for
hollowing out the lemons –
or make two quantities, freeze
in cake tins and serve in slices

CAKE
Christmas Cake with Marzipan
& Glacé Fruits (p.228), make two
Pistachio Butter Cake with
Marzipan Icing (p.232),
make two
Flourless Chocolate, Chestnut
& Rosemary Cake (p.234), make
two or three
Coffee & Walnut Cake (p.236),
make two
Summer Berry Cloud Cake (p.240),
make two or more
Chocolate Chestnut Meringue Cake
(p.242), make two
Lemon Meringue Cake (p.244),
make two

NO-BAKE CAKE
Coffee Mascarpone Biscuit Cake
(p.190), make two or more
Pistachio Panettone Cake (p.198),
make two or more
Pistachio, Mascarpone & Salted
Caramel Cheesecake (p.214),
make two or more

NO-BAKE PIE
Chocolate Chestnut Meringue Pie
(p.178), make two, or even
three, though it's an odd rule
of catering science that large
crowds eat less than smaller
ones, so I'd make two
Easy-Peasy Lemon Meringue Pie
(p.182), make two or more

OTHER SWEETS
Svergognata (p.202), serve in a
large trifle dish for everyone
to help themselves
A Very Good Vanilla Pannacotta
(p.206)
Lavender Honey Pannacotta (p.208)
Salted Caramel Pannacotta (p.210)
Chocolate & Rum Pudding (p.226),
make two or more
Meringues (p.238), make ahead
of time in batches

HOW TO
COOK
BY TIMINGS

Cooking in stages, preparing what you can in advance (and when it most suits you) is what makes cooking for friends not only doable, but also enjoyable… effortless, even.

Of course, you don't have to cook ahead of time; sometimes there is no need to. On Sundays, for instance, we almost always have friends over for lunch. I don't prepare in any way, as that would take away from the relaxed laziness that makes weekends feel like weekends. Instead, I make sure we have a well-stocked fridge to delve into, then I potter in the kitchen all morning, slowly and haphazardly bringing the meal together. It's rare we sit down much before 2pm, but then, on Sundays, we have all the time in the world.

Most of the time, however, you need to be more organised. Few things give greater comfort when embarking upon dinner than knowing that part of the meal is already made: a cake baked yesterday to be smothered in icing, or a bowl of panzanella in the fridge ready to be tossed and served.

I've grouped recipes together here by timings, so you can choose what to cook and when to do so, just as you like. There is nothing to stop you making a dish and serving it straight away, and, indeed, those dishes grouped together in the first section must be prepared at the last minute. But should you want to get ahead, you will find plenty of food you can make one, two, even three days ahead. Each is listed by the furthest ahead you can make it.

You'll notice that there aren't any sweet dishes in the first two sections here; this is simply because all the sweet recipes in this book can be made more than six hours before you serve them.

DISHES BEST THROWN TOGETHER AT THE LAST MINUTE

STARS

SALAD
Burrata with Preserved Lemon,
    Mint & Chilli (p.34)
Bresaola e Grana (p.44)

PASTA
Spaghetti with Creamy Lemon Sauce
    (p.60), though you can make the
    sauce in the morning, if that
    makes things easier
Tagliatelle with Gorgonzola,
    Pear & Walnut (p.62)
Rigatoni with Mascarpone
    & Pancetta (p.64)

MEAT & FISH
Sausages with Grapes (p.66)
Allegra's Pot-Roast Beef (p.68)

SIDES

VEGETABLES
Roast Red Onions (p.166)

FRUIT SIDES
Roast Grapes (p.168)
Roast Apples (p.172)

DISHES YOU CAN PREPARE UP TO SIX HOURS BEFORE

STARS

SALAD
Mozzarella with Celery, Olives
    & Pine Nuts (p.36)
Carpaccio of Figs with Lardo,
    Honey & Rosemary (p.42)
Panzanella with Garden Peas &
    Baby Artichokes (p.52), prepare
    the base of the salad and the
    dressing in advance, then
    add the lettuce and toss
    an hour ahead

MEAT & FISH
Aphrodite's Roast Chicken (p.90)
Buttery Lemon Roast Chicken
    (p.92), prepare the chicken
    and let it sit, uncovered, in
    its roasting tray in the fridge;
    bring it to room temperature
    before roasting

SIDES

SALAD
A Really Good Chicory Salad with
    Creamy Mustard Dressing
    (p.110), assemble the salad
    and prepare the dressing,
    then dress just before serving
A Really Good Green Salad (p.112)
    with Olga's Peppery Vinaigrette
    (p.260), assemble the salad and
    prepare the dressing, then
    dress just before serving

POTATOES
The Simplest Roast Potatoes
    (p.148), prepare and season, pop
    in the oven when you're ready
Roast New Potatoes with Bay Leaves
    (p.152), prepare and season, pop
    in the oven when you're ready
Pommes Dauphinoise (p.154)

VEGETABLES
An Embarrassment of Spring
    Vegetables (p.146)
Timballo of Baked Courgettes
    (p.162)

DISHES YOU CAN PREPARE *(largely, at least)* UP TO TWELVE HOURS AHEAD

STARS

PASTA

Tagliatelle Gratin (p.86), make up to the final stage, cover and store in the fridge, then bake when you're ready to eat

PIES & FRITTATA

Torta di Maccheroni (p.82), assemble the pie, glaze with egg wash, store in the fridge and bake just before serving

MEAT & FISH

Whole Poached Cold Salmon (p.74)

Buttery Lemon Roast Chicken (p.92), prepare the chicken and let sit, uncovered, in its roasting tray in the fridge; bring to room temperature before roasting

Honey-Roast Poussins (p.94), prepare the birds in the morning, store in the fridge and bring to room temperature before roasting

Roast Pork with Honey-Roast Persimmons (p.96), prepare the pork, then leave to dry out, uncovered, in the fridge over the day; bring to room temperature before roasting

Pork Wellington with Apple & Sage (p.100), make in the morning and store in the fridge until ready to bake

SIDES

SALAD

A Really Good Tomato Salad (p.114), slice and dress the tomatoes ahead of time and add the basil just before serving

Tomato, Red Onion & Mint Salad (p.116), slice and dress the tomatoes ahead of time and add the mint just before serving

Watermelon, Feta & Pistachio Carpaccio (p.120), slice the watermelon in the morning, assemble at the last minute

Baby Artichoke, Fennel & Pecorino Salad (p.122), assemble the salad in the morning, then, just before serving, top with pecorino and fennel fronds

Blood Orange, Red Onion, Black Olive & Basil Salad (p.124), add the herbs and toss to serve

POTATOES

The Simplest Roast Potatoes (p.148), these are best made at the time, but can be cooked in the morning and reheated

Especially Good Roast Potatoes (p.150), cook in advance and finish off in the oven when you like, allowing twenty minutes to crisp properly

VEGETABLES

Fried Broccoli with Black Olives (p.128)

Asparagus with Lemon & Toasted Almond Gratin (p.138), make the gratin and cook the asparagus in the morning. Store the asparagus in the fridge and the gratin on the side; warm the gratin in a frying pan before serving and sprinkle over the room temperature asparagus

An Embarrassment of Spring Vegetables (p.146)

Butter-&-Sage Roast Pumpkin (p.158), cook in the morning and store, covered, somewhere cool, then reheat in the oven for ten minutes before serving

Creamy Baked Leeks with Mustard & Parmesan (p.164), prepare the leeks in the morning, then let them sit in their tray and cook when you need to

MIGHT-AS-WELL-BE MAIN DISHES

Courgette Blossom & Taleggio Galette (p.160), bake that morning and serve at room temperature

SWEETS

FRUIT

Strawberries in Lemony Syrup (p.192)

Drunken Strawberries (p.194)

Melon in Grappa Syrup (p.196)

NO-BAKE CAKE

Pistachio Panettone Cake (p.198)

OTHER SWEETS

Svergognata (p.202)

DISHES YOU CAN PREPARE
THE DAY BEFORE

STARS

SOUP
Chilled Almond Soup (p.38)
Tuscan Spring Vegetable
    Soup (p.58)

SALAD
Tuscan Panzanella (p.50),
    at a squeeze
Panzanella with Tuna & Anchovies
    (p.54), at a squeeze, then just
    add the herbs before serving

PIES & FRITTATA
Torta Pasqualina (p.76)
Spinach, Mint & Melted Cheese
    Syrian Frittata (p.80),
    prepare the frittata, cover
    and store in the fridge, then
    cook before serving

MEAT & FISH
Poulet Anglais (p.72)
Cold Roast Topside of Beef (p.104),
    store in the fridge wrapped
    in foil, bring to room
    temperature and slice
    just before serving

SIDES

SALAD
Beetroot & Mint Salad (p.118),
    top with roughly torn mint
    leaves just before serving
Carrot, Cumin & Mint Salad (p.144)

POTATOES
New Potatoes with Lemon &
    Samphire (p.126), store covered
    somewhere cool, then just add
    the parsley before serving

VEGETABLES
Fried Broccoli with Black Olives
    (p.128), reheat gently in the
    pan just before serving
Saffron Fennel (p.134), store
    covered in the fridge, then
    gently reheat on the hob with a
    splash of water before serving
Asparagus with Lemon & Toasted
    Almond Gratin (p.138), store
    in the fridge, with the gratin
    in an airtight container, then
    assemble just before serving
Green Beans with Baby Tomatoes
    (p.140), store in the fridge
    and reheat gently on the hob
    before serving, or serve at
    room temperature
Roast Stuffed Tomatoes (p.156),
    serve at room temperature,
    or reheat in the oven
    before serving
Creamy Baked Leeks with Mustard
    & Parmesan (p.164), store,
    covered, in the fridge, then
    bake in the oven

FRUIT SIDES
Roast Plums (p.170), cook in advance,
    store in their roasting tin in
    the fridge or somewhere cool,
    then reheat in the oven for
    ten minutes before serving

SWEETS

FRUIT
Winter Fruit & Mascarpone Tart
    (p.180), store the base and
    filling, covered, in the fridge
    for up to twenty-four hours,
    then top with the fruit a
    few hours before serving
Frozen Berries with Hot White
    Chocolate & Saffron Sauce
    (p.204), make the sauce twenty-
    four hours in advance and store
    in the fridge, covered, then
    slowly reheat before serving

CAKE
Pistachio Butter Cake with
    Marzipan Icing (p.232)

NO-BAKE CAKE
Pistachio, Mascarpone & Salted
    Caramel Cheesecake (p.214),
    make the cheesecake the day
    before, store in the fridge,
    then drizzle with caramel
    on the day of serving

PIE
Apple & Walnut Crumble Pie (p.246),
    bake the day before and serve
    at room temperature, or cover
    with foil and reheat gently
    in the oven

DISHES YOU CAN PREPARE DAYS BEFORE

STARS

SOUP

Gazpacho (p.40), up to three days
    in advance

Carrot & Cinnamon Soup (p.56),
    up to two days ahead, store
    in the fridge, then reheat
    before serving

SALAD

Sicilian Couscous Salad (p.46),
    up to three days in advance
    and store in the fridge

Wintry Saffron Couscous (p.48), up
    to three days before, then add
    the pine nuts and pomegranate
    up to one day before

PIES & FRITTATA

Torta Pasqualina (p.76), up to two
    days before

MEAT & FISH

Ossobuco with Sage & Lemon (p.70),
    up to three days ahead and
    store, covered, in the fridge;
    reheat very gently in a pan
    before serving

Confit Duck Pie (p.98), prepare
    until the final stage up to
    three days in advance and
    store, covered, in the fridge,
    then bake when you are ready
    to eat

SIDES

SALAD

Beetroot & Mint Salad (p.118), will
    keep for up to two days in the
    fridge; add the mint leaves
    just before serving

Blood Orange, Red Onion, Black
    Olive & Basil Salad (p.124), add
    the basil just before serving

VEGETABLES

Fennel & Parmesan Purée (p.136),
    make up to three days ahead,
    keep covered in the fridge,
    then reheat slowly on the hob

Green Beans with Baby Tomatoes
    (p.140), prepare up to two days
    ahead, then store, covered,
    in the fridge. Warm in a pan
    before serving, or serve at
    room temperature

Buttery Carrots with Chestnut
    Honey (p.142), store in the
    fridge for up to two days, then
    serve at room temperature or
    reheat in a pan with a splash
    of olive oil before serving

MIGHT-AS-WELL-BE MAIN DISHES

Braised Lentils with Pancetta
    (p.130), make up to three days
    before, store in the fridge
    and reheat before serving

Wild Rice & Lentil Salad (p.132),
    make up to three days
    in advance, store in the
    fridge and add the mint
    at the last minute

SWEETS

FRUIT

Red Wine Poached Pears (p.212),
    up to three days before

Pink Rhubarb & Prosecco Jelly
    (p.222), make up to two days
    in advance

Ambrosial Apricots (p.224), keep
    happily in the fridge for three
    days, though may discolour

ICES

Rum, Raisin & Walnut Ice Cream
    (p.184), will happily keep for
    three months in the freezer

Salted Honey Ice Cream (p.186),
    will happily keep for three
    months in the freezer

Pine Nut Ice Cream (p.188), will
    happily keep for three months
    in the freezer

Honey, Fig & Walnut Semifreddo
    (p.218), make up to one month
    before and top with fruit, nuts
    and honey just before serving

Limoncello Semifreddo (p.220),
    make up to a month in advance

CAKE

Christmas Cake with Marzipan
    & Glacé Fruits (p.228), bake
    up to three months ahead and
    decorate up to two weeks
    before eating

Flourless Chocolate, Chestnut
    & Rosemary Cake (p.234), make
    up to two days before, store in
    an airtight container and dust
    with icing sugar before serving

→

Coffee & Walnut Cake (p.236),
make the cakes up to three
days in advance, wrap in foil
and store in an airtight
container; ice and decorate
on the morning you serve it;
if it's hot, once iced, store
in the fridge

Summer Berry Cloud Cake (p.240),
make the meringues up to
three days before, assemble up
to twelve hours before eating
and store in the fridge or
somewhere cool

Chocolate Chestnut Meringue Cake
(p.242), make the meringues up
to three days ahead and store
in an airtight container; a few
hours before serving, whip the
cream, assemble and decorate
the cake, then store in the
fridge until ready

Lemon Meringue Cake (p.244), make
the meringues up to three days
ahead and store in an airtight
container; a few hours before
serving, whip the cream,
assemble and decorate the
cake, then chill until ready

NO-BAKE CAKE

Coffee Mascarpone Biscuit Cake
(p.190), keep in the fridge for
up to two days

NO-BAKE PIE

Chocolate Chestnut Meringue Pie
(p.178), make the base and
filling up to three days ahead,
then top with soft meringue
on the day of serving

Easy-Peasy Lemon Meringue Pie
(p.182), make the pie crust and
filling and store in the fridge
for up to two days, then top
with meringue on the day

OTHER SWEETS

A Very Good Vanilla Pannacotta
(p.206), prepare up to three
days ahead, store in the fridge,
then unmould up to a few hours
before serving

Lavender Honey Pannacotta (p.208),
prepare up to three days ahead,
store in the fridge, then
unmould up to a few hours
before serving

Salted Caramel Pannacotta (p.210),
prepare up to three days ahead,
store in the fridge, then
unmould up to a few hours
before serving

Chocolate & Rum Pudding (p.226),
prepare up to two days in
advance, store in the fridge
and serve chilled; unmould
a short time before serving

Meringues (p.238), make up to
three days in advance and store
in an airtight container

INDEX

ACKNOWLEDGEMENTS

This is a book of recipes, but more than anything it is a book about the joy of eating with friends: at its heart is the belief that food tastes best when shared with others. And as it turns out, the very same principle applies to the business of book-writing: as much as I've loved the process of writing, sitting at my desk, it is those moments of collaboration with the brilliant team who made this book happen that have undoubtedly been the most fun. Without the many and talented voices that helped me create these pages, there would absolutely be no book at all.

A Table for Friends started with an idea and a list of recipes jotted down (literally) on the back of an envelope. For a long time it was simply a jumble of thoughts floating around in my head. I owe a huge debt to my agent, Caroline Michel, for her boundless enthusiasm and tireless energy in turning my dreams and aspirations into the book that sits proudly on the kitchen table in front of me today. Thank you also to the rest of the team at Peters Fraser & Dunlop - in particular, Laurie Robertson, Lucy Irvine and Daisy Chandley - for always being such a joy to work with. Likewise, Laura Creyke and Mark Hutchinson; this is the second book I have had the privilege to work with you on, and I remain, as ever, so grateful for your kindness, encouragement, wise advice and - above all - friendship.

A good editor does more than 'edit' a manuscript, they push, challenge and inspire you to write the best book you possibly can. Thank you to my editors, Natalie Bellos, Lisa Pendreigh and Lena Hall: it has been a true pleasure and a great privilege to work with you. As with the rest of the lovely team at Bloomsbury: Alexandra Pringle, Alexis Kirschbaum, Ellen Williams, Don Shanahan and Laura Brodie. I am so proud of what we have created.

Special thanks also to Richard Atkinson, not my editor for this book, but my friend. Thank you for being so generous in sharing your thoughts, listening patiently to mine, and for making the time to do so even when in the throes of writing your own magnum opus. I have treasured your advice.

At the heart of a cookbook is of course the food: thank you Aya Nishimura and Ellie Mulligan for creating the most magnificent dishes to illustrate these pages; so much of the beauty of this book is down to you, your tireless hard work and your brilliant eye.

Thank you also to Toni Musgrave, Nicola Roberts and Alice Ostan for all your help in the kitchen. Huge and heartfelt thanks to Stephanie Howard and Ioana Marinca for assisting me with the photography. Shooting an entire book was for me an intensely daunting prospect: you not only made it possible, but also so much fun. Special thanks to Anna Gilchrist for so beautifully capturing the images on p.43, p.61, p.137, p.161 and p.197.

Poppy Mahon, thank you once again for magicking my scribbles into reliable and foolproof recipes - I don't know what I would do without you - and Lucy Bannell, thank you for patiently and so artfully shaping my ramblings into words that actually make sense. It has been a true joy to work with you: the passion with which you have approached this project and your unparalleled attention to detail are inspiring.

Last but in no way least - indeed perhaps the biggest thank you of all - is to my family and friends who are the inspiration and the reason for this book. In particular, to my boys - Anthony, Aeneas and Achille - for allowing me the space to chase after my dreams, and for catching me when I stumble.

To my godmother, Olga Polizzi, I wrote a huge chunk of this book while staying with you at Tresanton: thank you for taking such loving care of me while I was suffering from morning sickness and in the throes of perhaps my greatest 'essay crisis' yet, and for always supporting me so generously in everything that I do.

Finally, my heartfelt thanks to all our friends who have, over the years, gathered around our dining table and indulged us with their delicious company. How lucky I am to have you in my life.

BLOOMSBURY PUBLISHING
Bloomsbury Publishing Plc
50 Bedford Square, London, WC1B 3DP, UK

BLOOMSBURY, BLOOMSBURY PUBLISHING and the Diana
logo are trademarks of Bloomsbury Publishing Plc

First published in Great Britain 2020

A catalogue record for this book is available
from the British Library.

ISBN: HB: 978-1-5266-1511-4
eBook: 978-1-5266-1510-7

10 9 8 7 6 5 4 3 2

Project Editor: Lucy Bannell
Cover Designer: Greg Heinimann
Photographer: Skye McAlpine
Food Stylist: Aya Nishimura and Ellie Mulligan
Indexer: Vanessa Bird

Printed and bound in Germany by Mohn Media Mohndruck Gmbh

To find out more about our authors and books
visit www.bloomsbury.com and sign up for
our newsletters.